Finding My Father

HIS CENTURY-LONG JOURNEY

FROM WORLD WAR I WARSAW

AND

MY QUEST TO FOLLOW

Deborah Tannen

BALLANTINE BOOKS

NEW YORK

2021 Ballantine Books Trade Paperback Edition

Copyright © 2020 by Deborah Tannen

Published in the United States by Ballantine Books, an imprint of Random House, a division of Penguin Random House LLC, New York.

BALLANTINE and the HOUSE colophon are registered trademarks of Penguin Random House LLC.

Originally published in hardcover in the United States by Ballantine Books, an imprint of Random House, a division of Penguin Random House LLC, in 2020.

All photos, unless otherwise noted, are from the author's collection.

LIBRARY OF CONGRESS CATALOGING-IN-PUBLICATION DATA
NAMES: Tannen, Deborah, author.
TITLE: Finding my father : his century-long journey from WWI Warsaw and my quest to follow / Deborah Tannen. Other titles: His century-long journey from WWI Warsaw and my quest to follow
DESCRIPTION: First edition. | New York : Ballantine Group, 2020.
IDENTIFIERS: LCCN 2020012964 (print) | LCCN 2020012965 (ebook) | ISBN 9781101885857 (paperback) | ISBN 9781101885840 (ebook)
SUBJECTS: LCSH: Tannen, Eli Samuel, 1908–2006. | Tannen, Deborah—Family. | Fathers and daughters—New York (State)—New York. | Jews, Polish—New York (State)—New York—Biography. | Jews—New York (State)—New York—Biography. | Lawyers—New York (State) —New York—Biography. | Warsaw (Poland)—Biography. | New York (N.Y.)—Biography.
CLASSIFICATION: LCC E184.37.T37 T36 2020 (print) | LCC E184.37.T37 (ebook) | DDC 305.892/407470922—dc23
LC record available at https://lccn.loc.gov/2020012964

Printed in the United States of America on acid-free paper

randomhousebooks.com

9 8 7 6 5 4 3 2 1

Book design by Barbara M. Bachman

BY DEBORAH TANNEN

That's Not What I Meant!

You Just Don't Understand

Talking from 9 to 5

The Argument Culture

I Only Say This Because I Love You

You're Wearing THAT?

You Were Always Mom's Favorite!

You're the Only One I Can Tell

Finding My Father

FINDING MY FATHER

In memory of my father

Born Schmuel Eliyahu Tenenwórcel

Warsaw, Poland
October 3, 1908

Died Eli Samuel Tannen

United States
September 20, 2006

Contents

FINDING MY FATHER

Its Hour Come
Round at Last

I ADORED MY FATHER. HE'S THE PARENT I FELT AN AFFINITY WITH, the one I thought understood me. I trace to him my love of words, of language, of reading, and of writing. When my father was home, he was often sitting at his desk, writing. That remained his favorite place to be, his favorite thing to do, until he died two weeks before his ninety-eighth birthday. I don't know if I was emulating him or expressing the genes he passed on, but when I was a child, the object I loved most was an old black manual typewriter with yellowing keys rimmed in tarnished silver. I typed poems and stories—and letters to my father, telling him what happened to me during the day, often laying out grievances against my mother.

I talked to my father through letters because when I was growing up he was rarely home. The strongest presence I felt in the house was his absence. A sense of yearning for him stayed with me long after I was grown. A dream I had in my thirties was typical: I'm having a birthday party. My father is there, but he's suspended about two feet off the floor, with his head near the ceiling. I don't know what he's doing up there; he doesn't seem to be doing anything, just floating in his own world. I can't reach him; he doesn't seem to hear or see me. I desperately try to make contact with him, but he's stuck up there, and I can't get him to come down.

After my father retired at seventy, he had time to spend with me and talk to me—and during the nearly thirty years left to us before he died, he did a great deal of both. Yet I'm seeking him still. A character in a story by Ethan Canin says, of a TV show he turned on in the middle, "I have entered too late to understand." That's what it's like to try to understand our parents: we came into their lives too late. But we keep trying, keep crafting our own personal creation story—maybe creation myth. By writing this book, I'm trying to figure out what happened in my father's life before I came in. My parents both helped by living to be very old: as they aged, their internal censors fell, and they told me things about their marriage that made me question everything I'd thought about their relationship; about relationships between women and men; and about the circumstances of my birth. My father helped especially, because he was ever eager to talk about his past—and because he left me mountains of words: not only the hours and hours of conversations we had, but also stacks of letters and notes that he saved, and memories that he wrote down for me.

I think I've come closer to understanding my father. I know I've come to see that his life story, as I heard it growing up and embellished it in my mind—the creation story I'd devised for myself—was, in many ways, a myth.

*

MY FATHER'S LIFE TRACES THE HISTORY OF THE TWENTIETH CENTURY: he was born in 1908 and died in 2006.

I've always been proud that my parents were born in Europe—my father in Poland, my mother in Russia. When I was a child, I thought it exotic. As I got older, I liked that it gave me a closer connection to my European roots, compared to most American Jews of my generation, whose parents were born here; it was their grandparents who came from Europe. But it wasn't until writing this book that I understood the significance of that difference, the ways that my parents' immigration reflects history: they came to the United States at the tail end of the massive influx that brought more than 2 million East European Jews to the United States between 1880 and 1924. The year my father came, 1920, was the last year there were few limits on immigration from Europe. The very next year the Statue of Liberty lowered her torch: in 1921 Congress imposed quotas, and in 1924—the year after my mother arrived—quotas were set so low that the doors effectively slammed shut.

My father was raised in a Hasidic household in Warsaw and had astonishingly detailed memories of life in that community before, during, and immediately after the First World War. He turned twelve two weeks after arriving in the United States with his mother and sister; his father had long since died of tuberculosis. At fourteen, my father became the family breadwinner: he quit high school and went to work in New York's garment district. He studied high school subjects on his own; passed a law school qualifying exam; attended law school at night; earned a master's degree in law; and passed the bar exam on the first try. But the Great Depression had descended, so he couldn't get work as a lawyer or build up a practice without first working for little or no pay. This he could not do—not then, and not for many years after—because he was supporting first his mother and sister, then his wife and children. He was a Communist, and was investigated by the FBI; I have a copy of his file. Disillusioned with Communism, he became active in New York's Liberal Party, a progressive third party closely tied to the garment workers' union, and ran for City Council and for Congress on their ticket. From the time he received his law degree at twenty-one to the time he began earning a living as a lawyer at fifty, he held a dizzying number and array of jobs, including prison guard, parole officer, gun-toting alcohol tax inspector, and, from the time I was born till I was in junior high, a cutter in the garment district. After that, my father was a partner in his own law firm.

His is an American story, an immigrant story.

*

IN WRITING THIS BOOK, I'M FULFILLING AN ASSIGNMENT I GAVE MYself more years ago than I can remember. Or maybe it's an assignment my father gave me. A year after he retired, in 1979, he began writing down memories of his life:

> This is an inauspicious spur of the moment beginning. I doubt I'll live long enough ever to read these pages, just as I don't expect to complete, nor even start, the myriad projects

I've set for myself, so this effort can only be for my children or grandchildren. Maybe one of them will some day peruse these notes, or jottings, and find a nugget—one that might even be incorporated in a book (as I ventured to suggest to Deborah recently).

Reading this now, I'm caught up short: was it my father's idea that I write this book? I was certain it was mine. And 1979? I often say I've been planning to write a book about my father forever, but I didn't realize that forever goes that far back.

I FIND A NOTE my father attached to a multipage dot-matrix printout of memories he's written for me, stamped with the date DEC. 5, 1992. (He always had a date stamp on his desk, and always used it; how I wish I had done the same.) In the note, my father encourages me to write this book: "D'you have an envelope for my stuff? You know many of us take seriously your suggestion that you'll write a booklet on the basis of my recollections after I'm gone." My father talks to me through notes like this, and through slips of paper on which I jotted down things he said. Through one such slip of paper he tells me, "If you write it while I'm alive, you'll have to be thinking of my feelings."

I say to him in my mind, You're no longer alive, but I'm still thinking about your feelings. I'm trying to understand what they were, and how they shaped your life—and mine.

I FIRST PLANNED TO write my father's life in the mid-1990s, while he was alive. It was going to be my next book after *You Just Don't Understand,* the book that became a surprise bestseller and changed my life, and the one that followed, *Talking from 9 to 5.* I started interviewing him regularly, recording our conversations and writing notes, but didn't begin shaping the material into a book. In 1995 I feared I was tempting fate by putting it off: my father was eighty-seven, and had a bad fall. Yet I went ahead and wrote two other books instead. When those were done, he was ninety-three and, amazingly, still fine. Why didn't I count my lucky stars and start writing this book then? I think in a way I felt like Penelope, who said she'd accept her husband Odysseus's death when she finished weaving a death shroud, but made sure she never finished it. So long as I was still gathering my father's stories, he couldn't die. If I were to start writing the book about him, it would be like writing his obituary, accepting, if not hastening, his death.

MY FATHER DIED MORE than a dozen years ago. The time for this book has come round at last.

*

IT'S 1995. I'M WITH MY FATHER IN THE WESTCHESTER CONDOMINIUM where he and my mother moved when his law practice was thriving, and my two sisters and I had long since moved on. We're in the room he uses as his office; he's telling me about his mother in Poland.

"She always sang," my father says. "My mother loved opera, and she sang arias from the opera. I remember she sang."

My mother comes in. I say, "Want to sit down?"

My father says, "Have a seat."

My mother demurs: "Well, frankly, I mean, I don't want to sit down to, you know, to hear all this garbage."

I laugh.

My father voices her perspective: "You heard it; you've heard it a hundred times."

"Yeah, I heard it. Over and over. That his mother loved opera and all this."

I laugh again.

"Haven't you, Deb?" she asks. "You've heard it."

"Some of it I've heard, some I haven't."

"Oh, well, that's your problem," she says.

My father and I both laugh.

My father says, "You haven't gotten sick of it yet!"

My mother concedes, "I guess if you're writing a book." Then she says, "You know I'd like to ask you a question. Are you planning to spend the rest of the day doing this? All day?"

"The rest of your life," my father offers—a comment that now strikes me as charmingly, or chillingly, prescient.

"Gee," my mother says. "I'll have to think of my biography."

WHY DON'T I CONSIDER writing about my mother's life in addition to my father's—or instead? She, too, was born in Eastern Europe, in Minsk—what's now Belarus. The story of her emigration is far more dramatic than his. Her father and three of her older siblings went first, and immediately began working and saving their earnings to bring the rest of the family to America. Because it was illegal to leave Russia, someone had to be paid to help them escape. The first person they hired took the money and disappeared, so her father and brother had to save up and send more. When my mother was nine, she, her mother, and a sister and two brothers climbed into a horse-drawn wagon to be driven by a Polish farmer through a forest over the border to Poland. It was a perilous journey. Forced to walk much of the way, her mother lost her shoe in the snow; they didn't dare stop to find it, and she suffered frostbite in her toes. It was 1921, the year the United States imposed quotas on East European immigration, so they had to wait in Poland for two years before they got permission to join the rest of the family in America. They finally arrived in September 1923, eight months before the Immigration Act of 1924 made it all but impossible for East European Jews to enter the United States legally.

How much easier was my father's emigration. His mother's oldest brother, who'd been in the United States since 1912, sent her money for the journey. She borrowed more from a colleague of his who was visiting Warsaw, and assured him her brother would pay him back. With the extra money, she bought second-class tickets on a ship from Antwerp, so they wouldn't travel steerage, as my mother did, and would be processed by U.S. immigration in Antwerp rather than being detained at Ellis Island, as my mother and her family were. The extra money also enabled his mother—and therefore her children—to visit her two sisters living in Switzerland and to see a bit of Europe on their way to the port.

I ASK MY MOTHER about her childhood in Europe: her first nine years in Minsk, and the two years her family spent in Vilna before coming to the United States.

"My memories really are mainly after I came to this country," she says. "This is where I grew up, and I was happy, and you know, just with my family. Very unexciting. I was not like your father. You know, I had parents, and brothers, and a sister, and we had a normal family life. Lots of friends and, I mean, we weren't—no hardships, we always had enough to eat, we weren't wealthy. But my father worked, and then my brothers went to work, and then . . ."

Thinking of my father's elaborate descriptions of his life in Warsaw—Friday night dinners, childhood friends and games they played, the apartments he lived in—I try to spark my mother's memories of similar scenes.

"Do you remember mealtimes in Russia?" I ask.

"Mealtimes?"

"Yeah."

"No."

"Do you remember any friends you played with in Russia?"

"Yeah, I remember playing in this backyard, you know, with kids?"

"Do you remember any specific friend you had?"

"No, I don't."

"Do you remember the house, and the layout? Who slept where?"

"Vaguely. I remember a dining room, and a table and chairs."

I press her with more questions about her childhood, but she waves them away: "That's it! We grew up, we came to this country, and went to school. We got married, and we had children and grandchildren. There was nothing really, too much."

I'M NOT PASSING ON stories of my mother's life because she hardly told me any. I'm writing my father's life because he bequeathed his words to me—all the words he wrote and saved; all the letters and documents and cards and notes that he gathered and held on to; all the stories he remembered, wrote down, and told me; and the hours upon hours of conversations we had when he was old, and are still having—are having now—through all the words he left me, as he himself promised and predicted.

*

MY FATHER, IT SEEMS TO ME, KEPT JUST ABOUT EVERY PIECE OF PAPER that came into his life. He must have believed, as James Salter put it, that "only those things preserved in writing have any possibility of being real"—and that they remain real only if you keep the paper they're written on. Discolored, crumbling documents disgorge my father's past: a Polish identity card shows a photograph of him as a child and his Polish name: Szmul Tenenwórcel (pronounced *shmool TENin-voortzil*). His Yiddish name was Schmuel Eliyahu, Samuel Elijah, but he was called Schmul-eli (it sounds like *shmool-ELLie*), Samuel Eli. His names were soon reversed and he became Eli Samuel, so he wouldn't be confused with an uncle who had the same name. In law school he shortened his last name to Tannen because his professors couldn't pronounce Tenenwórcel.

When I mine the cardboard boxes filled with documents, letters, cards, and notes that my father saved, along with the many pages of memories he wrote down for me and my own notes and transcripts of our conversations, I get a sense of how things I remembered came about and fit together; how things I knew little or nothing about fit in; and what it all meant for my father's life—both how he lived it, day to day, and how he viewed it, looking back. I see sides of him I couldn't have known and wouldn't have imagined. Some make me admire him more—but not all. Inevitably, my view of my father, and of the ways he influenced me, gradually changes. That view is changed most drastically by two stashes of written pages that my father saved—and hid—for sixty-five or more years, then gave to me.

∗

ONCE AGAIN I'M WITH MY FATHER IN MY PARENTS' WESTCHESTER condo.

"I guess I don't have them anymore," he says, referring to letters he received more than half a century before from the woman he might have married instead of my mother. "I saved them," he says, "but now I don't know where they are."

We all have alternate lives we might have lived had we made different decisions, including decisions about whom to marry. I suspect my parents are unusual only in how openly and casually they talk about Helen, my mother's "rival," especially when they're old. My father mentions her often in our many conversations about his past. Learning that he kept her letters is enticing: if I could read them, I would get to meet her, hear her voice—and feed my fantasies about the alternate life in which my father marries Helen* instead of my mother.

One day, while I'm again visiting my parents, my father says he's going down to the basement storage room. I offer to go with him. Once we're there, after he locates whatever he went down for, I suggest we look for Helen's letters. He readily agrees. We go through the shelves one by one, checking every bag and cardboard box; it doesn't take too long, because he's labeled everything. Disappointed, I reach for the last box. It's on a high shelf, far to the right, flush against the back wall. I pull the carton away from the wall—and hear a plop. Something was wedged between the box and the wall. Reaching be-

---

* Helen is not her real name. I have changed her name and the name of a friend she mentions in a letter.

hind the box, I pull out a bulky brown manila envelope, its sides creased and torn. Inside is a stack of envelopes addressed to Eli Tannen in a woman's neat hand. There is also a stack of unfolded typed pages clipped together, signed "Eli." I have found not only Helen's letters but also—a treasure I hadn't dreamed of—copies of letters my father wrote to her.

I clutch the envelope to my chest and jump up and down with excitement. My father smiles with calm amusement.

"Take them," he says. "I'd like to look at them someday."

We both assume we won't tell my mother about these letters. We're protecting her not from the letters themselves but from the fact that he kept them, and kept them hidden, for so many years, through so many moves—at least fifteen by my count.

*

ANOTHER DAY, ANOTHER CONVERSATION WITH MY FATHER. HE'S SITTING in his desk chair, which he's wheeled around to face me, telling me about his life. At one point, he swivels his chair toward the desk, and pulls open the large drawer to the right that holds file folders. He lifts out two notebooks, turns back to me, and holds them up. "These are journals I kept when I was young," he says. Then he hands me one: "You can have this one now." It has a soft mottled-brown cover, and is bound by a narrow strip of black cloth. Its pages are discolored, but its cover, with the word COMPOSITIONS preprinted in an ornate framed square, looks surprisingly new. He returns the other to the drawer and says, "You can have this one after I'm gone. It'll be here."

I've always kept journals, but I had no idea that my father did, too. I'm stunned to realize that he has handed me a window on his life, his thoughts, his feelings when he was young. I'm particularly intrigued by the journal he returns to the drawer: what's in it that he wants to keep from me? Before he dies, he gives me that one, too. These journals are the most precious documents my father leaves me: one that he kept from 1927 to 1928, when he was eighteen and a half to twenty; the other from 1929 to 1931, when he was twenty-one to twenty-three. Reading and rereading them, I get to meet my father before he was my father; hear his voice; and learn things about him that a daughter would never know about her father—including some I suspect many daughters wouldn't want to know. But I want to know everything. By giving me his journals, he's telling me that he wants me to know everything, too. Because he knows I'll write a book about him, he's giving me leave to include in this book the words—the views of him, whether favorable or faultable—that I find there. And that is what I do.

★

I MENTION TO A COUSIN—HIS FATHER WAS MY MOTHER'S BROTHER— that I'm writing a book about my father. He says, "Your father was one in a million. No, one in a billion." I ask him why. He explains, "Each of my parents had seven siblings, and your father stood out from all of them. He was by far the tallest, the biggest. I thought of him as a gentle giant. He was strong and determined, yet soft and compassionate. I took his intelligence for granted. It was his wisdom that stood out. He espoused very liberal ideas, but without any hostility to those who disagreed with him. He was a loving optimist. And he had so much charm."

I'm pleased by this reassurance: I'm not the only one who thinks my father was special.

★

THE NIGHT BEFORE I START WRITING THIS BOOK MY FATHER VISITS me in a dream. I've dreamed of him many times since he died, but this is different. It doesn't feel like a dream. It feels like a visit.

My father and I are sitting in a car. He's in the driver's seat; the car is stopped. I'm about to get out, but I linger. Deeply happy to be in his company, in his physical presence, I take his hand. It's the thin hand of his old age, but I notice how warm it is. "You're the best daddy in the world," I say, "except that you're dead."

When I wake up, I don't feel the desolation that usually sweeps over me when I awake from dreams my father has been in. Instead, I'm overwhelmed with gratitude to have been in his presence one more time. It feels as if, by visiting me in the dream, my father is setting me on the path of writing this book, saying to me, "Ready or not, here I come." But of course it's really me saying that to him.

Daddy Young and Old

M Y CHILDHOOD, IN MY MIND, IS AN ENDLESS TRAIN OF DAYS spent with my mother, missing my father. My father is a series of snapshots that I carry with me wherever I go.

I take out snapshots, one by one, and savor them.

DADDY LEAVES FOR WORK before I wake up in the morning, and often gets home after I've gone to bed. He works overtime as a cutter in a coat factory: extra hours on weekdays and all day Saturday. He spends most Sundays in the Brownsville–East New York neighborhood of Brooklyn, at the Liberal Party branch he's "active" in.

DADDY TRAVELS TO AND FROM work in Manhattan by subway. The station is a twenty-minute walk from our house on East Ninth Street in Brooklyn. On his way to work, he eats breakfast at the counter of the candy store on Coney Island Avenue. It's the store where I buy whatever the neighborhood kids are playing with that season: hula hoops or yo-yos or slinky balloons or brightly colored plastic-coated strings we weave into lanyards. When I'm in the store, I regard with awe the round counter stools, their seats upholstered in red leather with silver chrome encircling their sides, because Daddy sat on one of them that morning, eating fried eggs, toast, and bacon.

———

IF IT'S ONE OF the lucky days when he's coming home in time for dinner, my sister Mimi and I wait outside for Daddy to appear. As soon as we spot him, we run to him. He scoops us up, first one then the other, lifts us high off the ground, and engulfs us in a hug before gently setting us down to walk the last half block with a little girl fastened to each hand. I love the hard rough skin of his huge callused hand, a big safe house around my little one. At six feet, Daddy seems to me nearly as tall as the Empire State Building.

DADDY'S HEIGHT AND HIS CALM are comforting. His genius for order creates an aura of safety that clings to his places and possessions. One is his dresser, which he calls his chest of drawers. In the top drawer, he placed dividers so his socks are snugly nestled in front-to-back rows of compact little lumps sorted by color. Another is the drop-leaf desk he built himself. Its shelves and compartments are just the right sizes for what they hold: one wide compartment each for white paper, carbon paper, and Liberal Party letterhead; two narrower ones for the notepaper he creates by tearing into thirds any scrap paper that's printed on one side only; and tiny compartments for paper clips, thumbtacks, and rubber bands sorted by size.

THE CELLAR IS WHERE Daddy builds things. On one wall, tools hang in neat rows. Another wall is covered with narrow shelves on which baby food jars hold nails and screws in order of size. In a small adjoining room, there's a toilet he can use without risk of running into one of the five females who use the upstairs bathroom: my mother; her mother, Babi, who lives with us; and his three daughters: my eight-years-older sister Naomi; my two-years-older sister Mimi; and me.

I'M SITTING ON THE STEPS going down to the cellar, watching Daddy working.

"Don't you want to go outside and play?" he asks.

I don't. I want to be where he is.

———

IT'S A LUCKY DAY: Daddy got home before Mimi's and my bedtime, and he's tucking us into our side-by-side beds. My blanket is a jumble, so he stands at the foot of my bed, takes the blanket by two corners, spreads it between the enormous expanse of his outstretched arms, and gives it a great shake, so it billows in the air and comes to rest over me, smooth and comforting. Mimi and I beg him to tell us a "story with actions," one of the many he makes up himself. Daddy moves about the room, becoming each character as the story unfolds: A fire-breathing dragon threatens a town. A policeman, confident and brash with his puffed-out chest, confronts the dragon and threatens, "I'm going to kill you!" The dragon breathes fire, and the policeman runs away. The same ignominious fate meets the mayor and a succession of other big strong men. Mimi and I shriek with delight each time Daddy-the-dragon rushes at us, breathing mock fire in our upturned, laughing faces. Finally, Daddy mimes the movements of two little girls who take a different tack: instead of marching up to the dragon and challenging him, they take the long walk to the end of its tail, then tiptoe delicately along its back to slay the dragon from atop its head. The town organizes a parade to celebrate their saviors: two little girls, Mimi and Debby.

The story over, Daddy lies down with us, each in turn; with my head on his shoulder, I snuggle up to him and quickly fall asleep.

DADDY IS WORKING AT his desk on the second floor of our house. I approach him there and stand beside the desk. Absorbed in his writing, he doesn't notice me. To get his attention, I lift my plastic water gun and squirt him in the face. He erupts with a great shudder of fright, and roars like a tiger. I dart out of the room and down the stairs to the first landing, where I stop, ready to run the rest of the way down if he's angry at me. I'm scared because I've never before seen him angry. He appears at the top of the stairs, spreads his arms wide, and laughs; his laugh and his outspread arms invite me to run back up the stairs and into his huge hug. With his hug and his laugh reassuring, he apologizes for scaring me.

——

I HAVE A SPLINTER in my finger. If I give my finger over to my mother, she'll jab at it with a straight pin; it will hurt, and I don't trust her to get it all out. I insist on leaving the splinter in place until Daddy gets home. When Daddy takes out a splinter, he first sets up an operating table: he lays out alcohol, matches, pin, a razor blade, and tweezers. To begin, he strikes a match, holds the point of the pin to the flame, then wipes both pin and razor blade with alcohol. Next he turns to the operation. Using the razor blade, he carefully, painstakingly, shaves off thin layers of skin. The razor blade is a dangerous instrument only he can be trusted to wield. When the splinter is exposed, he loosens it with the pin, then lifts it out with the tweezers. It never hurts.

THE WAYS THEY REMOVE splinters capture, for me, my parents' ways of doing things: my father's measured and methodical, my mother's haphazard and impetuous. If a venetian blind cord fails to work, my mother yanks and swings it, hoping one of these movements will fix the problem. My father looks to the top of the cord to see where it came loose, then carefully maneuvers it back in place so it's reengaged. As a child, I feel that my father's approach isn't just more efficient but morally superior. When I'm grown, I frequently catch myself using my mother's approach; I remind myself to slow down and try my father's.

I'M SEVEN; MIMI IS NINE. One day we get home from school and find only Aunt Eva, my mother's sister, waiting for us. She tells us that Babi had a heart attack and our mother went with her to the hospital. Aunt Eva assures us that Babi will be fine. I don't believe her. I suspect—I know—that Babi died.

I'm standing in the street outside our house, beside my father's black Buick with its three chrome notches on the side fender. I'm watching the neighborhood kids, incredulous that they're playing as usual after such a dreadful thing happened. But it isn't only the loss of my grandmother that's shaken me. It's the fact of death: that I could go blithely off to school in the morning and return to find a person gone—

vanished, poof. If it could happen to my grandmother, it could happen to my father. He could go to work one morning and never come home. Part of the dread this knowledge brings is a fear I know is trivial, but haunts me nonetheless: when my teacher tells the class to look something up, I ask my father. He knows everything. If he dies, I'll have to look things up in books like everyone else.

SOMETIMES DADDY DOES LIBERAL PARTY work at home, and lets Mimi and me help. I love stuffing envelopes for political mailings. He's taught us to line up the flaps of multiple envelopes, moisten them all with a single swipe of a wet sponge, and quickly seal them one by one. He also takes us with him to distribute leaflets. In apartment buildings, we stand before the banks of mail compartments, and press a folded leaflet through the slot in each one. I love going with him on these missions, because they're important—and because it means spending the day with him.

IT'S 1956. I'M ELEVEN. Daddy is running for Congress on the Liberal Party ticket. I go with him to Coney Island, where he stands on the back of a flatbed truck to address a group of people who have gathered to listen. I stand beside an old woman wearing a worn coat over her housedress. She pulls from her pocket a small, tattered photograph of Franklin Roosevelt. She tells me proudly that she voted for him every time he ran. I tell her proudly that this man running for office is my father.

*

WHILE I'M AT COLLEGE, MY PARENTS SELL THE HOUSE I GREW UP IN and rent an apartment facing Prospect Park. I'm home on a break. Careless and chaotic, I'm always misplacing my things. But I always know where to find my father's possessions. This time I have taken his nail file, which he keeps at the front edge of the second shelf in his drop-leaf desk, to the right. It's a dependable metal file, slightly bent; he's had it, and kept it there, all my life. My father appears in the doorway of the room I'm staying in; he confronts me, not in anger, but in quiet exasperation. He doesn't chastise me, but simply asks where his nail file is. I feel found out. I don't remember where I left it. My father looms in the doorway like an implacable judgment. I am guilty. But I know he'll forgive me.

SEVERAL YEARS LATER, my parents buy a condominium in Westchester, a suburb north of New York City. It's the 1990s; in the room my father uses as his office, I'm interviewing him about his past. My mother comes in. She's frustrated because she can't find her keys. My father suggests she look in the pockets of the "garments" she wore in the last few days. He explains how he avoids misplacing his keys—or anything else he keeps in his pockets: "I have to have eight things. And I always count. Morning, evening, I always count. Two keys. My wallet. Handkerchief. Change purse. My watch, hearing aid, and glasses. Eight things. If I don't have eight things, I figure out what's missing, and I get it right away."

Hearing him say this, I see my father standing by the dresser in his bedroom as he prepares to go to work, taking items from the large marble ashtray where he put them the night before, and distributing them in pockets of his suit jacket and slacks. I now fill in that memory with the specific things he's picking up and placing, and hear him counting them in his mind.

AFTER MY FATHER RETIRES, my parents begin spending winters in Boynton Beach, Florida. Their small, sun-filled Florida apartment was never home to me, and the furnishings are not the ones I grew up with. But the order my father created in these scaled-down rooms makes me feel like I've come home. In my own coat closet, the shelf over the hanging coats holds a jumbled mass of hats, scarves, gloves, and small umbrellas. In my parents' coat closet, the shelf contains neatly folded scarves. My father's hats are arrayed on the wall above, each hanging from a nail he hammered in. My father's desk in Florida, painted a glossy white, is built in against a wall. He's added plastic trays with tiny compartments that hold tacks, safety pins, paper clips, and rubber bands—all ordered by size. Three identical dispensers, perfectly aligned, hold three different types of tape. On each dispenser, a small square of paper identifies the width and type of tape it holds.

———

FROM THE TIME I go off to college until my mother dies, four decades later—except for the two years I live in Greece—I call my parents often. Though I call my parents, my mother is the one I talk to. She almost always answers the phone, but even if my father answers, he cedes telephone conversations to her.

I'VE CALLED MY PARENTS, as I do each week. This time my father answers. Hearing his voice, I feel a lightness in the air, a giddiness. As soon as he recognizes my voice, he says, "I'll tell Mother you're on the phone. She'll be so happy to hear it's you." He calls to her, she picks up an extension, and we begin talking. Before long I realize I haven't heard my father's voice for a while.

"Where's Daddy?" I ask.

"He hung up."

ANOTHER TIME, I'M HAVING a phone conversation with both parents. When the conversation winds down, my mother hangs up. My father doesn't. We realize it's just the two of us on the phone. "Oh," he says, "I have a chance to talk to you. There are so many things I want to say. I can't think of them now." We find lots of things to say, and enjoy saying them till my mother picks up an extension: "Are you still on the phone?" she says. It sounds like an accusation. I feel as if my father and I have been caught in an illicit encounter. I assure her of our innocence: "We were just talking about . . ." My father disappears without a word, as if slinking away.

MY FATHER WILL TALK to me at length if I happen to call when my mother is out. One day I ask him why. "Maybe because it's pent-up words," he says. "I like to reminisce. I can't reminisce with Mother because she doesn't like it. She complains, 'You only want to talk about people who are dead.' Sometimes she makes a rule: No talk about dead people! She's like most people. They like to talk about things that are happening. They don't like to talk about old things. To me it's not real unless it's in the past." My father never tires of talking about the past, especially his childhood in Poland, and I never tire of listening.

IT'S 1996; MY FATHER is eighty-eight. I arrive for a visit at their Westchester condo. My mother greets me at the door. After we've hugged and kissed, my father appears at the end of the hallway. It's taken him longer to rise from his chair. He isn't carrying the cane he finally agreed to use after his last fall. He stumbles, but the wall catches him. Something inside me rebels: who stole my father and put this old man in his place?

A FEW MONTHS LATER, I'm visiting my parents in Florida. My father is recuperating from emergency bypass surgery on his leg. I walk beside him on the catwalk that runs from their apartment to the elevator along the outer wall of their building. How strange life is to bring things round to this: my father, who never walked up stairs but sent them flying behind him two at a time, now inching along. I'm grateful to time for having slowed him down. My father old has time for me as my father young did not. The skin of his hand is hard, as it was when I was little, only now the roughness is from not calluses, but age: the skin dried, the muscle between thumb and palm shrunk concave. Though my hand is almost as big as his, holding his hand gives me the same sense of comfort that it did when I was small: if I hold my father's hand, he can't run away, recede, or disappear. But there's another layer: I fear that if I let go, my father will fall, as he does in my bad dreams, thudding to the ground. So I firmly hold his hand, hold him in my hand.

WHEN MY FATHER AND I sit and talk, I forget he's old. But when he inches along beside me; when he stumbles on firm ground; when he tries to rise from his chair and the chair pulls him back, I'm reminded with a jolt that the man who looks to me like my father, to the world looks like an old man.

MY PARENTS MOVE PERMANENTLY to Florida. My father, in his early nineties, is in the hospital there, following emergency surgery. He had septicemia for days, with a fever of 103, caused by an infected gallbladder that his doctor misdiagnosed as gastritis. The hospital hematologist is incredulous that my father survived; septicemia, the doctor says, unchecked for so many days, would likely have killed even someone much younger. I walk with my father down the hospital hall, accompanied by the IV pole on wheels. When we come to an alcove with chairs, we sit and continue the conversation we've been having all afternoon. Though it breaks my heart to see him so weak, I treasure the hours—the days—that the hospital gives us to talk.

MY FATHER GRADUATES FROM a cane to a walker. The walker makes him seem younger, because with it he moves quickly and surely. Without it he takes halting, tentative steps. Yet I hate the walker because it hogs my father's hands: I can no longer hold his hand as we walk, and he can no longer greet me with his arms spread wide, can't wrap me in his hug.

I'M WALKING WITH MY FATHER, his hands on his walker. I keep him on my left, because I hear better in my left ear. He tells me he's breaking a private rule he's observed his whole life: with people on his left, he keeps the upper hand. If he lets someone walk to his right, he yields power to them. I understand this private way of ordering the world as a facet of his personality related to his drive to save everything—and to organize and label all that he saves. I hear his telling me this as trust, confirming and creating closeness by sharing something so intimate. And I interpret as love that he lets me walk on his right. I hold his trust and love in my palm, where his hand would be if it wasn't grasping the walker. As I tell this story now, I wonder: was he asking me, gently, to please move to his left?

MY FATHER OFTEN MAKES requests in that indirect way because he's reluctant to impose. Once, when I'm driving my parents home from a family gathering in upstate New York, my father asks if I have enough gas in the car. I assure him I do, pleased to allay his concern about whether I've thought ahead. But that's not why he asked. After a brief pause, he says, "If you were going to stop for gas anyway, I'd use the restroom."

MY FATHER ALSO SHRINKS from being the center of attention. This reticence extends to the physical mishaps that come with old age. My husband and I are visiting my parents in the Florida retirement community they've recently moved to. The four of us pay a visit to another couple they've befriended. As the couple are showing us their dining room, my father says he'll wait for us in the adjoining living room. Suddenly I see my husband running toward the living room: my father's legs are dangling over the edge of a large upholstered chair, his knees pointing to the ceiling. The rest of him is lying on the floor against the back of the chair, which tipped over when he plopped into it. My husband and I manage to right the chair, with my father in it, seemingly untroubled. "Why didn't you say something?" one person after another exclaims. My father says, "There was no need to interrupt your conversation. I knew someone would notice eventually."

WHEN MY MOTHER DIES, my father, ninety-five, moves to an assisted living apartment in Saratoga Springs, New York, to be close to my sister Naomi, who is retired herself. We now have hours and hours and hours to talk, as I call every day and visit often.

I'm talking to my father on the phone; he's lying on his bed. He thinks of something he wants to tell me, but the paper it's written on is on his desk, across the room. "I'll get it," he says.

"That's okay," I say, "I don't need to know now." The thought of him rushing to his desk—I know he'll rush so as not to keep me waiting—frightens me. He's so unsteady, and he never locks his walker before lunging for it, never makes sure that a chair is stable before plopping into it.

"It's no problem," he says. "I'll get it and I'll call you back from there."

I can't talk him out of it, so I caution: "Be careful! Don't rush!"

I await his call, my anxiety rising. The phone doesn't ring. Maybe he's looking for the paper, or having trouble finding his glasses. Still I wait. Finally, I dial his number. The phone rings and rings. At last he answers.

"Daddy!" I say. "Where are you?"

In an unruffled voice, he says, "Lying on the floor under my desk."

"Are you hurt? Are you okay?"

"I'm fine," he says. "I slipped off the chair when I sat down."

Damn chair! I think. I told him he shouldn't have a chair on wheels!

"I'll call the office," I say. "They'll send someone to help you up."

"Don't call! Don't bother them. They have plenty to do. They're busy."

"But you need help to get up! I'm going to call!"

We argue back and forth—"Don't call!" "I'm calling!" Finally he relents, but says, "Make sure you tell them it's not an emergency. They can come when they have time. I'm fine."

DURING OUR MANY CONVERSATIONS—the ones we have on the phone and the ones we have when I visit—I write down things my father says. I'm not the only one who does this. One of the assisted living aides tells me that she keeps a computer file titled "Eli-isms."

"How do you feel today?" I ask.

"With my hands, like always."

I ask if his arthritis hurts.

"I don't believe in pain," he says. "Who needs it."

"Daddy," I say, "you never complain."

"I tried complaining once. It didn't help."

"I can't believe I'm sixty years old," I say.

He says, "Were you surprised to turn sixty at such a young age?"

"Daddy," I say, "you're so witty."

"My friends would say I'm dimwitty."

There's a small table outside the dining room with a flower in a vase and the names of residents who recently died. Passing this table on his way to dinner, my father says, "Look to see if my name is there. If it's not, I guess I'm still alive."

"How old am I?" he asks.
   "Ninety-seven."
   "Ninety-seven? That's ridiculous! What's a ninety-seven-year-old man doing walking around?"

A few months after his ninety-seventh birthday, he says, "I didn't expect to be here."
   "Are you glad to be here?"
   "Yes. I wouldn't have much appetite if I were dead."

I begin my daily phone call by asking, as I learned from him to ask: "What am I interrupting?"
   "Nothing," he says. "I'm lying down."

It worries me that he says this so often when I call.
   "I keep busy," he reassures me. "I study the ceiling."
   "That's not enough!" I object.
   "It's not the only thing I do," he says. "Sometimes I get up and look at the floor."

"You can't lie in bed all day!" I say.
   "I lie in bed because the floor is too hard."
   Another time he says: "So if I die, I'll be in position."
   And yet another: "I'm practicing. I'm going to be lying underground for a long time."

I arrive for a visit. My father is delighted to see me—and surprised.
   "But I've been telling you every day when we talk—I'll be there in six days, I'll be there in five days, I'll be there in four days—right up to yesterday!"
   "No wonder I forgot," he says. "You keep changing it."

"Dealing with memory loss must be strange," I say.

"Yes, it is strange," he says. "But it's better to be alive and not remember than to remember and not be alive."

"How are you feeling?" I ask.

"I always feel well," he says. "I can guarantee I'll feel well for the next thirty years. Twenty-nine of them may be under the ground."

As we eat pizza at a restaurant, my father says, "I expect one morning to wake up and find myself dead, and I wouldn't mind. I wasn't alive before I was born, and I didn't mind at all."

"I'll take some wonderful memories with me," he says.

I say, "You'll leave some here with me, too."

My father and I are talking about how long he's lived, and then about how long I'm going to live—and how I'll like living that long.

"I don't know," I say. "I guess I won't know till it happens."

"I'll have to talk to you from upstairs," he says. "I'll be watching over you from up there."

CHAPTER

THREE

A Man of Words

My father is telling me about his childhood in Warsaw. Talking about his aunt Ruchcia (her name sounds like *ROOK-cha, with the vowel in "spook"*), he mentions a Yiddish expression, *Chas VeChalila,* which, he explains, is used more or less the way we might say "Heaven forbid." "Only she said *Chalila veChas,*" he tells me. "I remember because she was the only one who said it that way." Ruchcia died when my father was ten, yet he noticed—and recalls nearly ninety years later—this slight difference in how she uttered a common phrase.

My father is a man of words. His attention to them, their nuances, is a sensibility that connects him to me. It was from him that I learned to always have a dictionary nearby, and to look up any word whose meaning or pronunciation I'm not sure of. Now the dictionary resides, like so much else, in my phone. I appreciate the convenience, but I miss the walk across the room, the anticipation of grasping the dictionary's whisper-thin pages, first in thick wads, then a few at a time, till, turning a single last page, I close in on the word. When I walked across a room to the dictionary, my father was by my side. Tapping a word on a screen, I'm on my own.

When my father is eighty-three, I hire a woman who interviews older people about their past. Encouraging my father to talk about his grandfather, she asks, "How do you like to remember him?" He re-

sponds, "Like it or not, I remember . . ." I delight in the way he cali-
brates his reply to the wording of her question—and subtly corrects it.

IT WAS ALSO FROM my father that I learned to listen for unspoken
meanings in people's conversation. When I was a child, and the family
gathered after guests left, my father would comment, "Did you notice
when she said . . . ?" and go on to explain what meaning he gleaned
from the guest's tone of voice, intonation, or wording. So I trace to
him what became my life's work: observing and explaining how subtle
differences in ways of speaking can lead to frustration and misunder-
standings between New Yorkers and Californians, women and men,
and people of different ages, regions, or cultures.

MY FATHER SPEAKS POLISH, Yiddish, and English and reads Hebrew,
but his native language is writing.

I'M TALKING ON THE PHONE to my parents in Florida. They tell me
that a distant relative paid them a surprise visit.
    "Did you enjoy the visit?" I ask.
    My father replies, "Did you say 'enjoy'? That word does not belong
alongside his name under any circumstances."
    My mother adds, "Your father likes relatives to write letters to, not
to spend time with." We all laugh, because she has his number.

AFTER HE RETIRES, my father writes long letters to relatives, friends,
and the grown daughters—yes, they're all daughters—of relatives and
friends who have passed away. These women seek my father out to
learn about their own fathers, who never talked about their pasts. After
my father answers their questions, some continue the correspondence.
I have many bulging folders with letters my father got in return, and
letters—or copies of letters—he wrote, that his correspondents sent
me after he died.

IT'S 1993. I'M SITTING in my parents' Westchester living room, my
mother beside me on the couch, my father in an adjacent upholstered
chair. I'm reading aloud a play I've written, based on a trip to Poland

that my husband and I took with my parents several months before. The play interweaves my father's memories of his childhood in Poland and my memories of my childhood with him. When I finish reading, my mother is weeping. She hugs me, and tells me that the play is wonderful—and I am, too. My father starts talking about something else. I'm crushed. I've written a play about his life, full of his words, and he doesn't seem to care. The next day he hands me a letter in which he tells me how moved he was, and explains that he changed the subject because he didn't want to show his emotion. I'm sure he means he was afraid he'd cry. Wanting to write his feelings rather than speak them shows how strongly he feels about—and how deeply he appreciates—my putting his stories of his childhood into a play.

THIS LETTER IS ONE of many that my father writes to me from the time I leave for college. After he retires, the letters increase exponentially in number and length. When he's eighty, I help him buy a computer, and he begins sending emails in addition to the letters he writes on paper. The emails begin "Darlin'," "Dearest," "Doll," or "Dearest Darlin'." At ninety-one, responding to an essay I wrote about him, he writes:

> Precious little Deborah, You glorify me beyond my worth. You paint your father in splendid colors and describe him in far more complimentary fashion than he deserves. I can never live up to the picture you paint of me and I don't recognize myself in it, much as I may enjoy it. I thank the gods for giving me such a brilliant and beautiful daughter and blinding her to my faults and limitations. For all this, I thank you and God both. Your loving, devoted, admiring, worshipping dad.

And I thank God and my father for his effusiveness, his love, and his inclination and ability to put them in writing so I can hear his words today—and keep them in mind as I write this book, opening my eyes to the faults and limitations I didn't always see when he was alive, and putting into words some of those that I did see, but left out of that essay.

———

WRITING LETTERS FIGURES IN many of the stories my father tells from his past.

We're sitting in the Westchester condominium. My father is telling me of his grievances against Norman, my mother's rough-hewn brother, who, two weeks after arriving in the United States with his family, went to work at the same coat factory where my father was already working full-time. They were the same age—fourteen—and quickly became friends. (That's how my parents met: Norman brought his new friend home, and introduced him to his brothers and sisters, including the youngest, the twelve-year-old sister my father would marry a decade later.)

"If I talk to him," my father says of Norman, "I don't talk to him personally, because I'm angry with him, all my life."

"Now, too?" I ask.

"Always. And I cover it up, and I do him favors he asks me. He doesn't know that I'm angry. I think there should be a record of it, because I'll never tell him."

Laughing, I promise to comply: "Let's get it on the record." I'm keeping my promise by writing this now.

"One time we were still friends," my father goes on, "and he asked me to go someplace, see him or something. And I said I can't, I have to take my mother someplace. So he opened up a big mouth on me. 'What do you mean that bullshit with your mother? You don't have to go with your mother! I'm asking you to do this and we're friends.' He gave me a whole business. I was very offended."

"I hope you didn't listen to him," I say.

"No, I wrote him a letter: 'I'm finished with you.'" Then my father laughs. "I wrote him a long letter showing him how wrong he is. So what did he do? He comes with the letter, unopened, to the house, and brings me the letter. So he didn't read anything I told him. 'What are you mad about this? Let's be friends.' I said, 'I told you. We're finished.' He talked me out of it. But the funny part of it is later I found out that he did open the letter, and he did read it. And he reseals it! He didn't want to answer because he knew he was wrong. He couldn't defend himself; he couldn't say he was right."

Norman won the argument because he refused to fight on the turf where my father could win: the written page.

ONE OF MY EARLIEST BOOKS is a collection of academic essays I edited that I titled *Spoken and Written Language: Exploring Orality and Literacy*. I dedicated it "To my mother and father, who introduced me to orality and literacy respectively." When I wrote this, I was thinking of my mother's ease in social conversation and my father's ease with writing.

I began writing poems, stories, and letters when I was very young.

```
                                                        Jan. 1o, 1953


        Dear Father,

        I am being bad lately, mowt of my resens are becaus Iam
        Unhappy.  I am not sqying that I feel sorry for myself, for I
        know that there are mush les forshanet children then I am.
        I am just saying that your wife, and my mother are treating me pretty
        bad I think.  As I said I think, but I guess it is probably good
        for me, after all, I never forget, Mother Knows Best.
        You will be angry to when you hear what I did.
        So I will skep the rest of things I was going to say,
        I will get to the part.
        Now I can tell you what I did.
        I did not go to school today, becaus I did not like the way my hair
        lookst.  Of course your wife and my mother gave me a betting
        Oh! oh! Yes! I have a quesyion to ask you.
        Did you join another Club?
        I hope you did not, for I think you have anov
        on your mind.  And I also think you have anof to do.
        Again I think you have anof metings to go to
        being the sakara-tary of the Lebrel Party in East N. Y.
        being the Chirmen of your shap.
        And being a member of the Unoin.
        I wrote a pretty long letter, I am prabably useing your very
        valuble time.
        I won'nt use any more of it.

                                Good-by
                                Lovey-Dovey Eli



        Love
        Debby
```

Letter I typed to my father when I was seven

Long before I could spell properly, I typed letters to my father and other relatives. Here's one I wrote when I was seven. (I don't know what I had in mind when I wrote that my mother "gave me a betting." Neither of my parents ever hit me.)

It was always obvious that my inclination to write traced to my father. When I realized, to my surprise, that as an adult I also found it easy to talk to people, I assumed that came from my mother. She was unself-conscious, comfortable talking to anyone. I still smile to recall a scene from one of my first television appearances. In 1990 I was a guest on Phil Donahue's television talk show, and my parents were in the audience. After the show, Donahue came backstage to thank me, and I introduced him to my parents. My father courteously shook his hand, but my mother grasped both his hands in both of hers, looked up at him—she was under five two; he was six feet—and began telling him how often she watched and how much she enjoyed his show. Whenever she attended talks I gave and I opened the floor to questions, my mother's hand would be among the first to go up. My father would never say anything before a roomful of strangers without first thinking through what he would say and how he would say it. Yet claiming—as I do in the dedication to my book—that my mother introduced me to orality isn't quite right. My father was full of words in private conversation, too.

THE WOMAN I HIRED who interviewed older people about their past spoke to both my parents. My mother's interview takes two and a half cassettes. My father's fills six; it's nine hours long. Later, I ask him if he feels he left anything out. "Yes," he replies, "my whole life."

I'M YOUNG—PROBABLY TEN or eleven. It's late at night; I'm with my family in a car, on our way home from a trip. My father is driving; my mother is beside him; Mimi and I are in the backseat. Mimi is asleep; I'm talking to my father. My mother tells me that she is going to sleep, too, so I should keep my father talking, to make sure he stays awake. This will be easy, I think. I'm always happy to talk to my father. But then I start to feel sleepy. I struggle against it. My father tells me I needn't fight sleep; there's no chance he won't stay awake. But the responsibility to keep my family safe weighs heavily on me—the responsibility to keep talking to my father.

HAVING LONG, SERIOUS TALKS was something I shared with my father from the start. I know this from the notes my mother wrote—and my father saved—when I was seven and had what I'd now call a panic attack, soon after my grandmother died. Both my parents wrote notes about the incident, probably thinking of the social worker they would take me to afterward. My mother wrote, "Husband has academic, analytical mind. Goes into long explanations with her." Clearly she thought my father's long analytical explanations were inappropriate for a child, maybe even contributed to my distress. I'm grateful to her for letting me know, through these notes, that my father had such conversations with me—and to him for having them. I especially treasure the words "academic" and "analytical." They tell me that my life as a linguistics professor, so distant from both my parents' lives, so different from any life they wanted or could have imagined for me—my mother's only concern was that I marry; my father thought I should be a teacher because teachers get summers off, and their workdays end at three—may have grown from a seed my father planted.

REFLECTING HIS ACADEMIC, analytical mind, my father often views and discusses his circumstances with philosophical distance. When he's old, he talks often about aging and death, as he does in another email that he writes to me when he's ninety-one:

> Re my forthcoming demise: Overall I'm against it. Why not live forever. Other times I feel too much is enough. . . . When we meet we can explore it further. I am not sensitive about it at all. I am conscious I am living on borrowed time.

I share this sensibility, and draw on it in our conversations. When my father is ninety-four, after we've been talking on the phone for nearly an hour, he asks, "How can you spare the time to talk to me?"

"I love to talk to you," I say. "I'm going to miss you so much when you're gone, I won't be able to stand it."

My father and I laughing together when he's ninety-seven

"I'll just be a memory," he says. "There are so many people who were so real to me in their lives, and now they're just memories."

NOT LONG AFTER, I'm in the midst of a long, laughter-filled telephone conversation with both parents. I burst out with the same comment I made to my father: "I'm going to miss you both so much when you're gone!" My mother shrieks, "WHAT KIND OF THING IS THAT TO SAY?" I tell her that it's "counterphobic," a word I wouldn't use if I were speaking only to her. Sure enough, she responds, "WHAT?" I explain that "counterphobic" means "against fear. It's a way of warding off what you're afraid of, trying to make sure it doesn't happen."

"Well no one lives forever," she says, "but why talk about it? We're here now."

"Your sister lived to a hundred and two," I say. "Why not you?"

"It's not likely," she says.

"Well, I want you to," I say.

"You won't want me around when I'm old and decrepit."

My father chimes in: "You're old and decrepit now."

"What about you?" she fires back. "You can't walk without that pushcart. I can!"

The word "pushcart" sets us all laughing again.

I love the way my parents tease each other and laugh together, and with me. But the conversation reminds me how differently I talk to each of them, and how uncomfortable my mother is with the counter-phobic talk of death that my father and I find comfort in—and how annoyed she is by words like "counterphobic." I think it's because of my parents' so-different relationship to words that I feel comfortable talking to other academics and writing articles and books for scholars—and just as comfortable talking and writing about the same ideas in everyday language for everyone else.

MY FATHER IS NINETY-SEVEN, in the assisted living facility that he moved to after my mother died. I hire a college student named Ryan to interview him about his life and record their conversations for me—but really to visit and talk to him. In one of their conversations, Ryan asks my father how he met his wife. My father replies, "I would say I first took her out when she was seventeen. She liked me because I talked a lot. If a girl likes you, you're in trouble. She was the only woman I knew carnally."

"That was her name?" Ryan asks. "Carly?"

Ryan is tripped up by the same linguistic habit—using big words—that my parents often said had attracted my mother, but, when they're older, makes her angry.

What my father said wasn't true, but that's another story—one I'll tell later.

I'M A CHILD, SITTING in the back seat of our family car beside my mother and her friend Thelma. Thelma's husband is in the front seat with my father, who is driving. Something my father says prompts Thelma to remark that Eli talks like a book. I realize she's right: my father uses words in conversation that others don't—words he knows from reading.

———

MY FATHER'S BOOKISH VOCABULARY is obvious to others even when
he's young. He recalls a conversation that took place in the factory
where he went to work when he quit high school at fourteen: "Not
long after I started working there, one of the owners took a trip to
Europe for his summer vacation and was telling a group of us at the
end of a day following his return all about the wonders of his trip. He
used the word 'utopia,' remarking, 'Eli will tell you what it means.' I
nodded knowingly and felt so grateful nobody asked me to explain
because I didn't know it till I looked it up that night."

This was only two years after he arrived in the country knowing no
English at all.

IN ADDITION TO HIS FACILITY with words and his comfort with writing, my father has a novelist's sense of story and detail.

In 1931, eleven years after she emigrated with her two children, my
father's mother makes a months-long trip to Warsaw, to visit her father
and three siblings who still live there. I find in my father's files letters
he wrote to his mother during that trip. (Did he ask for them back
when she returned? Did he find them in her apartment after she died?)
In one, he tells her of a chance meeting with someone she knows, a Mr.
Herman:

> I was very much surprised to hear him remark all of a sudden
> that I should pursue a literary career. I inquired why he thinks
> so to which he replied that he once saw a translation of mine
> from Yiddish to English and he liked the way I brought out the
> thoughts.

I'm pleased by this evidence that my father's literary talent was apparent early on—and that someone thought he might pursue the life I
lived: a writing life.

It's fitting, I find myself thinking, that I'm paying tribute to him—
in a way, paying a debt—by writing.

———

IN ANOTHER LETTER HE writes to his mother during her visit to Warsaw, my father thanks her for sending postcards home regularly, but
admonishes her for their brevity. The list of questions he wishes she
would answer sounds like an outline for a short story:

> How did your father look when he first greeted you. Who
> awaited you at the station. What exactly has made the town
> seem so dilapidated and disgusted you so. How did the environ-
> ment from which you have been away so long strike you upon
> your first encountering it? Did the dress, the language, the car-
> riage of the people impress you as being radically different from
> the people here? Did the buildings, the pavements, the advertis-
> ing signs, the lights of the city call forth memories in you?

After listing many more such questions, he writes:

> The above are just a few of the innumerable questions I
> would like to bombard you with. I realize that you would have
> to spend almost all your time writing in order to jot down your
> impressions in such detailed form. Although your cards are so
> meager they nevertheless are very interesting and give me much
> pleasure. I await each new card with the same pleasure and an-
> ticipation that I used to feel when following the serial pictures
> that they used to show in installments every week at the "Em-
> pire," the little moving picture house on DeKalb Ave.

By naming the theater and the street it's on, he models for her how
specific details create scenes and bring them alive.

FINDING EVIDENCE IN my father's letters and journals of his attunement to and facility with language and writing is satisfying. But it
doesn't surprise me. Something else I find there does. Though it, too,
involves attention to words, it connects him to me in a way I don't

treasure: excessive attunement to words' power to hurt. My father describes, in his journals, being hurt by others' words in ways that make me question my lifelong assumptions about his temperament—and the source of my own.

MY FATHER IS "SENSITIVE." That is a given in our family: my sisters and I are always afraid of hurting his feelings. When Naomi is a teenager, he stops talking to her for a day, because he thinks she cursed him. She was calling down to him from the attic of our house in Brooklyn. He was two flights below, on the ground floor, and couldn't make out what she was saying. After repeating herself several times, she murmured, in frustration, "Shit." That he heard.

My sister Mimi is in high school when she hears a friend address her parents by their first names. She thinks this is impressively mature and tries it with her father. She greets him by asking, "Eli, how was work today?" Looking wounded, he says, "If you ever want to hurt me, you can call me Eli."

I find, in a letter I wrote to my best friend when I was sixteen, a record of my father's silent retribution for a word I used. (My friend saved my letters and returned them to me when we were sixty.) "My father isn't speaking to me," I wrote, "because I told him he was boring me (situation too complicated to describe). My mother agrees that I did a terrible thing, but she's magnanimous enough to forgive me since I didn't mean it viciously. She regrets that 'daddy is so sensitive' and that I 'hurt people without realizing it.'"

THAT MY FATHER WAS easily hurt by words is something I knew. I never suspected that his sensitivity tapped into a deep well of unhappiness.

In all my memories, my father is unfailingly cheerful. It's my mother who is often unhappy, whose unhappiness I dread because I absorb it, as if I were a lightning rod grounding her sadness in my chest. When I call home, I'm on guard: which voice will I hear when my mother answers? If she says, "Hi, honey. How *are* you?" her greeting high-pitched and ending with a level tone, I'm safe: she's in a good mood. But if she says, "Hello. How are *you,*" I know from her low pitch, and the way her intonation falls at the end, that she's feeling down, and my own spirits plummet. My father never sounds down, not even if he's in pain, which he often is: from extensive dental work, from arthritis, from frequent surgeries, and throughout his life and chronically when he's old, from his back. Small things make him happy, like the foods he loves: herring, anchovies, oysters. The cars he feels lucky to own make him happy. During my childhood, he buys a big used Buick and exults in what he calls its "suuurging power." When I'm at college, he announces with excitement, on one of my weekly calls home, that he bought a new car, a Lincoln Continental! He allows himself this extravagance because all three law partners bought them, paid for by the firm, since the cars will be used in the course of their work.

My father takes particular joy in singing. When I'm a child, he teaches me Polish songs he recalls from his childhood and delights (as I do) in our singing them together. He often sings when he's alone, right through his last years in the tiny assisted living apartment, where the aides hear him singing the melancholy folk song "Greensleeves" and the theme from his favorite film, *High Noon*. After he retires at seventy, it makes him happy to do the things he didn't have time for before: playing tennis and riding a bicycle. And when he can no longer do these things—even when he realizes he can no longer drive safely and gives his beloved last car to Naomi—he utters not a word of regret. Throughout everything, my father's cheerfulness, his optimism, is palpable in his ever-present sense of humor. Yet I'm struck by a comment he makes in a conversation with Ryan: "If there is no humor, you find sadness. Sadness appears. No humor isn't followed by nothing. It's followed by sadness." I see in his journals and written memories that my father's perennial good humor and quick wit may be a cover for his sadness, which reminds me of my own.

I WAS A TROUBLED CHILD. Though the panic attack that struck me when my grandmother died was unique—unusual enough for my parents to take notes and my sisters to remember—I was often deeply unhappy. I was hurt by small slights, afraid of invisible threats, difficult because I found life difficult. I refused to go to school when my mother braided my hair with unequal strands because they made lopsided braids. I refused to eat food my sister Mimi had stared at because I could see poison flowing from her eyes. I couldn't fall asleep because I could hear voices saying things I didn't want to hear: voices of what I referred to, without irony, by my father's name for them: my imaginary friends. I assumed that being terribly unhappy was the universal condition of childhood, until I reached my teen years, when I was amazed to learn that my close friends were happy as children. My search for reasons why I wasn't, always led to my mother. When psychological explanations were in vogue, I came to the conclusion that because she didn't want a third child—something I always knew—I must have picked up her antipathy as an infant. Or maybe I picked it up in the womb, since she commented often that I cried more as a baby than my sisters ever did. Later, when psychological problems tended to be seen as biologically based, I decided that she had an inborn tendency toward misery—I still think that's true—and I'd inherited it from her. As I cycled through theories, I never considered tracing my unhappiness to my father. But there it is, in his journals.

AT EIGHTEEN MY FATHER describes being out with Norman in Coney Island:

> We plodded onward along the boardwalk, I wanting to sit down and brood as is my wont and Norman pushing me along with the encouraging words "Come on we'll pick up a couple of broads." But there were no broads to be picked up, and when some girls did answer us they addressed Norman and entirely disregarded me and my remarks. My extremely sensitive nature always on the lookout for insults was hurt, and I was plunged into deeper sorrow and inward mourning. Who knows what it is to suffer this?

In my mind I reply to his rhetorical question, aware—and amused—that it makes me sound as laughably self-dramatizing as his journal does him: I know, Daddy! I know!

I know because he sounds so much like me, overreacting to slights,

so that even the most insignificant snub from a stranger can plunge—
yes, that's the word I've used myself, "plunge"—me into despair. I'm
sad to learn that he, too, felt such despair. But in a way I'm pleased,
too, as I'm always pleased to find evidence of ways we're similar.

I'M WITH MY FATHER in the assisted living apartment where he moved
two weeks after my mother died. It's his fifth day there. He's been writing letters to people in Florida he and my mother were close to. When
he finishes the first letter, to their friend Sam, he hands it to me, and I
read it aloud. When I read his description of how much he misses my
mother, we both begin to sob. At first, he covers his face with his hands,
but when he sees me crying, he reaches out to comfort me.

"You lost your mother," he says. "That's worse."

"No," I say. "It's worse for you."

Later, he hands me a copy of the letter he's written to Jo Anne, a
nurse he and my mother were particularly fond of.

"I won't read it out loud," I say, "or we'll cry again."

"You and I are sensitive," he says. "Not like Americans, who are
cold."

CHAPTER FOUR

"I Have Always Felt Myself Part of That Life"

A CHILD IN WORLD WAR I WARSAW

O F ALL THE CONVERSATIONS I HAVE WITH MY FATHER, THE ONES I love most—and I believe they're his favorites, too—are about his life in Warsaw before, during, and right after World War I. Like a child who begs to be told the same stories again and again, I never tire of hearing my father's memories of the neighborhood he lived in and the people he knew before he came to this country at twelve.

In 1934, my father wrote to his aunt Magda, who was still living in Poland, "My memories of Warsaw and the large part of my life which I spent there are very sharp and sentimental. I have always felt myself part of that life and not of the life which I have led since I am in this country."

What an astonishing statement. When he wrote this, my father was twenty-five and married, and had passed the bar. I think he never stopped feeling that way, though he lived in the United States seventy-two more years. This letter helps me understand why his memories of the Warsaw of his childhood are so uncannily detailed and vivid, and why he tells them again and again. By telling me these stories, my father invites me into the world, so different from the one I know, that shaped him—a world of gas lighting, horse-drawn carriages, and, most of all, the Hasidic Judaism that gave meaning and structure to everything else. As he speaks—and, after he's gone, as I read what he wrote and transcripts of what he said—I find my way back to that world and settle in.

"TWARDA ULICA," HE BEGINS, pronouncing it *tvARda ooLEEtsa*.

Twarda Street, Twarda Twelve. That's the address of the apartment building where I lived till I was seven. "Twarda" means "hard," so it's Twelve Hard Street. It was my grandparents' home. I was born in that apartment, and my mother was born there, too. The Hasidim had a tradition called kest. When a couple married, the bride's father would let them live with him, and support them, for a number of years. So after they married, my mother and father lived in a room in that apartment. After we were born, my sister Ella and I lived in the same room, too.

I have no memory of my father living there. From the time I can remember, it was just the three of us. My father moved out when I was two and Ella was three, because he had tuberculosis. Mother told people she asked him to leave because she didn't want him to infect the children. And she always said she didn't remarry because she didn't want her children to grow up with a stepfather. Maybe it was true. But I always believed she preferred to live on her own. She wasn't the kind of woman who wanted to spend her life waiting on a man.

PUTTING OFF MARRIAGE AS LONG as she could, my grandmother rejected several potential matches. When she was eighteen, dangerously close to unmarriageability, her father won a lottery and used his winnings to provide her a substantial dowry, so she agreed to a match he arranged with the son of a wealthy family named Tenenwórcel. She met her husband the day before the wedding, a progressive indulgence: by Hasidic tradition, they should have met the moment they married. My grandmother straddled tradition in another way, too: to make sure a married woman would not be attractive to other men, Hasidic brides had their heads shaved, and kept them shaved for the rest of their lives. My grandmother submitted to this the day before her wedding, as two of her younger sisters pounded on the door, begging her not to let them do it. Before long she broke with tradition and let her hair grow back.

EVEN BEFORE HE CAME down with tuberculosis, my grandmother never liked the man her father had chosen for her. My father says,

> My father wasn't a good businessman, and he wasn't practical. He opened a leather goods store with my mother's dowry, and lost it all. She used to tell with disgust how she'd bring him the wholesome lunch she'd prepared for him and find him eating lox and chocolate. Somehow that captured for her what she scorned in him. She never told me directly that I was ugly, but she'd often say that I looked just like my father, and whenever she spoke of him, she'd say how she hated his looks, especially his long hooked nose. She'd say, "He had a *nokh!*" She pronounced it that way, instead of *nos,* to show how much it disgusted her.

As he says this, my father lifts his hand and traces a long nose in the air in front of his face as if drawing his own nose out, mimicking the gesture his mother made as she said this. His nose is neither hooked nor particularly long. That's because he had an operation to reshape it when he was twenty-three. I know the date because he writes of it in his journal: a plastic surgeon agreed to perform the operation at a discount, and let him pay for it over time. I once asked my father if he ever regretted having this operation. His answer was swift and definite: "Never!" Before the operation, he was always aware of—and ashamed of—his nose. After, for the first time in his life, he felt like a "normal" person.

"It wasn't only my father's looks that disgusted my mother," my father says.

> Whenever I did something she didn't like, which was just about anything I ever did, she'd say, "Just like your father." If I slept late; if I stayed up late; the way I ate, what I ate, the time I

ate, how I dressed, if I spent money, how much I spent, what I spent it on—it was all the wrong thing, all the wrong way, and all "just like your father." It wasn't until I was an adult and talked to people who knew him that I found out my father was a wonderful man. They said he was kind, gentle, sensitive, and intelligent. Everyone loved him, except my mother.

Those adjectives, "kind, gentle, sensitive, and intelligent," describe my father, too, but apparently they were not qualities his mother valued.

My father died when I was six. He was twenty-seven years old. Since I didn't know him, I wasn't sad; I thought it was an interesting piece of news. I ran into a neighbor on the staircase, and boasted excitedly that I knew something she didn't. "What is it?" she asked. "That your father died?" I saw from her manner that my excitement wasn't the right emotion to have. "No," I lied. "That isn't it." But I wouldn't tell her what it was.

HIS FATHER'S DEATH WAS just an interesting piece of news to my father, because it didn't change his life. He continued to live where he always had: his grandparents' home:

My early memories are of life in that household, with my grandfather and grandmother and my mother's sisters and brothers, my aunts and uncles. My mother had a great many siblings. I was always told there were twenty-three born of whom sixteen lived to adulthood. There were nine that lived there when I did. That was what I loved most: the liveliness, the warmth, of so many aunts and uncles. I felt bad because I wasn't a Kornblit. Everyone was named Kornblit. I was a Tenenwórcel. I wanted so much to be part of that large family.

Hearing my father speak of longing to be part of a large family, I get a flash of understanding why he wanted lots of children. It explains why I'm here. From very early on, I knew the story of my birth: my father wanted a third child; my mother didn't. One night he talked her into forgoing birth control, saying, "Let's leave it to chance." The next day she asserted herself: she wouldn't do that again. But it was too late. He wanted a fourth daughter, too, and spoke of her, using the name he'd picked out. Sometimes, when I was visiting, he'd say to my mother, "Aren't you glad we had her?" and sometimes he'd add, "Aren't you sorry we didn't have Rachel?" After my mother died, when I visited him, if the aides in his assisted living facility remarked on his having three daughters, he'd say, "I wanted more, but I couldn't get my wife to agree."

IN 1993—MY FATHER IS eighty-five—my husband and I travel to Poland with my parents. First thing, after checking into our hotel in Warsaw, we all take a taxi to Twarda Ulica. It feels surreal to be standing under a sign with the street name I've heard my father say so many times. The apartment house he grew up in is gone; in its place is a grim gray building with a cement wall covered in obscene spray-painted graffiti. That wall and that graffiti are what I see, but my father is seeing the building it replaced, and the household he grew up in. For him—as for all of us, I guess—the home he lived in isn't a building but a family: the people who lived there, the people he loved, and the neighborhood they were all part of, the heart of Hasidic Warsaw. For many people, Hasidic men with long beards and side curls, wearing long black coats and large wide-brimmed hats, still represent the stereotypical image of Jews, but only a tiny fraction of Jews alive today are Hasidic. When my father was a child, there were 300,000 Jews living in Warsaw—over a third of the city's population—and two thirds of them were ultra-orthodox Hasidim. When my father describes the building he grew up in and the neighborhood surrounding it, he's seeing a world that still lives in his memory—that he still lives in when he recalls it.

Our apartment was in an old building. Actually it was three oval buildings each surrounding a cobblestone courtyard. You entered through a *brama,* a huge archway with a wooden gate. Then you crossed the first courtyard. There were entrances to apartments on both sides, right and left. To get to our house, we would go through a second archway to another courtyard.

There was also a third courtyard with some mechanic shops and a lot of junk, like rusted machinery. I was first introduced to a spider back there when I was very little.

The balcony of our house looked out on the second courtyard. I had my friends there and we had our fights there. On the ground floor were factories. One made frankfurters and delicatessen. It fascinated me because of the smells, especially after the war broke out, and we couldn't afford to eat any of it. Vendors came into the courtyard, shouting about what they had to sell. One man had a grinding wheel. People brought him knives and scissors to sharpen. Another man would push a wheelbarrow in and set up shop. He took iron pots blackened from cooking and returned them sparkling and shiny. One time my grandmother sent my uncle Bernard down with some pots. When he brought them back she showed him that part of one pot wasn't done, so she sent him back down. He got into a loud argument with the man. An audience gathered to watch, but I was stuck in the house because I was sick. I had to strain to see what I could from the tiny balcony. I couldn't get over the injustice. All my friends got to enjoy the show, and I missed it—and it was my uncle!

To get to our apartment, you entered a staircase on the left side of the second courtyard and went up three flights of wooden stairs covered with rubber. There were twice twelve steps between each floor. I remember because when I ran up and down with Ruchci Leibele—my aunt Ruchcia's son Leibl—we always counted them. Above the third floor was an attic. It had a dirt floor with wooden planks you walked along. That's where our clothes were taken to be hung, to be dried. On the street level, you went into a cellar. Each apartment had a little section inside the cellar. I would go down there with my uncle Bernard to bring up food that had to be kept there so it wouldn't spoil. They used to buy a block of ice and keep it in a pan, to keep things cold, and that would last maybe a day or maybe less than a day, maybe eighteen hours or so.

The apartment appeared huge to me, although actually there were only six rooms. Ours was small, long, and narrow, with two beds head-to-head along the left wall. It was painted pale blue. My sister slept with my mother in one bed. I slept in the other. In most of the rooms you had an oven for heating, built with tiles—a tiled oven that went into the ceiling so the smoke could go out through the roof. We had gas lighting. It was quite adequate. People could easily read in the evening. We took hot baths, so we were able to heat water.

I treasure these details because they invite me into the day-to-day life of my father's childhood. They also bring back to life the Jewish community of Warsaw that he grew up in. Keeping that world alive is, in my father's mind, the main purpose of the book he expects me to write. I'm reminded of this when I come across a letter he writes to a friend when he's eighty-seven, where he says, "Deborah is planning a book on life of the Jews in Poland based on my recollections." Though my purpose is to write about his life, I did long ago form the idea that by preserving his detailed memories of his childhood, I'd be helping to preserve the Jewish community of Warsaw that was wiped out by the Nazis in World War II. I was still thinking of it that way when I began writing. Then I read, in an essay by the Polish historian Piotr Wróbel, that the First World War, not the Second, brought "the twilight of Jewish Warsaw," because it was followed by a rise in Polish anti-Semitism and a decline in political and economic opportunity for Jews—the reason so many left for America. I can see this decline in my father's account of his family's experiences after the war. This makes even more poignant, more urgent, the assignment he gave me to write his life. The details he recounts bring back to life the Jewish community of Warsaw just as its lights were going out. As I listen—as I write—I see that the structure and meaning of my father's young life, and of the lives of those who made up that community, come from the strict requirements of Hasidic Judaism.

"DURING THE DAY," my father goes on,

especially in preparation for the Sabbath, there was fearful activity in the kitchen. Before the war, there was a servant, sometimes two. After the war, it was my grandmother doing everything herself, though sometimes the children helped. Tremendous *challahs* had to be baked at home: long, braided, shiny white loaves of bread. I've never seen anything like them in this country. Live chickens, sometimes a duck or two, were running around the kitchen. They were kept at home until they were taken for kosher slaughtering and brought back home to be plucked and prepared, cooked in tremendous pots on a very large stove. Goose, too. For Jewish holidays, the activity was even more elaborate, everything done according to strict rituals.

My grandfather was a stickler for protocol. I felt the brunt of this when we all sat down to dinner during the war. The meal began with my grandfather saying a prayer over the *challah.* No one could eat anything till they said a prayer, too. But you couldn't say the prayer until you had a slice of the bread. My grandfather took the first long *challah* and gave the first slice to his wife. Then he gave a slice to each of the children in order of age. As soon as they got the bread and said the prayer, each person would start to eat. I was the youngest, so I was the last to begin eating. During the war I was always hungry. I had to watch every aunt and uncle get a slice of *challah* and begin eating. My tongue was literally hanging out by the time I got mine, and could say the prayer, bite into the *challah,* and start devouring the piece of fish which usually started the meal.

My grandfather went to the synagogue across the street every day. It wasn't what you'd think of as a synagogue. It was called a *shtibel,* and was a little below street level, a partial basement. Most of the men who went there were poor. Some of them spat on the rough, unpainted wooden boards of the floor. That turned my stomach, when my grandfather took me there. My grandfather and the men he went to shul with were all dressed the same way, like most of the men in the street. There were plenty of those who wore ordinary clothes; they were called the enlightened Jews, the progressive Jews. But the majority wore the long black caftans and black boots up to the knee with trousers tucked into the boots, and the *tsitsit,* the ritual fringes, peeking out from beneath their vests. And they wore round black hats with *yarmulkes* underneath them. Everybody who could grow one had a beard.

The "fearful activity" of preparing for the Sabbath meal that my father describes in his grandparents' home was also going on in the streets outside. The level of detail that he recalls of the neighborhood, and the people who filled it with life, astonishes me again. And again, I'm grateful that he's helping me see this world that no longer exists—except that it does, in his memory.

When I was growing up there was so much life, so much commotion, on the street. Friday was an especially busy, festive day. People were rushing about to get home in time to prepare for the Sabbath. They took baths in the public bathhouses and put on their holiday clothes. At dusk you saw men dressed in their finest: silk caftans, newer-looking black hats, and shiny black boots. They carried their prayer books and folded prayer shawls.

But it wasn't only Friday. Both sides of the street were lined with stores, and the sidewalks were always teeming with people—working men, women shopping, men going to and from the synagogue. People loudly haggled about prices. There were *tragers*—carriers—men hired by people too poor to hire a wagon. They walked about with ropes around their waists, which they used to tie amazing loads on their backs—a desk, a bed. Rarely did an automobile come through, but there were quite a few *droshkis,* horse-drawn carriages that took passengers, and open wagons for trade. The drivers were beating and yelling at their horses, and yelling at pedestrians to get out of the way. Occasionally a *kareta* drove by—a fancy carriage that rich people rode in. That caused a stir, as people wondered whether a rich person might get out, and what he might be after. Epileptics would fall down and have convulsions in the street. No one stopped, because it was common.

MY FATHER'S DESCRIPTION OF life in the neighborhood he grew up in gives me a sense of the terrible poverty that helped drive so many Polish Jews to America during this time. It also lets me see the extreme effects of class differences in that society, which my father didn't question until he saw how different things were in America.

Many children had *krzywica,* rickets, which gave them bow legs, from malnutrition. And many, especially children, had *parokh,* a condition where the scalp was covered with scabs. That was unsightly, and sad. Missing or rotten teeth were common. And beggars, everywhere beggars in torn clothes. Some wore clothes sewn from sacks, some had rags on their feet instead of shoes. Some of the beggars went to the houses, but they didn't ask for money, only for leftovers, especially pieces of dried bread. They carried sacks, and put whatever they could into the sacks. These conditions were prevalent before the First World War. After the war started, they grew worse.

Streetcars ran in both directions, their bells clanging. The tracks ran down the middle of the street, so people waited at the curb and walked out to the streetcar when it stopped. One day an old Hasid stepped off the curb just as an automobile came rushing into the space between the streetcar and the curb, and its wheel ran over the old man's foot. As the man shrieked in pain, the driver stopped his car, got out, rushed over to the old man, and began loudly berating him for getting in his way. Soon after I arrived in America, I saw a cabdriver and his passenger standing by the cab, arguing. I couldn't get over the contrast. In Poland, if you were rich, you had the right to yell at anyone. In America, a cabdriver in his worker's cap was shouting at a rich man in a silk top hat.

The fare on the streetcars was minuscule but to me it was a fortune. I recall the first time I took a trip away from the street all by myself. I must have been five years old, yet I had enough money for a trip on a streetcar. I boarded, rode for some distance, and got off at a little park. I sat down on a bench but was nervous. After a few minutes I took a streetcar back to Twarda, to home, feeling as Marco Polo must have felt on returning from his travels.

*

I'M SITTING WITH MY FATHER IN MY PARENTS' WESTCHESTER CONdominium. "I was thinking about my grandfather while trying to sleep last night," he says. "I could tell you about him."

"Yes, yes, tell me."

"I'm so happy to share my memories with someone without bothering Mother, who hates the past so enthusiastically."

I laugh. "I can hear Mommy saying, 'I've heard enough about your grandfather!' I think when she says that, 'your grandfather' is shorthand for all your memories of Poland."

He laughs, too. "That's because she's heard it all a thousand times."

"I haven't. Well, maybe I have. But not a thousand times. Tell me about him."

My grandfather was the closest I ever came to having a father. I called him Zidishi, from *zayde,* which is Yiddish for Grandfather. He called me Eliyue [this sounds like *ay-lee-YOO-uh*], the diminutive of Eliyahu, Elijah, which is my full name.

To me, my grandfather was an imposing giant of a man with his flowing gray beard and black Hasidic attire. Years later, when I was an adult and saw a picture Uncle Jack brought back from a visit to Poland, I realized that my grandfather was actually rather short. I was in awe of him. I felt that he was omnipotent. I remember how surprised I was when the czar was spoken of as being more powerful than my grandfather, someone he might have to obey. He had deep blue eyes, piercing eyes. I thought that he was scaring people, but I'm sure he wasn't.

Maybe that's where you got your blue eyes, I think, and why my eyes are light—not blue exactly, but hazel, greenish. Somehow, this feels

My father's grandfather Chazkiel Kornblit

like a tiny connection to the great-grandfather I never knew. And through his description of his grandfather—the scenes he brings to life with the details he remembers—my father connects me to the Hasidism that shaped his life and the lives of the majority of Jews living in Warsaw when he was a child.

He was up at five A.M. each morning and sat in the kitchen studying a large tome which must have been a Talmud. Next to it was a samovar and a pyramid of sugar cubes. He held one in his mouth while sipping tea from a glass. Judging by the number of cubes in the pyramid he must have drunk a great many glasses of tea before it was time for him to have breakfast and depart for the synagogue. He sniffed tobacco. He'd put some in each nostril, then he'd sneeze. Tobacco came wrapped in very heavy lead wrapping. He'd take it carefully, smooth it out, and save it. I wonder what he did with all those wrappings.

He was always serious. I don't remember his ever smiling except one time. He brought along some impressive-looking rabbis from the synagogue and took them into his bedroom for privacy. After some time the door opened. My grandfather came out and took me back with him into the room. The door closed again behind us, and a venerable-looking rabbi addressed me. I don't remember what he said, if he asked me any questions. It was all very mysterious to me, especially when he blessed me with a rather long prayer and his hands outstretched over me. I'd never been blessed before, so I'm afraid I kept gazing at him instead of downcasting my eyes before being escorted out of the room. I guess my grandfather wanted to take advantage of the presence of the holy man to help my future. I would not have guessed then that I was that important to him. I do remember his smiling then.

He was severe and authoritarian with his children. Most of them ended up detesting him. But he was always gentle and kind to me. One Yom Kippur, I may have been five, I took it into my head to fast. Mother brought me something to eat in my bed, but I remained adamant. She enlisted my grandfather to persuade me. He explained that I didn't have to fast because I wasn't bar-mitzvahed yet. If I fasted, it wouldn't please God, but it would displease my mother.

He once took me by the hand to the *mikvah,* the ritual bath. As we walked, I asked him why paper money had value, but other paper didn't. At the *mikvah,* I was struck by the number of naked, bearded men in the dim light. My grandfather patiently instructed me on how he covered his facial openings while immersing himself in the water: thumbs on the ears, index fingers on the eyes, middle fingers on the nostrils, and ring fingers on the mouth. I guess the pinkies rested on the chin. I remember because I was amazed to see him naked.

For years I thought my grandfather's name was Zahzogit, because that's how my grandmother addressed him: "Zahzogit, would you pull out that chair?" "Zahzogit, may I have some money to buy food?" Then I found out that *zahzogit* meant "be so good." She began that way to be properly deferential to her husband.

This misunderstanding—an amusing example of a child's learning to interpret the world—is a chilling reminder of the place of women in this community. It gives context to my father's comment that his mother wasn't the kind of woman who wanted to spend her life waiting on a man, and why she put off getting married as long as she could. It also helps me see how dramatic a departure from his upbringing were my father's expectations of his wife, and himself. My sister Naomi tells me—she knows because he told her—that when she was a baby, he took on the task of hand-washing her diapers: "He knew it was twelve diapers. Every night he'd come home from work and wash the twelve diapers. And he used to iron my little dresses. He told me that he knew how to iron the puffed sleeves."

MY FATHER'S MEMORIES OF his grandfather also show how differently the Germans who occupied Warsaw in the First World War behaved than the ones who flowed into the city in the Second.

> Here's something that placed in some little doubt my belief in my grandfather's omnipotence, and to that extent diminished my sense of security. When the Germans first appeared in Warsaw in 1915, they fumigated every apartment in the city. They sealed the windows and doors and exploded within a kind of antiseptic bomb which killed every type of insect, and indeed every apartment was infested with bedbugs and lice. When they did our house, my grandfather's house, we spent the time at neighbors', and we accommodated them when their turn came. The Germans also compelled all adults to go to delousing stations where they had to strip and bathe and have all their clothes fumigated. I remember the comments, some favorable, others critical, but what I couldn't fathom was my grandfather submitting to such indignities.

When he talks of his grandfather during and after the German occupation, my father focuses on the realization that all children eventually confront about elders they see as all-powerful—as I saw my father when I was small: his grandfather was not the godlike authority he seemed to be at home. But my father's recollections also show how the war and its aftermath impoverished his grandfather, as it did most of the Warsaw Jews at the time:

> At one time, my grandfather had a furniture store. He sold his share to his partner so he would have more time to study Talmud, and made his living lending money. All payments were suspended during the war. When it ended in 1918, he made efforts to collect debts owed him. Of the few people he located, none agreed to pay. All his investments were a total loss. He took me with him on one of his attempts, to the home of an ex–Polish general. What remains in my memory is that he removed his hat in the man's home, leaving on his head only the *yarmulke* resting beneath it. What shocked me is that my grandfather would doff his hat to a mere mortal.

I suspect the grandfather brought along his grandson in hopes that the blue-eyed, towheaded little boy might soften the ex-general's heart and encourage him to repay even a fraction of the money he'd borrowed. Though my father remembers the encounter because of his grandfather's deference, I see a man who no longer has a way to earn a living and support his family. His grandfather came to depend on what his oldest son could send from America.

> There were only two times I remember seeing my grandfather show any emotion other than anger. When my grandmother died in 1919, I went to my grandfather's house as soon as I heard. I found him framing the door to their bedroom, where she was lying in the prescribed manner, on the floor with her feet toward the exit. He seemed to me gigantic and to fill the entire doorway, while tears were rolling down his cheeks.

I was with my parents in Florida when my mother died at home. As we waited for the funeral director to retrieve her body, my father said, "In Poland, we would have put her on the floor, with her feet toward the door." I heard this, at the time, as an observation about an odd custom. Now I realize he must have been seeing, in his mind, his grand-mother laid out that way.

My father continues,

After having so many children with my grandmother, no doubt he had more feeling for her than he displayed in his be-havior. The next year we left for America. When we were about to leave, he called me to him and took me on his lap. Tears streamed from beneath his gold-rimmed glasses, down his cheeks, and into his long white beard. He knew he would never see me again. With his arm around my shoulders, he said, "Never forget that you are a Jew." He believed that when Jews went to America, they ceased to be Jews, because they stopped being Hasidic. Those were my grandfather's last words to me: "Never forget you are a Jew."

*

NOT ALL MY FATHER'S MEMORIES OF POLAND ARE OF LIFE IN WAR-saw. Many of them take place in small towns outside the city where he spent summers. Apparently it didn't cost much; they rented rooms from the gentiles who lived there year-round. The thought of War-saw's Jews escaping the city heat reminds me of a similar exodus of New York City Jews to resorts and bungalow colonies in the Catskills, which my parents were part of when they were young. Only recently—very recently—did I learn that the resort areas my parents referred to as "the Jewish mountains" were developed because Jews weren't al-lowed in other resorts.

"My mother was proud that we never spent a summer in Warsaw," my father recalls.

It happens here, too. The women and children leave the city to escape the heat, while the men stay, trying to make a living. One summer we rented a room in a cottage close to the river Wisła—Vistula—in Kazimierz. It was maybe 80 percent Jewish. A neighbor, a gentile, suggested to Mother that he take me for a boat ride. He had a rowboat and rowed it with one paddle while standing the entire time. The river was rather rough. Thinking back, I could have drowned if there had been a mishap. I couldn't swim and of course there was no life preserver.

While we were there, Mother took me with her to buy a chicken. The butcher had a place off the main square, a rather large, famous square with tradesmen and stores and stalls all around it, all Jewish. Yet I felt as if I were in the midst of gentiles, probably because of the neighbor who befriended me. The bearded butcher had an open space behind his store where he killed chickens, and that's where we went for Mother and another woman to make their selections. He slit the chickens' throats nonchalantly. In each case the chicken didn't drop dead as I had expected but flapped its wings and hopped around crazily before finally dropping to the ground lifeless. The scene made a terrible impression and the memory of it never left me. I have since imagined having my throat slit on many occasions.

Now I have an image to match the expression "running around like a chicken without a head"—and I'm no happier to have it than my father was. I'm not surprised that he identified with the chicken. It's the kind of reaction I would have had as a child—and have now.

I have another memory from a summer that involves a chicken. It was another town. There was a fire in one of the barns or little buildings. They had a volunteer fire department that came, these young boys, and I loved watching them. I got closer and closer, to watch. I had a wonderful time, but I burned my big toe on a cinder. It was pretty badly burned so I came home to Warsaw with a burned toe. My mother was changing the dressing on my toe in my grandmother's kitchen. The kitchen was very large with a stove that you could almost sleep on at night. And my mother put me there, then went out of the room. My grandmother had a chicken running around, which wasn't unusual in preparation for Friday. I taunted it, tried to provoke it, and sure enough the chicken came over and pecked at my burned toe. I was looking for action, and I got it!

My father is eighty-seven, but when he talks to me about his child-hood, he's ageless. He becomes the little boy in his story, then laughs at the way the little boy saw the world—at the humor he now can see. As he laughs he hunches his shoulders and crinkles his eyes in a disarming way. I see in that gesture the affection he feels for the child he was, together with the indulgence of an adult who knows better. His laugh seems to say, "How foolish I was then, but sweet."

We were in the country when the war started in 1914. I wasn't six yet. This was in August; I became six in October. Of course there was no radio; we had no telephone, and we weren't getting newspapers out in the country there. So I remember my grand-mother, my mother, and others went to the fence along the road, and when passersby came from the direction of Warsaw, they asked, "Anything new? What happened?" They stood there every day looking for news. In a short time they decided to go back to Warsaw because they didn't know what happened with the war. We packed all the things onto a wagon, with an old broken-down horse, and all the things we brought out were piled up on the wagon. There were pieces of furniture—beds and mattresses. And they carried all the dishes, everything nec-essary: towels, linens, clothing, everything belonging to quite a number of people all on that one wagon. It was piled so high, there was no place for people to sit, because all they could afford was that wagon and that old horse. So everybody walked along-side on the road, except for me. I was the youngest, and I was placed on top of it. I had a beautiful view, and it didn't bother me that everybody was walking. I didn't think there was any ef-fort on their part. My grandmother, too. She must have been along in years. She must have been sick already. We went through towns, and the trip took all day long with that horse going along.

When we got home, my grandmother started putting in sup-plies in expectation of shortages. I recall we had a barrel of her-rings, a barrel of sauerkraut, and a barrel of white flour. I recall these three things for particular reasons. To make the sauerkraut

a woman was engaged who brought a machine in which she put
heads of cabbage, several at a time, into this machine, then by
moving it up and down, she was shredding the cabbage to make
sauerkraut. I recall the barrel of herrings because later on when
it was nearing the bottom—this was quite a while later—I took
surreptitiously a herring into the bathroom and closed the door
and finished it to still the hunger without ever disclosing this
horrid deed to anyone. The memory of the white flour is so
fresh in my mind because I contracted scarlet fever and heard
later that I almost died. Obviously, I didn't. During my recu-
peration I was given white *challah,* which was always made at
home of course, with butter and tea and milk. No one else was
allowed to have any flour because there wasn't enough left. They
all had to eat black bread, which was bought.

MY FATHER'S MEMORIES OF the war years are of hardship caused by
hunger, cold, and poverty, but not by the occupiers' cruelty.

It wasn't long before the German soldiers arrived. So unlike
the Nazis of the Second World War, they were civilized, well
behaved. They walked about unarmed in their silly hats, often
carrying maps of the city. But they were thorough in exploiting
the country. They visited every single apartment in search of
copper utensils, which they confiscated and paid for in pennies
when they were worth dollars in the open market. But they
were very methodical in weighing copper by removing any iron
parts. I recall them removing laboriously iron wires around the
rims.

My father recalls his family crowding onto the tiny balcony of his
grandparents' apartment to see a German zeppelin (he pronounces it
TSEPelin), an early airship, and an early delivery system for bombs:

We all stood at the balcony looking up at the sky in which a
German zeppelin was slowly flying. It dropped a couple of
bombs, which no one seemed to fear, at least not those around

me, though one of the bombs fell perhaps a half a mile or a mile away from us on a church which my friends and I went to inspect the following day. We saw a huge bell which had fallen from the top of the church onto the ground.

If bombs didn't cause great suffering, the occupation did.

Hunger was not long in coming and disease followed quickly. And cold. When there was no coal or wood to burn, they kept enough in the stove for cooking, and that's the only room that was warm. I remember what a terrible thing it was at night to go into the cold room to go to sleep. My mother used to carry me wrapped in a blanket and put me in there. To take a bath in those times, first of all it was the same water we used for several people—first one then the next, because you couldn't have enough hot water for everyone separate. And then out of the bath to go to the bed, was such a painful experience, that to this day I shudder when I think of coming out of a warm shower and going to a cold room, although it doesn't happen often. All this did not completely cease until we left in 1920 for America.

Mother had only rich and prominent friends. She avoided uneducated or uncultured or poor people. So I was always in wealthy homes and trained to be oh so polite and always feeling inferior, which I was.

My grandmother must have met her rich and prominent friends at college, the advanced secular education she and her sisters got. Before the war, her father was comfortable, if not rich, as the owner of a furniture store and then a moneylender. But during the war their circumstances changed.

Once Mother took me with her to visit a friend who had boiled an egg and was trying to get her daughter to eat it. The little girl kept refusing. I hadn't seen an egg since the war started. I was so hungry. I wanted so badly to say that I'd eat the egg. But I didn't dare. I knew that my mother would kill me.

Aha, I think, that must be why my father loves eggs. When the anti-cholesterol craze sweeps the country, my mother, falling in line with expert advice, limits him to four eggs a week. After she dies, he begins every day with two fried eggs, and most days has an egg salad sandwich for lunch.

His mother's education was also key to a major change in my father's life: the move to a school his mother established and ran. The way his mother became principal of a school is also a reminder of how different the German occupation of the First World War was from the Second. Many Jews served in the German army during the First, and a German rabbi who came to Poland in hopes of improving education for Polish Jews was appointed a chaplain in the army.

It was indirectly because of the war that when I was seven, we—my mother and sister and I—moved out of my grandfather's home and into a large apartment in a new building at 74 Wielka Ulica, where my mother became the principal of a school. The Germans came in in 1915. Along with them was a major in the German army who was a Jewish chaplain. He went around to some rich Jewish businessmen, and told them that he wants to open a school for girls, who will be educated and prepared for college but who were at the same time to be trained to be Jewish wives. This Dr. Carlebach, in association with another gentleman called Dr. Auerbach, undertook this, and they chose my mother to head it because she had the combination of being a religious observant Jew, and at the same time she had the college education that was necessary. She found and rented the space—the entire fourth floor, two apartments, in a new building; negotiated with the Board of Education; and became the principal. I recall her boasting frequently that she had bought every last nail and ordered cubbyholes where the students could keep their books; she hired the teachers and took care of the office, supervised the curriculum.

The name of the school was Havazelet. In Polish it was spelled Chawaceles. We moved to a room at the school where we also had the use of a kitchen and, when school was out, the use of all the classrooms. The building was quite fancy, with a self-service elevator, electric lights, steam heat, and telephone. It was such a novelty to me, that I invited my friends to witness all the wonders. One of them kept turning the lights on and off in amazement until it broke. Mother at the time was entertaining a friend and I came over to her, crestfallen, worried, in great fear, and confessed that the electric was broken. She hauled off and smacked me right in the face. When I came to America, my friends wouldn't believe me that our apartment in Warsaw had an elevator and electric lights. I couldn't convince them. It frustrated me. It still does.

I remember my grandmother's sister, Mime [pronounced *MEEmuh,* it means "aunt"] Yochvitel, visiting us at the school. She was fairly tall, vivacious, progressive, relatively modern, interested in current events. She was *too* affectionate. I dreaded her visits because of the enthusiasm with which she pinched my cheek, which was a customary gesture toward children.

This is a gesture I know from experience. I dreaded visits to my father's uncle Max for the same reason. He'd press the backs of his first two fingers into my cheek, catching the flesh between them, then squeeze. "There's another visitor I remember," my father says.

I'll tell you why. There was no heat in the house. It was so cold but we were used to it; we didn't expect any heat, because there was no heating material. We used to bundle ourselves up as much as we could. When this relative visited, tea was served in order to warm themselves up, and I noticed that everybody loved the hot tea. I don't know whether there was sugar; sugar was scarce. We had a system; if there was a little sugar you drank the whole glass without sugar. And then the last bit you sweetened. And then you drank that and you felt like you had a whole glass of sweet tea.

I was very shy. I remember one incident when the school celebrated Chanukah with a big party and a show. Since I was the only boy in the school, I was designated to light the first candle and recite the prayer. I was so shy that while doing it I refused to face the audience or lift my eyes despite the frantic motions of my mother.

You didn't change all that much, I think. When my father's ninety-sixth birthday is approaching, I ask, "Would you prefer that we celebrate here where you live or at Naomi's house?"

He says, "I prefer to hide under the table."

LONG AFTER MY FATHER is gone, I look for Dr. Carlebach in historical accounts from the period. To my surprise and delight, I find mention not only of him but also of the school he hired my grandmother to run. In an article revealingly titled "A German Rabbi Goes East," I learn that Dr. Emanuel Carlebach, a prominent orthodox rabbi from Cologne, was sent to help improve the educational system among the Hasidim in Poland, who were viewed as backward by German Jews. He was appointed a chaplain in the German army after arriving in Warsaw. The essay about Dr. Carlebach's mission includes letters he wrote to his family back in Germany and describes the school he helped establish as "an orthodox school for girls (whose education had been entirely neglected by the Chasidim hitherto)." The letters provide glimpses of the dreadful conditions—extreme poverty and near starvation—in which the vast majority of Warsaw's Hasidim were living during the war. In a letter dated February 1916, Dr. Carlebach writes that he visited a *cheder,* a school where Hasidic boys learn to read Hebrew and study the Talmud, "with 1000 children and 25 teachers. The children's clothes were in rags, and most of them hadn't eaten in days."

Among my father's papers I find letters that Dr. Carlebach wrote to my grandmother after he returned to Germany, apparently responding to her pleas that the teachers' salaries were not enough to buy food. In October 1918 (one month before the war ends), he wrote (in German), "It is simply not possible that a higher salary than 600 and 200 for the service is paid. I would therefore ask you to not talk about this again." He also chides, "Some fathers already complain to me in the morning that many classes do not take place. You are responsible for the upkeeping of the class schedule." He concludes, "Please tell all the teachers in my name that considering the situation I have no obligation other than paying them timely for the last month. Quitting is not at all possible."

My father is unaware of these circumstances. He often says that his mother gave up a secure, well-paying job at the school when they emigrated. But he recalls,

> So much happened during that period: the war, and the hunger, and the disease, and the fear that you felt all around, and the cold that you had to suffer. You didn't have enough of anything. Getting clothes was a problem. Everything was a problem. The fear, and the attacks. One time my mother made a long trip outside Warsaw to find food. She managed to buy a sack of potatoes from a farmer. She lugged that sack of potatoes home, though it was very heavy and it took her many hours. But when she got home and tried to cook the potatoes, she discovered they'd been frozen. Have you ever tasted a potato that was frozen? It's inedible. It has a sickening sweet taste. I've never been able to eat a sweet potato, because it reminds me of that taste.

*

THOUGH MY FATHER'S MEMORIES OF THE WAR ARE GRIM, MOST OF the time, when he talks about Warsaw, he talks about family—his extended family—with affection and longing. He says little about his sister; I get the sense she was not much in his day-to-day life. He mentions his mother mostly to say how others protected him from her: at the school, a series of housekeepers who took a liking to him—a series because his mother would inevitably fight with and fire them. In his grandfather's household, it was his mother's youngest sister, Magda, and, above all, his grandmother.

> The one I loved most, the one I was involved with every day, was my grandmother, Bubishi. Her name was Leah but everyone called her Leiele. I called her Bubishi. That's an endearing form for Bubbe, "Grandmother." She was my grandfather's second wife. His first wife was her sister, Chana. He was married to Chana when they were still children. He was thirteen. They

FRONT ROW, LEFT TO RIGHT: *my father, his grandmother Leah Kornblit,*
his sister Ella. BACK ROW: *my father's mother, his aunt Magda,*
Ruchcia's daughter Topcia, his aunt Ruchcia

didn't live as man and wife right away, of course. He was well
into his teen years before he became a father. That was his first
child, Jack. Chana died a few weeks after Jack was born, from
childbirth. Hasidic custom required that he marry her sister, so
he married Leiele. He didn't marry her immediately. She was
only fourteen when Chana died; he waited till she was fifteen.

Bubishi was the one who looked out for me, who showed me affection. One time when I was very small, my mother was going out. She was a young woman herself, I realize now. She was only twenty-two when I was born. She loved the theater; she loved concerts. And my grandmother scolded her: "The child is sick!" Apparently I had a cold or something. "And you're going away and leaving the sick child?" My mother paid no attention. She left with her friends.

I remember one summer we went to the country and arrived toward evening. I must have been quite young, maybe four. A crib was prepared for me with a mattress filled with straw that stuck you as you laid down on it. I was put to bed early in a poorly lit room, while the family was busy settling in. For some reason I felt depressed, felt like crying in the gloomy surroundings, feeling ignored by everyone. Bubishi came over. Did she guess how I felt? And she sang me to sleep. My mother never sang to me. She was strong and she gave orders.

As he tells me about Bubishi, my father's eyes fill with tears. For a moment, I'm surprised that a man could be moved to tears recalling someone who died over eighty-five years before, when he was eleven. I'm immediately ashamed of my surprise. Of course. Bubishi, more than anyone else, made him feel loved.

When my aunt Magda came to visit here in 1959, the first time I saw her again after I left Warsaw, I had one request of her: what were the lyrics of a song my grandmother sang to me. It was a song that made pictures in my mind of a beautiful girl in a house, and a handsome young man outside and it was a dark night and he came to the fence and sang to the girl. Magda didn't remember it. I was very disappointed.

It's a blessing, I think, that Bubishi died the year before my father left Poland. It would have been so hard for him to say goodbye to her, and so hard for her. She'd already said goodbye to nearly all her many children. Two sets of twins died at birth; two died of disease when they were still very small: a little girl at four, a little boy at one and a half; and a daughter burned to death at fourteen when she was cooking and her apron caught fire. Of the children she saw grow to adulthood, the first she gave birth to, Ruchcia, died in the 1918 flu epidemic; two daughters were living in Switzerland; and five—another daughter and four sons—had already gone to America. Seeing yet another daughter depart, and with her the grandchildren she all but raised, would surely have brought back the pain of all the other losses.

With his beloved grandmother and most of his aunts and uncles gone, as my father tells it, he was not sad to leave Warsaw. In explaining why he was glad, he talks about school:

The whole time I was in Poland, I was in school, day and night. At first I went to Hebrew school—to *cheder*—all day, and in the evening I took private lessons from a university student in secular subjects. When I was admitted to Gimnazjum Szwarc-mana, a Jewish boys' high school where secular subjects were taught, Mother arranged for me to continue studying Hebrew after school. The tutors hadn't given me enough preparation to enter the third year of high school. The other kids had already been there two years in *wstępna* and *podwstępina,* introductory, and preintroductory classes, so I found it very hard. They used words that weren't in ordinary Polish, language that wasn't familiar to me, so I felt out of my depth.

All the kids had friends, and felt at home. In gym I felt lonely, and in the manner of kids, instead of making me feel at home, one of the tough kids called me *orli nos,* "eagle beak." I already was very sensitive about my long hooked nose because Mother had predisposed me, that a man with a long nose is an ugly man. She would say, "I hate long noses. Your father had a long nose." So being called eagle beak devastated me. I wanted to hit him, demolish him, but he was so much huskier than I, and tougher, that I only walked away, trying, and failing, to show contempt for him while holding back tears with difficulty. The pain of this incident stayed with me all my life. I struggled at the school and was always behind.

After 1918, we reestablished communication with relatives in America, and they started sending us packages. I remember they sent Kolynos toothpaste, and it created such a foam in the mouth when you were brushing your teeth with it. The talk then was that you don't have to bring anything to America because you could just pick up coal with a shovel in the streets. After so many years of privation and shortages and hunger in Warsaw, the affluence in America that we heard about seemed impossible. Mother put to me the question of whether we should emigrate to America, claiming that as a man, I was the head of the family (though she always ignored my opinions). I opted enthusiastically for immediate emigration. She didn't know I was only thinking about how I might flunk out of school.

*

IN NOVEMBER 1927, SOON AFTER HE TURNS NINETEEN, MY FATHER writes in his journal that a friend of his mother's visited their home with her husband; then he adds:

> They are not important but it is important to me in so far as it recalled to me a life different from the one I have been leading till now, of a sociable life, surrounded by friends and relatives, as for example the environment on Greene Ave. which was to me a taste of such a life.

Greene Avenue is where my father and his mother and sister lived when they first came to this country: an apartment they shared with a cousin; his mother's two brothers Max and Bernard; and her sister Eva—a household made up of extended family, like the home in Warsaw that was his until he was seven. The arrangement was that his mother would keep house while all the others worked, but it didn't last long; she railed against her fate, reduced to cooking for the brothers she scorned as *analfabeta*—illiterate! And they weren't happy with the arrangement, either. Max later told my father that some days he'd return from work and find nothing to eat in the house at all.

My father also describes in his journal a moment when he's re-

minded of the life he was part of in Warsaw that is now out of reach:
the family and community that came with Jewish observance in his
grandfather's home and his Warsaw neighborhood. It's a Jewish holiday, Rosh Hashanah. He writes,

> I didn't feel the holiday spirit that some do on this occasion.
> Ah! how I envied those who had bought clothes anew and im-
> bued with the warm holiday atmosphere paraded around with
> faces lighted up with smiles, and entered houses swarming with
> friends, relatives and all the members of the family. The kitchen
> is stuffed with victuals and the table in the dining room is cov-
> ered with fruit, cake and wine. The atmosphere is filled with
> contentment, the feasting is enlivened by talk and laughter. . . .
> Ah, under such conditions a holiday is a pleasure, something to
> look forward to. And I who love such scenes missed them so
> much the more. Nearing the synagogue I saw many people, old
> men, young men, women and girls, greeting each other congre-
> gated in groups, rejoicing, happy, and I, I, lonely being that I
> am, could but watch and envy. So I didn't go in, just as I failed
> to go in for 3 previous consecutive years, and went to the mov-
> ies.

Seeing Jews of all ages gathering to observe the holiday must have reminded my father of the extended family and Hasidic community he
left, and lost, when he came to America. This contrast adds layers of
meaning to a comment he made after one such description of his childhood in Warsaw:

> Even when I was very little, I recognized that it was a closely
> knit community, almost everyone knowing everyone else, rela-
> tives all living in the same area. You could hardly step into the
> street without encountering a relative. When young people got
> married, after the kest period was over and they got their own
> homes, it was usually on the same street, certainly no more than
> a few blocks away. The chief source of entertainment was visit-
> ing, especially on the Sabbath.

I think again of the historian Piotr Wróbel's observation that World War I brought "the twilight of Jewish Warsaw." My father's Jewish Warsaw was darkened by a final sunset when he emigrated to America. But it lived on—vividly, poignantly—in his memory. And he kept it alive by describing it in detail, and by talking about the people who still walked its streets in his memory.

It dawns on me that this is why my father writes to his aunt Magda in 1934 that he still feels part of life in Warsaw and not of the country he's been living in for fourteen years; and why, when he's old, he keeps returning to these memories in his mind and his conversations: his years in Warsaw are a paradise lost, when he was the youngest member of a household made up of grandparents, aunts, and uncles, with cousins and neighbors going in and out of each other's houses. Reading these comments in his journal, and rereading his memories of Warsaw, I see how deeply my father missed being part of that community—and how deeply I misunderstood him, foolishly believing he was happiest sitting alone at his desk.

Einstein's Lover and Her Sisters

THE STORIES OF
MY FATHER'S AUNTS (AND UNCLES)

I N THE NOTEBOOK WHERE MY FATHER BEGINS WRITING DOWN memories when he retires, the very first entry says he visited his mother's sister Eva in her senior residence, and "we reviewed, between us, all the sisters in order of age." I smile to see him doing with his aging aunt exactly what I do with him when he's old: going down the list of his mother's many sisters, recapping their astonishing life stories and remarkable professions, and then, almost as an afterthought, adding her brothers. (I've listed them all in the appendix.)

If I wonder why my father is ever eager to talk about his mother's siblings, I recall his comment about growing up in his grandfather's household: "That was what I loved most: the liveliness, the warmth, of so many aunts and uncles." I think he's recapturing that warmth by naming them and remembering them. But why do I never tire of listing them with him? Why do I want to tell their stories after he's gone? Getting a sense of their lives helps me understand the world that shaped his: both the household he grew up in and the cataclysmic social changes that were taking place at the time: the decline of Hasidism, the rise of Communism, what was possible for women in the Jewish community of Warsaw and the communities they dispersed to.

I'm fascinated by the lives of my grandmother's sisters, which were so different from their brothers' lives—the brothers my grandmother contemptuously referred to as "illiterate." Like all Hasidic boys, her brothers were protected from the corruption of a secular education, expected to spend their lives in religious study. Such study was not to be wasted on girls. And because they didn't matter, my father explains, girls were allowed to get a secular education. It still stuns me to think of the professions these women, born in Poland in the 1880s, attained: my grandmother, a school principal; Eva, a periodontist; Bronia, a philologist; Magda, a high-ranking official in the Polish government; and Dora, a mathematician and physicist who was a student—and lover— of Einstein, became pregnant with his child, and had an abortion.

LET'S STOP RIGHT THERE. Or start right there. Student of Einstein, lover of Einstein—just the sort of myth that families puff up, or make up, about their forebears. But my father knows specifics—and I find more after he's gone—that make this seem possible, even likely. Dora's story is the most captivating of the sisters', but it's also heartbreaking, because it shows how little can come of a stellar education when a brilliant student is forced to emigrate—and when she's a woman.

"I remember her from Warsaw," my father says,

though she left for Switzerland when I was very young, maybe five. She was the shortest of the sisters. I remember her standing in front of a full-length mirror, combing her hair, and the tips of her hair touched the floor. Usually she wore it in a braid wrapped around her head. She was trying to comb it and was having trouble with it. Like all the brunette sisters, she had long thick hair. My mother, too. Not the blond sisters.

We saw Dora in Switzerland on our way to America. She met us at the Zurich train station wearing a red hat made of paper. I guess that was all she could afford. She came to the United States after we did. I remember her talking with Eva and my mother, and Sam's [his mother's brother's] wife was there. I was only thirteen, so I didn't participate in the conversation, but I listened. Dora was saying that Einstein said she was one of the ten people in the world who understand the theory of relativity.

But what about Dora being pregnant and getting an abortion? How likely is that to be true?

"Eva told me," my father says, "when she was old, that she had a letter from Dora—well, she didn't have it, she didn't save letters like I do. That she got a letter from Dora saying that she was pregnant with Einstein's child and was asking Eva's advice about getting an abortion." It makes sense that Dora would seek such advice from Eva, the first sister to come to this new country, and a dentist, a medical professional.

Dora settled at first in New York, but in the 1930s she moved to Princeton to be near Einstein, and rekindled the affair they had begun in Switzerland. My father explains that Dora thought Einstein would marry her after his wife died. When he didn't, she left Princeton and went as far away as she could: Los Angeles, where she worked as a governess. "I never understood why she didn't go into teaching," my father says. "I never asked her, which I regret."

I'm intrigued that Dora's Yiddish name, Dvoyra, is also Yiddish for Deborah—and that she chose an academic life, though she didn't live out her life as an academic. The end of Dora's story is sadder than sad:

> She committed suicide. She was eighty years old. In Los Angeles she was friendly with only one member of the family, one of Jack's daughters, Sylvia. After Dora committed suicide, Sylvia went into her room, and she saw that it was covered with icons and crosses, and from the papers she could see that Dora had been a lifelong Catholic. She probably converted when she was still in Poland. She was in love with a Polish poet, so maybe that's why she converted. But she never told her family. And this also might explain why she changed her name from Kornblit to Corlitt. And it explains why she never let anyone from the family into her home.

After my father dies, I try to find evidence that might corroborate or belie Dora's connection to Einstein. University of Zurich records confirm that a Dorothe Kornblitt, born 1887, matriculated in chemistry in 1911, when my father was three. That meshes with his memory of her living in his grandfather's house when he was very small. The records also show a Dorota Kornblitt, born 1887, matriculated in physics in 1919. This explains why she was in Zurich in 1920, when my father saw her on his way to the United States. Did she switch to physics because of Einstein, or did her switch bring her into contact with him? He took a position as professor of physics at the University of Zurich in 1912—one year after Dora's first matriculation. Though he moved to Berlin in 1914, he returned to give a series of lectures at the University of Zurich in 1919, the year of Dora's second matriculation. So she could have been romantically involved with Einstein during either or both of his times in Zurich.

Public records also include traces of where Dora lived and the work she did in the United States in the twenties and thirties. These corroborate the story, too. A 1924 Declaration of Intention to apply for citizenship and a 1928 Petition for Naturalization are both filed by Dorothy Corlit, a teacher living in New York City. Einstein settled in Princeton in 1933, and his second wife, Elsa, died in 1936. Dorothy Corlett, a teacher, is listed in 1938 and 1941 Princeton directories. The 1940 census lists her as a houseworker in a private home. Houseworker? Could that be what my father recalled as her working as a governess?

All these dates give credence to my father's recollection that Dora went to Princeton to be with Einstein and expected him to marry her after his wife died. That she was in Einstein's orbit while she lived in Princeton is corroborated by a very different—and very serendipitous—source of information. My father's cousin, his aunt Eva's daughter, lived in a retirement community in Connecticut. There she met an elderly man named Thomas Bucky, who was a good friend of Einstein's in Princeton. She asked if he knew Dora Corlitt, and he said he did: she was called Corly and was "one of the girls, one of Einstein's girls." Though I cringe to hear Dora's connection to Einstein trivialized in this way, Bucky's recollection confirms that she had one.

The most astonishing evidence of Dora's relationship to Einstein comes to me via email. When Walter Isaacson publishes a biography of Einstein, I email to ask if he came across any reference to my great-aunt. Almost immediately, he sends me a link to an item in the Einstein archive: a letter of recommendation handwritten by Einstein.

© THE HEBREW UNIVERSITY OF JERUSALEM, ISRAEL.
DIGITAL IMAGE PHOTOGRAPHED BY ARDON BAR HAMA.

Here's an English translation:

> Miss Dorothea Corlitt studied mathematics in Zurich and I have known her very well for many years. She has frequently and successfully taught mathematics, physics and chemistry on various levels, also French. I consider her a hardworking educator with an extensive educational background and a remarkable intellectual ability.

Einstein did not date the letter, but someone typed at the top, "[Pasadena, winter 1931–32]," a year or two before Einstein moved to Princeton.

SO I KNOW THAT this much of my father's account is true: Dora studied with Einstein in Zurich; had a relationship of some sort with him that continued when he came to the United States; lived in Princeton, where he lived, after his wife died; and eventually moved clear across the country. I haven't substantiated that she was his lover and became pregnant with his child, but whether or not it's true—and I think it most likely is true—what startles me is that my grandmother's sister, born into a strictly observant Hasidic family in Warsaw in 1887, studied mathematics, physics, and chemistry in Zurich; knew Albert Einstein "very well for many years," in the words of his own handwritten letter of recommendation; and sought work as a teacher, but became instead a "houseworker" in a private home.

I get to hear Dora's own voice, and learn more about her life, in letters that I find in my father's files. There's a copy of a letter Dora wrote to her sister Eva, dated June 11, 1946. Now living in Los Angeles, Dora writes that she has hit upon a way to earn a living:

> Baby things is my new craze and I may make more money with them than with anything else. I have a heck of a time to get the yarns, cross stitch canvas, and the DMC threads. I had already a couple orders as the people simply rave about them. Primarily I am concentrating on baby jackets. . . . It is really a set—Mama and baby—crochet in a most lovely stitch and colors with all sorts of variations in decoration. The baby jacket I am selling $6 apiece for the baby and Mamma's. I didn't figure it out as yet. I made the same pattern as a sweater blouse and get for the work alone $12—it is quite a little. The idea is to break into the movie colony and then everything will be OK. My main idea is to work a mail order enterprise and then I can stay anywhere I please in USA. It will depend upon how easy I can get the material. . . . It would make me free and quite independent from people—even more than teaching or anything else.

It's shattering to see Dora, her academic training and accomplishments receded to a distant past, hoping to sell her crocheted baby jackets to people working in the Hollywood movie industry.

The second letter that fills in a detail of Dora's life is dated 1992 and addressed to my father. It's from Dora's youngest sister, Magda, who was still living in Warsaw and is apparently—once again!—answering my father's questions about her sisters. Magda writes (in Polish), "Dora was in Warsaw in 1928 probably seeking her lover. She was beautiful, intelligent, highly educated, spoke six languages. I agree hers was a wasted life. What a pity nothing's left of her save the photo you sent me."

I think I have the photo my father sent, as I have only one of Dora.

*My father's
aunt Dora*

*

IF MY FATHER'S AUNT DORA BRUSHED HISTORY THROUGH HER RELA-
tionship with Albert Einstein, her sister Magda didn't just brush history; she helped make it. And if Dora's life has a roller-coaster quality,
as she went from being a physicist to crocheting baby jackets she hoped
to sell, Magda's life takes a roller-coaster ride in the other direction:
from eight years locked up as a political prisoner to a position high up
in the Polish government, living in a spacious apartment with a house-
keeper to help clean and cook, and a car and driver provided by the
Party. Magda's life reads like—is—a chapter in the history of Poland.
She's everywhere in my father's memories of his childhood—and a
huge influence on him: the youngest of my grandmother's many sisters
and brothers, she was only six years older than my father, more like an
adored and admired older sister than an aunt. Of all his aunts, Magda
is the one who returns most often and most vividly in my father's
stories—and because she visited us in the United States and we visited
her in Poland several times, she is the aunt I knew best, too.

———

"I LOVED MAGDA," MY father says. "Before the First World War, when I lived with my grandfather and all my aunts and uncles, Magda was my protector against my mother. I didn't care for my mother. I was afraid of her mostly. She used to lash out. I was always getting beatings. Magda saved me quite a few of them."

Magda figures in one of my father's earliest memories:

> One time when I was very little, I must have been about four, I was sitting in the stairwell crying all day. It couldn't have been that long, but that's how I remember it. I was crying because my mother had made me wear one of my sister's outgrown dresses. I didn't want to go outside like that, because the other boys made fun of me. Magda found me there and convinced my mother to take the dress off me and let me wear pants.

I've heard my father tell this story from the time I was very young. While still a child, I wrote one of my first short stories based on it. I didn't know what the stairwell in Warsaw looked like, so I pictured my father as a little boy on the stairs of the apartment building across the street from our house in Brooklyn. But it isn't until he's old, and we're listing his mother's sisters, that my father tells me it was Magda who rescued him.

PEOPLE ARE ASTONISHED TO learn that I have relatives in Warsaw. Nearly all the 3 million Jews living in Poland when the Second World War began were killed during the war. When most American Jews make heritage trips to Europe, they visit the places their forebears came from; they don't find relatives. They don't even find graves, since Jewish cemeteries were desecrated and destroyed. Only 11,500 of the 300,000 Jews living in Warsaw before the war remained alive when the city was liberated by Soviet troops. But not all the troops that liberated the city were Soviet. Along with them were Polish troops led by Polish officers, members of the Polish army constituted in Russia during the war. My father's aunt Magda was an officer in that army.

*My father's aunt
Magda in Polish
army officer's
uniform
(photo taken in
USSR, 1944)*

How did my father's aunt survive the war? How did she become an officer in the Polish army in exile, and, after the war, a high-ranking official in the Polish government?

Here's what I know from my father, which he learned from Magda herself.

When the Germans invaded Poland in 1939, Magda was five years into a term in prison for her Communist activities. It was her second time in prison. Earlier, she had served a three-year sentence in a Warsaw jail. This time, she had a daughter who was two when she was arrested. The child's father was Christian, and she stayed with his parents in their village. Magda was imprisoned in a town near the Russian border. When the Germans were about to overrun the town, the prison guards let the criminals go but left the Communists in jail, hoping the Germans would get them. But the townspeople let them out, too, and they escaped over the border to Russia. The last detail I knew from my father—and from my own acquaintance with Magda and her family—is that Magda met and married a fellow Polish Jewish Communist in Russia; they returned to Poland together after the war, and both joined the newly constituted postwar Communist government.

I learn more details—including many surprises—from Magda's daughter, the little girl who survived World War II in a village with her father's family. She was in her seventies and still living in Warsaw, but I caught up with her when she was visiting her own daughters, who live in the United States. As she fills in Magda's story, I'm reminded of how much human experience, how much insight into history, is erased by summaries of events in people's lives. My first surprise is that Magda's making it over the border to Russia—and then to Lvov—was not in itself an escape to freedom. Most Polish Communists who turned up in Russia during the war were immediately arrested and sent to Siberia. Magda avoided that fate by showing an affidavit, given to her by Ukrainian Communists who had been imprisoned with her, attesting to her loyalty to the Soviet Union.

I'm also surprised to learn that the son I know, only a year younger than I, is not Magda's second child but her third. In Lvov, Magda became editor of a Polish language Communist journal; met a man who was also a Polish Communist; and they had a baby. Tragically, the man drowned in a swimming accident. When the Germans invaded Russia, Magda and the baby were evacuated to the Ural Mountains, but Russia was in the grip of famine, and the baby died from malnutrition.

Yet another surprise lies behind Magda becoming an officer in the Polish army in exile. I'd assumed she simply signed up. Hardly, her daughter explains. When Magda heard that a Polish army was being formed in the Soviet Union, she wrote to the authorities and asked to join. They refused. She applied three or four times, and was rejected each time. It turned out they didn't want too many Jews. Finally, she wrote to the Union of Polish Patriots in Moscow, and there found friends from before the war, also Polish Jews, who arranged for her to be accepted. Magda was wearing the uniform of an army officer when she sought out her twelve-year-old daughter in the village that had been the child's home for so long, it was the only one she knew. The little girl guessed that this stranger must be her mother—and had no desire to go with her. Magda wanted to take her immediately to live with her in military barracks, but agreed to wait until she moved to a proper apartment with her new husband, and before long another child that she had with him.

Polish Communists, most of whom Magda had known or been imprisoned with before the war, were now in power, so it was natural for her to join their government. She went to work for the Communist Party central committee as vice secretary for human relations. Later she was head of cooperative national farms. Her husband was undersecretary of the treasury. In 1967 the Polish government turned on the Jews: most lost their jobs and any perks that went with them. A small article in *The New York Times* reported that only two Jews remained in positions of power in Poland; one of them was Magda's husband. (She had retired by then.)

After the war, Magda contacted her relatives living in the United States and later, when the Cold War began to thaw, visited them—visited us—twice, first in 1959 with her thirteen-year-old son, and again in the early 1970s with her husband. On that second visit, the FBI made us aware of how important Magda's husband was. Before they arrived, an agent visited my father in his law office to make a proposal: my father should take his Polish visitors on a bus trip, sit beside his uncle, and ask questions about the Polish economy. That was all. A Polish-speaking FBI agent sitting in the row behind them would do the rest. My father declined. After Magda and her husband arrived, my parents planned a dinner for them and several other relatives, including me. We arranged—by telephone—to meet at Mamma Leone's, an Italian restaurant in Manhattan. Amazingly, one of the waiters spoke Polish. He stood by our table with a white cloth napkin draped over his forearm, but ignored requests for waiterly services. He was too busy engaging Magda's husband in a conversation about the Polish economy.

ANOTHER OF MY GRANDMOTHER'S SISTERS was also swept up in the Communist dream of a just society that drew Magda away from her parents' religion. Bronia, too, played a part in trying to fulfill that dream. Her life story ends very differently from Magda's, because it intersects with something else that was pervasive at the time, the disease that rendered my father fatherless: tuberculosis.

During the same trip to Switzerland on their way to America, when my father and his mother and sister visited Dora, they also visited another sister, Bronia. She, too, was educated. My father calls her a philologist: "I heard her telling my mother that she knew ten languages thoroughly, and had acquaintance with about twenty." I'm predictably pleased by this connection to my own profession, though "philologist," like "linguist," now refers to someone who studies language, not someone who speaks many languages. Bronia wasn't in Switzerland to study. She was there, my father explains, "because of her lungs. They used to say she had one lung collapsed. She only had one functioning lung. That's why she was sent to the mountains in Switzerland. She was living in Mont Pèlerin, above Lake Geneva."

Hearing this, I think that a collapsed lung was Bronia's disease. I learn later that collapsing a lung was then the standard treatment for tuberculosis. The confluence of these two forces so emblematic of the times—one medical and one political—cost Bronia her life. But before they did, she took part in the era's dramatic events. My father tells me that Bronia went to Russia at the time of the Bolshevik Revolution to work for the cause. She knew she was taking a chance, because of her lungs. Sure enough, she died there and was buried in the Crimea.

BRONIA'S STORY, TOO, IS filled in for me by a letter from Magda to my father. She writes that her sister Bronka surprised her by turning up in Warsaw shortly after my father left for America, in 1921:

> Apparently in the course of the year 1920 she made a friendly connection with a leftist in Switzerland and decided on permanent emigration to the Soviet Union. She wasn't in the best of health. She took her temperature several times a day. But she was full of enthusiasm, impatient to participate in the great events taking place in Russia. She was very happy to learn that at that time I, too, was connected with the Communist Movement. She cautioned me to be very careful not to get arrested. Among others, Chicherin, the past foreign minister of the Soviet Union, was with them and she was sure that as a Polish citizen they will promptly grab her off the train and send her to Siberia. Luckily she reached Moscow happily. There she got herself very much involved in political work, got married. In the meantime I got myself arrested, received a three year sen-

tence. This worried Bronka very much and she engaged herself with it, often helped me as much as she could, wrote me frequently, even sent quite large sums of money for efforts to free me through bribes. Nothing came of it and I served my sentence to the end in a Warsaw jail as a political prisoner. Unfortunately her fate also was unhappy. Her husband, if memory serves, was a Swede named Rutgers. He was charged with Trotskyism and sent to Siberia and, though this was for her life threatening, she followed. There she fell ill with the tuberculosis which had been cured in Switzerland. They tried as much as they could to save her, sent her to a sanatorium in Yalta in the Crimea. It did not help. She died there. News of this was sent to me in prison by her husband together with the legend on her monument: "A will of iron, a heart of gold." I held onto these pitiful mementos for a long time, but my prison sentences and the war caused the disappearance of her letters and yours as well. I was in Yalta in the '50s. I tried to find the cemetery in order to locate her grave. But I was assured that it was totally destroyed and persuaded to abandon the effort.

FROM LEFT: *my father's aunt Eva, Ruchcia's daughter Topcia, my father, his sister Ella, his aunt Regina (standing), his aunt Magda, his aunt Bronia*

Though Magda is telling here about her sister's sad end, she is also reminding me of her own hardship and losses—and those of others who lived, and died, through the wars and political upheavals that convulsed Eastern Europe in the first half of the twentieth century.

THE THIRD SISTER WHO played a role in history, though a small one, is my grandmother, who, in 1915, established and became the principal of the first school for Hasidic girls in Warsaw, and probably in Poland—and ran it for the next five years. Though she's my grandmother, and I was twenty-eight when she died, the woman who did these things is as distant from me—as much a historical figure I know only from my father's stories—as her sisters Dora and Bronia. In a way, I have two grandmothers: the one I knew and the one in my father's memories of Warsaw. They are such different people, I have to remind myself that they are both my grandmother.

In my memories of my childhood, my father's mother visits our home in Brooklyn most Sundays. She appears at our door, an imposing (to me) stocky old woman with a thin white-and-yellow braid wound atop her head. I assume that the yellow means she was blond, like my father and me, but years later he tells me that her hair was dark; the yellow tinge came when it turned white. To greet me, she leans down and thrusts her chin toward me to kiss. She has an acrid smell about her, a smell that clings to the bathroom after she uses it. In my memory, she never shows any interest in me. I remember only one time that she spoke to me. I'm in junior high school; her usual Sunday visit is coming to an end, and it's time for my father to take her home. I volunteer to go along. As we drive through Brooklyn, she half-turns to me in the backseat and asks, "How many languages do you speak?" I reply "Two" with some pride, knowing how impressed my Spanish teacher is that I've actually learned to speak and write that language in his class.

"Hmph!" she scoffs. "I speak five languages! Polish, Russian, German, Yiddish, and English!"

I'm sure I remember this conversation because I was hurt by her scorn, and thought it unjust: her life served up those languages to her.

I have no other memories of her talking to me, and none of her showing me any affection, so I didn't have much affection for her.

But I admire the grandmother in World War I Warsaw, and I'm proud to discover that the school she established and ran, Chavaceles, is mentioned in history books and on the website of the Warsaw Museum of the History of the Polish Jews. The website describes the founding of the school during the German occupation of World War I and names my grandmother, spelling her name Salomea Tenenwurcel, as its first principal. I learn there that the school remained until 1931 in the building where my grandmother established and furnished it, and where my father lived until they left for America in 1920. I learn, too, that it moved to a different location in 1937 and—a chilling glimpse of the life, and death, my father escaped by emigrating when he did—the school continued to operate in secret in the Warsaw Ghetto until 1942, shortly before the ghetto was liquidated, and anyone still living within its walls was sent to concentration camps.

The essay I found about Dr. Emanuel Carlebach, the German rabbi who raised money for the school and hired my grandmother to run it, also places the school in historical context. "A German Rabbi Goes East" explains that Rabbi Carlebach encountered a lot of resistance in Poland to his goal of improving education for the impoverished and backward East European Jews. He regarded establishing the Chavaceles School as his most significant achievement. And a mention of the school in a book by Shoshana Pantel Zolty about the history of women and the study of Torah helps explain how my grandmother and her sisters came to be educated despite their father's devout Hasidism. Zolty explains that Rabbi Carlebach's efforts to improve education among the Jews of Warsaw were rejected by all but one "more broadminded" group: "It was the *Gerer Hasidim* who initially endorsed . . . the education of Orthodox girls." My father's grandfather was a Gerer Hasid, a follower of the rebbe of Ger. Maybe that's why he tolerated his daughters' pursuing secular education and even, I assume, paid for it, since no schools in Poland at the time were free.

THIS MIGHT EXPLAIN, TOO, how my grandmother's sister Eva studied dentistry in Poland. She came to the United States at twenty-one, in

January 1914, just before the First World War broke out. Retraining at Temple University, she became the first woman periodontist—and the first woman dentist—in Newark, where she continued to practice until she retired at eighty-four. So Eva was a pioneer, if not a revolutionary. As late as the 1950s, only 1 percent of dentists were women. Yet she was representative of her times, too. I'm intrigued to learn that many of the first women dentists in the United States were immigrants.

Talking about Eva, my father recalls a scene from his very young childhood that helps me imagine the Warsaw apartment he grew up in. He says, with his usual self-mocking irony:

> I remember Eva from Warsaw, though I was only five when she left. One thing in particular I remember. We used to have those chifforobes, freestanding wardrobes. There were no built-in closets until later. I climbed up on top of one of them—I must have been four years old—and I was waiting for someone to come in, to see me. A few people came in and sat there, but nobody noticed me. Eva was sitting there at the table and I wanted her to take note of this great thing I'd done, climbing up on top of that wardrobe, so I made some noise and she looked up and saw me and started yelling, "Get down from there!" She made me cry. I had expected to be praised!

OF THE EIGHT SISTERS whose fates I know, only the oldest lived the life of a Hasidic wife. Ruchcia's life represents the one that Eva, Dora, Bronia, and Magda rejected, and my grandmother escaped—or was deprived of—because her husband died so soon after they married: Ruchcia married the Hasidic man chosen by her father, kept house for him, and raised their five children. She also adhered to the custom of keeping her head shaved after marriage. In all the photos I have of the sisters, Ruchcia is the only one with short hair; it's obviously a wig.

My father tells me many stories about Ruchcia, stories suffused with his affection for her. He says,

> I could talk about Ruchcia for a long time. She was beauti-
> ful, taller than my mother, and unlike my mother she was al-

My father's aunt Ruchcia and her daughter Topcia

ways happy, always smiling. And very talkative. I loved listening to her and watching her. . . . I remember her saying—there's a saying, *Kawałek chleba z masłem zawsze spada masłem do dołu*. It means, "When a piece of bread falls, it always falls with the butter down." I never forgot that. It's a very important thing to know.

She was a cardplayer, the only one in the family to play cards. She did not get an education, like the other sisters, but she was smart in other ways. I remember hearing her say that her husband may be the king in the entire home but in the kitchen she's queen and would not allow him to set foot in it without her permission.

Ruchcia's death is emblematic of the era, too: she fell victim to the 1918 flu epidemic. She was thirty-eight.

The remaining two of my grandmother's sisters had tragic fates, too—and, in one case, a tragic life. A sister named Dina died three years before my father was born. "She was only fourteen when she burned to death," my father says. "She was cooking, and her apron caught fire. Her sisters poured water on her. They didn't know that makes it worse." The other is Regina, a sister who had epilepsy so severe she never left the house. My father remembers her as always unhappy, often the object of her siblings' anger because she'd snitch on them to their father, who would beat them with his cane. In 1927, seven years after my father left Warsaw, Regina went out on the balcony of their third-floor apartment and jumped.

Because Regina and Dina died and were buried in Warsaw before World War I, I have records of their deaths and photographs of their gravestones, retrieved from a database of Jewish cemeteries in Poland. Though my father always referred to her Polish name, Regina, she's identified on the cemetery records by her Yiddish name, Rivka.

Of the five brothers who lived to adulthood, all but one emigrated to America. The first to come, my father's uncle Jack, is the one who sponsored all those who came after. He worked most of his life raising funds for an organization whose name has nearly mythic overtones for many American Jews: HIAS (pronounced *HIGH-us*), the Hebrew Immigrant Aid Society. Founded in 1881, this is the organization that helped the great wave of East European Jewish immigrants who arrived in New York between 1880 and 1924. The oldest of all the siblings, Jack was thirty-three when he arrived in the United States in 1912. My father says,

I didn't know Jack in Poland. When I was born, he was already married to a woman from Łódź, and was living with her there. I heard that he went into business, but it didn't work out. He had to declare bankruptcy. The law was that he'd have to pay out whatever was left; he'd have nothing. So he went to America. He took what was left when he declared bankruptcy and emigrated.

The youngest brother, whom I knew as Bernard or Bob, was the uncle I knew best. Only seven years older than my father, Uncle Bob, and his wife, Mary, were very much a part of our family's life in the United States. It wasn't until our conversations about his childhood that I understood how large a role Bob played in my father's young life. In Poland, my father tells me, "His name was Boruch Zishe. When I was a kid, I thought it was one name, Brookzeesha." In many of the stories my father tells, he's a frightened little boy and Bernard is the older brother who makes him feel safe.

> One time when I was little—I must have been about six—I was walking with him and one of his friends. They would have been fifteen or even fourteen. We came to a bridge, one of the three bridges that cross the Vistula. I guess I was hesitant, though it wasn't very high above the water or very long either, nothing compared to our bridges in New York. Each took an arm and they carried me across the bridge. I don't know why it made me feel more secure to be carried rather than walk between them but it did.

Though Boruch Zishe had no secular education, he didn't remain Hasidic, either:

> Bernard rejected religion, refused any kind of study when he became a teenager. He refused to wear the Hasidic uniform. All the sons, except one, doffed traditional clothing, but Bernard also violated the Sabbath by carrying a cane—it was forbidden to carry anything on the Sabbath—and traveling while his father was in shul. I saw Bernard catch a blow from the old man more than once. He was the sort of fellow about whom we used to say, it's a Yiddish expression, "Every nail started up with him." In other words, he was always getting into fights, but it was never his fault, others started up with him and tore his clothes. He got plenty of beatings from his father, but it never did much good.

The oldest brother, Jack, got his younger brother a job working for HIAS in Poland. My father recalls, "He was handling money, riding around in carriages, and he dressed well. He spiffed himself out with long pants and spats. That filled me with wonder and longing. He used me as a messenger to take notes to and from his girlfriends. He had a lot of girlfriends." It's funny to imagine my father doing for his uncle what young people today do by text.

My father goes on:

> Bob came to America in 1919; he was just eighteen. Right away he went to work for HIAS in New York. His job was to meet immigrants when they came off the boats, and help them get settled. That's how he met Mary. She was a young girl, Russian from Odessa, and was brought over by a man she had agreed to marry. That man was supposed to meet her, but he was com-

My father's uncle Bernard as a boy in Hasidic garb between his brothers Max (on the left) and Sam

Bernard as a young man in Warsaw working for HIAS

ing from Canada, and he got delayed, so Bob met her instead, and he married her.

For our family, this is a happy ending: Bob and Mary fall in love at first sight and live happily ever after. But I can't help thinking how disastrous this must have been for the man who made it possible for Mary to come here, expecting to marry her. Whether he would have been a better or worse husband for Mary, or she a better or worse wife for him than the one I hope he eventually married, I don't know. I guess all our lives are shaped—or misshaped—by chance, but the story of Bob meeting Mary reminds me how much is unpredictable and confused when people leave their home countries to establish new lives in another.

His father's beatings probably helped drive Bernard away from his father's religion. They did that for his brother Sam, who came to the United States in 1912, when he was eighteen or twenty, depending on which of the documents I have seen online is accurate. According to his son, Sam never spoke of his life in Poland, except for one incident that he described when explaining his antipathy for religious fanaticism: his father beat him for carrying something on the Sabbath, too—something even smaller than a cane: a comb!

The third brother who came to New York is Max. He, too, had epilepsy, though not as severe as his sister Regina. He left Warsaw for New York in 1913, at twenty-two, and went to work in the garment district, as so many East European Jewish immigrants did. When my father quit high school at fourteen, Max was the one who helped him get a job in a factory there. Though Max managed to get jobs, he often lost them because of his epilepsy. My father tells me, "One day I came upon Max at the top of a staircase leading down to the subway. Just as I greeted him, he had a seizure. He would probably have fallen down the stairs, maybe even gotten killed, if I hadn't been there to grab him."

There's one more brother, the only one I never met, because he never came to the United States. Instead, he followed a path completely different from the others': "I don't remember much about my uncle Joshua, Schia," my father says, pronouncing his nickname *SHEE-uh*, "even though he lived in Warsaw the entire time I was there.

He was the brother just above Bernard and Magda, and I was very close to them. He remained a Hasid, like his father, except he was more so. I heard from those who visited Warsaw before World War II that their father complained that Joshua was too religious." My father says this with a sense of disbelief: how could anyone be more religious than his grandfather? And how odd, since all the other siblings except the oldest sister, abandoned Hasidism and most abandoned religion altogether. It occurs to me that becoming even stricter in observance could be Schia's response to seeing the faith, the way of life he was raised in, crumbling around him.

"I never got close to Joshua," my father explains.

He didn't have much to say to me. He was always busy with his theological studies. That must have been why he didn't follow his sisters and brothers to America. Same with his father. They believed that when Jews went to America, they ceased being Jews, because they ceased being Hasidic. Joshua's life was tragic, too. When he was twenty-one, his father arranged a marriage for him with a widow who was quite a bit older and had two children, but it was considered a good match because she had a little store, a tobacco shop, and my grandfather felt that at least he would be fed adequately, after having been hungry for so long. I remember during the war he got a job watching a warehouse during the night, and he was bitten by a rat. After he had the tobacco store—he'd only been there a short time—I visited him there, and he had a telephone, which he let me use to call my mother at the school. That was exciting. But then the government made a monopoly of tobacco, so selling it became a civil service position and Jews were not allowed, so he lost that business. And his whole fortune was gone, the fortune probably consisting of only enough to eat.

When my mother visited in 1930, he had a shop selling seltzer. He was poverty-stricken. I heard that he kept after his father to share with him the money he received from America, which the old man was reluctant to do. By then Joshua and his wife had three more children, so there were five children to feed. They all died in the gas chambers—Schia, his wife, and their five children.

I GET TO SEE a photograph of one of those children, a little girl, and to hear Schia's voice in Yiddish on the back. Schia sent the picture to his sister Chai-Sura, my grandmother, in America, apparently hoping that seeing the child named after their mother might inspire her to send money. He writes:

> Dear sister Chai=Sura: I'm sending you a special photo of my lovely daughter Leah, a dear child (named after her maternal grandma). I wonder why you had completely forgotten me, although I don't wonder, because (even) my father in Warsaw thinks of me very little.
>   (signed) Your brother Jehoshua Leib Kornblit

Cruelly, the religious devotion that kept Schia in Poland condemned him and his family to destitution—and led to their deaths.

                              *

I'M GRATEFUL THAT MY FATHER'S NOSTALGIA—HIS LONGING—FOR the liveliness and warmth of his childhood in Warsaw spurs him to preserve his aunts' and uncles' stories. I'm fascinated that their fates tell the history of the era they lived in, and that some of them played roles in that history. But, by a grand stroke of irony, my father's obsession with reviving these lives forces him, and therefore me, to see that his sweet memories of that household are far from the reality of that family. If I'm tempted to idealize the large family and Hasidic community that made my father feel loved and safe when he was a small child, a letter his aunt Magda writes in 1985 shatters that illusion. Answering my father's questions about the family he left behind when he left Warsaw, Magda tells a very different story of the aunts and uncles and the grandparents that my father felt such affection for—and from. The brief, plaintive note his uncle Schia wrote on the back of a photograph is a way into the truer story.

The money Schia knew his father was receiving from America was sent most faithfully by Jakub Rachmiel, my father's uncle Jack. Magda's letter explains why, of all his many children, Jack was their father's favorite. She begins by responding to my father's fond memories of his aunts and uncles and grandfather: "I can't share your nostalgia. It's not easy for me to reminisce warmly, the family warmth, his warmth, because there was none of it in our home." She traces this sad truth to the Hasidic tradition that required her father to marry his wife's sister when his first wife died giving birth to Jack. Magda writes that her father "truly grieved after the first wife, whom he, I guess, truly loved. Father did not like and did not respect our mother, he treated her as someone imposed on him." So it's not a surprise that "the only son, whom he really worshipped, was Jakub, his firstborn son of this beloved deceased wife."

The wife that her father "did not like and did not respect" is my father's beloved grandmother, who gave birth to all but one, and raised all, of the siblings—fourteen whose stories I know, twenty if I include those my father mentioned who died at birth or as toddlers. Magda, too, adored her mother, and blames her father for the way he treated her: "I faulted him, that he ruined the life of our wonderful mother. His coldness to her did not stop him from producing new children and making her a slave. She endured this quietly and obediently, her only satisfaction was great love for her children." The tragedy of her mother's life, Magda goes on to say, was losing nearly all of them: to illness, accidents, and, most of all, emigration.

My father, too, said often that his grandfather loved his first wife but never loved his second, though she bore and raised his many children, including the one born to her sister; kept his house; and slept by his side her entire adult life, including most of her teens. I always saw this as calamitous for her, my father's adored Bubishi. Not until I read Magda's letter do I realize that their forced marriage was calamitous for his grandfather, too—and for their many children. My father tells Magda that, though, as a child, he idealized her family, he recognized, as an adult, how far from ideal the family really was: "It was always so painful to me to observe how little sympathy there existed among the siblings, to say nothing about the parents. Rarely was there a loving relationship between any of them, or a feeling of closeness." He says this after telling Magda that he attended a gathering of another branch of the family and saw grown siblings who were close and enjoyed each other's company. "I was filled with envy and regret that this was never the case among the Kornbliths." (The *h* was added to the name in the United States.)

What an unlikely confluence of circumstances allows me to see both the idealized family of my father's memories of his childhood and the family's actual dark underbelly. I see the romanticized liveliness and warmth thanks to my father's obsessive recollection of the Hasidic community at the turn of the twentieth century in Warsaw. And I see the vast and varied legacy of that community reflected in the many children of his mother's Hasidic family. But it's only because the youngest of those children remained in Poland and survived the war that I learn the true story of how the strictures of that community could circumscribe, even ruin, the lives of its members. I find myself thinking that the lack of warmth Magda describes might explain not only the lack of closeness among the aunts and uncles but also—even more disastrously for my father—the lack of warmth that his mother created in the three-person household she headed. This knowledge makes more poignant my father's bringing his mother's Hasidic family together once again, and keeping them together, by remembering and telling the stories of his many aunts and uncles.

"I Feel Like a Jew"

"DADDY," I ASK MY FATHER WHEN HE'S OLD, "DO YOU FEEL MORE American or more Polish?"

He says, "I feel like a Jew."

I FEEL LIKE A Jew, too. I feel Jewish in the same way that I feel I'm American and a woman. They're all part of what I guess would be called my identity: immutable, fundamental, defining. For my father, being Jewish is immutable, fundamental, and defining in a way that nationality can't be. Though his fealty to the United States is deep and unwavering—he says often that this is the best country in the world—he never feels quite American because he lived the first dozen years of his life in Poland. Yet in Poland he never felt quite Polish. In our conversations about his childhood in Warsaw, when he says "Pole," he's referring to Christian citizens of Poland. Jews were not regarded as, or treated as, full citizens. They were seen, first and foremost, as Jews. They didn't have the rights or opportunities that Christians had. Their participation in government and civil service, in business and civil society, was restricted or forbidden. In the America my father came to, there was nothing like that level of discrimination, but even here, there were places Jews couldn't go, jobs Jews couldn't have.

AFTER I GRADUATE FROM COLLEGE, I get a job at Metropolitan Life Insurance Company. When I announce this news at dinner, my father says, "In my time, they didn't hire Jews. It wasn't only MetLife. Most companies didn't. Someone I knew whose last name wasn't obviously Jewish, she got a job, but as soon as she stayed home on a Jewish holiday, she was fired."

I never felt that being Jewish barred me from anything.

I'M TALKING TO A British friend. I tell her that an illness I contracted tends to afflict tall, thin Caucasian women. I expect her to share my astonishment that such a serendipitous array of characteristics would render me vulnerable to a disease. Instead, she says, "But you're not Caucasian." I'm baffled until she explains, "You're Jewish."

My father wouldn't have needed an explanation.

If I don't think Jewish is a race—though in 1987 the Supreme Court ruled that it is, so Jews are protected by laws against racial discrimination—what is it? A religion? Yes, but I'm not religious. A culture? I hear people talk about "cultural Jews," but that term feels inadequate to me; "culture" doesn't go deep enough. I'm more comfortable with the term "secular Jew"; that feels like a reasonable way to describe Jews who aren't "observant," but it still doesn't say what Judaism is. Is it a nationality, as the executive order issued by President Trump in 2019 decrees, so educational institutions can be found in violation of the Civil Rights Act of 1964 if they discriminate against Jews? Though this is a worthy goal, I feel that my nationality is American. Is Judaism an ethnic heritage? For me, that comes closest. I'm Jewish because my parents and grandmothers—I never knew my grandfathers—and my parents' sisters and brothers, were formed by the Yiddish-speaking orthodox Jewish communities of Europe they were all raised in, and they formed the community that raised me. Especially my parents. Especially my father.

EVERYTHING ABOUT MY FATHER is Jewish: his love of reading, of ideas, of learning make him much like a Talmudic scholar; his wry, self-deprecating humor; the jokes he tells; that he's a master joke teller who knows a joke—a Jewish joke—for nearly every circumstance and topic that arises when he's in a social situation. Even his distaste for pets—he put up with my adored cats, but never approved of them—

reflects a discomfort with the very notion of animals in a home, which, I learn as an adult, is common among orthodox Jews. (When my new kitten mistakes my father's long leg for a tree and tries to run up it, using claws to hang on, I fear she's proving him right.) For almost all his life, the people my father is close to are Jewish. The Warsaw community he grew up in was entirely Jewish. The street whose name I heard so many times, Twarda Ulica, was one of the main streets in the Hasidic community of Warsaw. The families who live on the block in Brooklyn where I grow up are almost all Catholic, but the two couples who become my parents' close friends head the two other Jewish families living on our block. When my parents move to Westchester, most of those who live in their condominium complex and all their friends are Jewish. The same is true when they move to Florida.

My sisters' and my biblical first names reflect our father's devotion to Jewishness: Naomi, Miriam, and Deborah—and Rachel for the fourth daughter he wanted—were his choices. Our mother's preference, reflecting her desire to be a modern American Jew, shows up in our middle names: Louise, Barbara, and Frances—names none of us use. The foods we ate at home were Jewish. Not just lox and bagels but chopped liver, gefilte fish, borscht, blintzes, and matzoh ball soup. Except in our house there weren't any matzoh balls; there were only *kneidlach*. The English I heard at home growing up was part Yiddish, though I didn't always recognize it. We called my mother's mother Babi, which rhymes with "lobby," and my father's mother Bubi, with the vowel in "book." Throughout my childhood I thought these were completely different names. It wasn't until I grew up and heard others refer to their "bubbees" that I realized Babi and Bubi aren't names at all, but different ways to pronounce the Yiddish word for "grandmother."

My English is still Yiddish-rich. I save my father's witty quips in a file I call "Dad's *chochmes*." That's the Yiddish word my father uses when he tells me the funny or charming things my little nieces and nephews say. "Have you heard the latest *chochmes* from . . . ?" he begins, then recounts something worthy of *Kids Say the Darndest Things,* like when my sister's little boy asked, "Grandpa, why are you bald? What happened to your hair?" and he replied, "It fell out." The boy then grabbed a fistful of hair on top of his own head, tugged it, and said, "Mine's stuck!"

I automatically use Yiddish words and expressions in conversation. I describe someone as a *nudnik* or a *schnorrer,* then have to explain what the word means. But the English translations—a pest, a sponger—never capture the words' true meanings, which is why I use the Yiddish words in the first place. I say, "You needed that like a *loch-in-kop,*" to show sympathy when someone tells me about an inconvenience or stroke of ill luck. I could say, "You needed that like a hole in the head," but in English it sounds lame, and flat. When I say it in Yiddish, I hear my mother's voice, then I see her, and I like bringing her into the room by echoing what she would say.

THE OLDER HE GETS, the more Yiddish my father uses in conversation. When he's ninety-seven, he says, "*Malokh hamoves,* the angel of death. I feel he's hovering over me, sending me signals saying 'It's time. Come on.'"

His using Yiddish words and sayings is one of the things I love about talking to my father—and miss most poignantly after he's gone. But the Yiddish words I hear are misshapen by my English ears. One day my father remarks, "It's halomoid, the plain days of Passover." "Halomoid" is the way I write it down, because that's how it sounds to me. Reading my notes, I turn to Google and find the Yiddish term *Chol Hamoed*—the days between the beginning and ending holy days of Passover. I like this phrase, though I'm not sure how to pronounce it. I also like the concept, though to me Passover is a one-day holiday: the first or second night, when I attend a seder. (Here I confront the merging of Yiddish and English. At first I think I should put "seder" in italics, because it's a foreign word. But to me it's an English word, so I don't.) The literal translation of *Chol Hamoed,* Google tells me, is "the weekday of the festival," but I prefer the way my father defines it: "the plain days of Passover."

This phrase reminds me that my experience of Passover is a pale trace of what my father's was, when life in his grandfather's home was shaped by the elaborate preparations for, and strict observance of, Jewish holidays. But there's a connection, too: during my childhood, Passover brings my extended family together as holidays did when my father was a child in Warsaw, though the tone is different. Our annual seders were joint productions of my mother's sisters and brothers and their families. With fourteen adults and eleven children who otherwise rarely gather all together, it feels more like an exuberant celebration than a somber religious observance. Though Uncle Albert makes a heroic attempt to read aloud the Hagaddah—the text telling the story of Exodus, as tradition requires, before dinner begins—he never manages to make it through, because Uncle Norman keeps interrupting with irreverent jokes and asides, till it all breaks down with everyone talking and laughing and demanding to eat. It was at a seder that I had my first public speaking experience. When I was five or six, I stood on a chair and called out an injustice: everyone was telling the children to stop making noise, I announced, but the adults were making more noise than we were.

DURING MY CHILDHOOD, we don't talk about being Jewish; we just are. The vast majority of my classmates at public school are Jewish, because most of the Catholic kids in my neighborhood go to Catholic school. All my teachers are Jewish, too, so the school closes on Jewish holidays. But I feel connected to Christmas, too. I look forward to it, because I love the way houses in our neighborhood are festooned. I know what decorations each house will have, and I have my favorites among them: the colored lights that fringe the entire porch of the house next door, and the Santa aboard a sled pulled by reindeer on the lawn of a house a few blocks away. At home, we open gifts Christmas morning—a ritual our parents observe so we children won't feel left out or deprived—but we know they come from our parents, not Santa. And we don't have a tree, except one year when my father's mother goes away for the season—my mother's mother has passed on—and we have a small one, which we call a Chanukah bush. We know that's funny, and that it captures the way we adapt aspects of Christian culture while remaining thoroughly Jewish.

MY FATHER'S SKEPTICISM ABOUT religion makes the world a safer place. While I'm in elementary school, my Catholic friend Claudia

moves to Long Island and invites me to spend a weekend there. On
Sunday morning, the family goes to church, and I go with them. I'm
excited to experience something new, and am glad that Claudia's
mother gives me a coin to put in the plate that will be passed around
during the service. When I get home, I eagerly tell my parents about
my visit. My mother listens with calm interest until I mention that
everyone kneeled in church, and I did, too. "Why did you kneel?" she
demands, her voice thick with alarm.

"What else could I do?" I ask, mortified to learn I did something
terrible.

"You could have stood at the back!"

My father absolves me: "It's a meaningless ritual, so there can't be
any harm in doing it."

MY FATHER'S JEWISH IDENTITY is inseparable from the experience of
anti-Semitism. "We were a fairly self-contained Jewish community,"
he recalls,

> but I remember the dread everybody felt when a troop of Cos-
> sacks on horseback would ride through, wielding leather whips.
> I was told they would sometimes use them to strike Jews who
> were within reach. I personally never witnessed that, but I
> caught the attitudes of the others and felt fear, though at the
> same time I admired the horsemen.
>
> One time—it was before the war, my sister and I may have
> been maybe seven and five—Mother had taken us to a big cele-
> bration. It must have been a religious, Catholic celebration; they
> were very colorful and interesting and there were parades we
> used to watch on occasion. That's why I remember them so well.
> The Poles, on their holy days, used to bring out the priests in
> their full regalia with the fancy crosses and gilded accoutre-
> ments. This time we were in the midst of a plaza, with thou-
> sands of people, and my mother had my sister and me by the
> hand, and we were enjoying the parade. I couldn't see too much,
> I was too small. And all of a sudden Mother said, "Let's go." She
> took Ella's hand and mine and we ran home. It frightened me. I

couldn't understand why. But I learned later when she was explaining it to the adults, that they started anti-Semitic talk in the crowd, and she was afraid they were going to start attacking Jews. It had an effect, that I was in danger, that we were in danger. That was the atmosphere in which Jews had to live in Poland.

Another scene my father recalls from his childhood also ends without incident but is a reminder that it might not have:

> In 1919, in the summer, we were staying in the country, in Michalin. My uncle Bernard came to say goodbye; he was leaving for America. At the time it didn't occur to me that we'll be following him a year later. Bernard was eighteen, only seven years older than I was. He took me and a friend of mine, the three of us went to a brook. And of course nobody had any bathing suits, or had thought of bathing suits. We were naked. We saw coming along three other boys, bigger boys than I, but not bigger than Bernard, and we were a little concerned that we were going to have trouble with them. We knew that they were gentile, and they knew that we were Jewish, because only the Jewish boys were circumcised, and none of the gentile boys were circumcised. But they didn't start up with us. Very often they did.
>
> When I went to school—schools were not free, education was not compulsory, in those years, when Poland was under the Russians. So Jews and gentiles had their own schools. And sometimes we'd get out at the same time from the schools, and fights would break out. And we had some, but they weren't too serious. But these boys—we used to call them black eyes—I used to try and avoid them.

The image of trying to avoid threatening boys from another school brings back a scene from my childhood. When I walked to and from elementary school in Brooklyn, I hoped to avoid the tough boys who went to a nearby Catholic school, Holy Innocents. I saw irony in the school's name; to me these boys were holy terrors. In the winter, they threw snowballs at the public school girls. But I didn't think they picked on us because we were Jewish. I assumed they picked on us because we were girls.

IN POLAND, ANIMOSITY AGAINST Jews was endemic, a perennial physical threat. Though he didn't experience pogroms—rampages where Christian mobs destroyed Jewish homes and shops, killing any Jews they could find—my father knew they were taking place elsewhere, and sensed adults' fear that attacks against Jews could occur closer to home. How lucky I am to never have felt that. When I first heard that the white supremacists attending the infamous demonstration in Charlottesville, Virginia, chanted, "Jews will not replace us," I had never heard that expression before; it sounded bizarre, and I was uncertain what it meant. I now know it's a theme common among white supremacists. During that year, 2017, according to FBI statistics, 60 percent of religious hate crimes were anti-Jewish (17 percent were anti-Islamic and 5 percent anti-Catholic).

Then there is a massacre in a Pittsburgh synagogue: eleven people killed and many others wounded because they're Jews. There follow attacks on Jews in California, New Jersey, and New York. My feeling of safety starts to seem like complacency.

MY FATHER IS PERPLEXED when my sister Naomi's husband, Joe, converts to Judaism, and together they join a synagogue, observe the Sabbath, and become interested in Jewish spirituality. He asks Naomi, "Why would anyone want to join a despised people?"

The assumption underlying this comment finds its way into my father's humor. He also says, "I like converts. They're less likely to be anti-Semitic." If I tell him of a minor frustration—say, another driver grabbed a parking spot I was heading for—he quips, "Maybe he's anti-Semitic." It's funny because it's so obviously absurd, but it's revealing, too: that anti-Semitism is ubiquitous and inescapable, is part of the landscape of my father's world.

I'M READING ALOUD TO my parents a commencement address I'm going to give at a community college in upstate New York, where few

Jews live. In it, I refer to being Jewish. "You shouldn't mention that," my father says. "It might turn some people against you." But being Jewish is at the heart of my academic research: my doctoral dissertation and first linguistics book are about New York Jewish conversational style. So I don't take the reference out of my commencement address, and I don't think it could turn anyone against me. I'm no longer certain I was right.

MY FATHER'S ASSUMPTION THAT anti-Semitism is ubiquitous grows out of his experience—and underlies his commitment to Israel. When he's ninety-three, having just returned home from the hospital, he says, "I had a great opportunity to have a good death. Unfortunately, I passed it up."

I ask, "Are you really sorry you didn't die?"

"No," he says. "If asked, I'd stick around. Israel is in such a difficult situation. How can I leave her in the lurch?"

DURING MY CHILDHOOD, I remember setting foot in a synagogue only once. I don't recall why we went; maybe my father thought it would be a good way to remind us kids of our Jewishness.

We all got dressed up and walked to the synagogue off Coney Island Avenue. I was excited about getting dressed up and about the prospect of seeing the inside of the synagogue, which I passed on my way to school every day. When we arrived, the service was already under way, so we filed in, my father first, the rest of us behind him in a line, and stood along the back wall. After a very short time—I remember it as only a few minutes—a whisper went down the line, from my father at the far end to me, at the other: "We're leaving. Daddy wants to go." Since I was the youngest and the last one in, I had to lead us all out. Once outside, my father told us that hearing the Hebrew prayers brought back the hours, days, years he suffered in religious study throughout his childhood, starting with *cheder*.

CHEDER (PRONOUNCED HAY-DER)—the religious school for Hasidic boys—is key to an irony: my father is why I feel deeply Jewish and also why I grew up without ever attending a synagogue. "I was sent off to *cheder*," my father recalls, when I was four years old, and I hated it. I hated parting from my friends and hated them for being able to continue playing while I had to sit at a desk every day from nine to four, listening to things I didn't understand and didn't want to know. I did get some satisfaction when a visitor came. I was taller than the others, so I was sitting in the back, which was fair so I can see above them. But when they expected an examiner, the rabbi put me in the front seat. And then, to show the examiner, he said, "Well, we'll take one of the boys and have him read." And I was the boy that he picked. You know [*he laughs*] just by coincidence, he picked me—any boy. And I read very fast. *Ivre* they called it, reading. I must have been still under five, because the rabbi was showing off that I could read fast, the Hebrew, Genesis. I did get some satisfaction from that.

But most of the time I got punished. I got punished because I used to look out the window wistfully. Among my earliest memories—I must have been five—is looking out the window. It was winter, and growing dark early, and a man was lighting the tall streetlamps with a long pole that had a flame at its end. I guess I remember because I wanted so badly to be outside myself.

My father describes this scene often. And he always uses the word "wistfully" to convey how forlorn he felt.

Cheder turned me against religion. I could see that what they were teaching wasn't logical. One time the rabbi was telling us about a great holy man. He was so holy, the rabbi said, if you looked at him you'd go blind in one eye. If you looked at him again, you'd go blind in the other eye. And if you looked at him a third time, you'd be struck dead. I asked, "How can you look at him if you're blind?" He didn't say anything. He just walked over and smacked me.

I often got punished for asking bad questions that I shouldn't have asked, and for pointing out contradictions. Another time the rabbi was telling us that the good people are rewarded and the bad people are punished, and I said, "But that isn't the way it works here!" He came over to me, picked me up by the ear, and he tore it away a little bit. There was a drop of blood—a little bit came out. When I came home I complained to my mother what he did. She said, "You must have deserved it." But we had a servant at that time, Salka, who liked me. The next morning Salka took me to the *cheder,* and she went over to the rabbi, and she said, "If you ever touch that child again, I'm going to come back here and I'm going to tear your beard out! Hair by hair!" I was in such awe of the rabbi, that it amazed me to see him cowed by our Salka. After that, the only punishment I got was a smack with a ruler on the hand.

The misery my father associates with Hebrew prayers and texts leaks out when I send my parents my first published academic paper. My father calls to tell me he read and admired it. He praises my close analysis of language, then adds that the way I pick apart the subtle meanings of words reminds him of studying the language of the Talmud, which he was forced to spend so many hours doing—all day in *cheder* when he was little, and all evening with a tutor when he was older and attended high school during the day. As describing these experiences brings them back, he blurts, "I don't know how you can stand it!"

THERE WAS ANOTHER WAY that my father was forced to sit through interminable, incomprehensible Hebrew prayers when he was very young. He recalls:

> After my father died, my grandfather took me by the hand every single day for a year to say *kaddish*—the prayer for the dead—in the synagogue. Not the *shtibel* across the street from our apartment, but a real synagogue, a big one, some distance from our house. I had to stay there for the entire service. I guess it was this experience, more than any other, that predisposed me against attending a house of worship for the rest of my life. But

I can understand the sentiments and feelings of religious people of every faith. When I was very young, my sister, Ella, was in the hospital having surgery—an appendix operation—and I spent the entire day praying, reading *tehillim,* with such fervor and concentration, I had the absolute conviction that God was listening and will be moved. I must have been under six because I became an atheist at that age.

THOUGH MY FATHER BECAME an atheist at six and remained one for the rest of his life—in an impassioned, not a casual way—that early fervor and conviction, the devout faith of his grandfather and the Hasidic community he was raised in, are an indelible part of him. Sometimes it underlies his wry humor, presuming the existence of the deity he doesn't believe in, as when he says, "I can imagine how God hates me, the way I talk about him," or ridicules the rules that render some foods kosher and others not: "Why should God care if I eat a shrimp?" He mocks Hasidic rituals that he learned in his grandfather's home: they'd say a prayer over every little thing—before you eat, before you wash your hands, before you use the toilet. Yet he absorbed the spirit of Hasidism, even as he abandoned its forms: saying prayers over every little thing means you're reminded, again and again, to be grateful; my father never loses that stance. He says, "Aren't we lucky to have plenty of food?" "Aren't we lucky to have clean water, flush toilets?" When he has excruciating pain from sciatica all along his left side, and people ask how he is, he says, "I'm wonderful. The whole right side of my body doesn't hurt." My father knows that his gratitude is a form of prayer. Telling me how much he enjoys his new walker, he says, "I tell you I feel so wonderful when I use it. I want to pray to God, to thank him, but I can't, so I'll have Naomi and Joe do it for me."

I ONCE HEARD A RABBI say that atheism is the fourth denomination of modern Judaism, the other three being orthodox, conservative, and reform. My father's life shows a way this is true. Though he turned against religion, he never turned against Judaism. He felt proud of being Jewish, and taught us to be proud of it, too.

My father's atheism came with his Communism, which was rooted in a wish to make the world, and the lives of the people in it, better—and that, too, is deeply Jewish: the classic rabbinic injunction to repair the world, *tikkun olam.* This insight is brought home to me by—of all people—an Episcopal priest. In her book *Holy Envy,* Barbara Brown Taylor describes aspects of religions other than her own that she deeply admires. She is drawn to Judaism, she explains, because Jewish identity doesn't reside, as Christian identity does, in what you believe, but in how you live: Jews are called to make the world better, and to consider the effects of their actions on others. From this perspective, my father hewed to the Jewish religion, even as he distanced himself from his grandfather's Hasidism. Yet in a way, he hewed to that, too. The word "hasid" derives from the Hebrew word for "kindness," reflecting the focus on actions that help others, which Reverend Taylor describes as fundamental to Judaism. When I ask relatives and friends about their impressions of my father, nearly every one of them, in describing him, uses the word "kind."

WHEN MY PARENTS ARE OLD and my sisters' children grown, we have family reunions at a resort still owned and run by the Workmen's Circle, an organization my father joined as a teenager and remained a member of till he died. "Workmen's Circle" is the English translation of Der Arbeter Ring, the name given to the organization when it was founded in 1900 by people just like my father: Jewish immigrants in New York, dedicated to helping workers and to Yiddishkeit—everything Jewish, except religion. At Circle Lodge, everyone in my family appreciates the Yiddish-culture focus of the activities, but to my father it's something more: a remnant and reminder of his early life in this country. And gathering his large loving family in this place must also remind him of his early life in the vibrant but already waning community of Jewish Warsaw, and of everything that happened—to him and to that community—from the time that he left it. I think when my father chose this Jewish setting for our family reunions, he was recalling what his grandfather said to him, in their last meeting before my father left for America. Holding his grandson on his lap, as tears rolled down his cheeks and into his beard, the old man said, "Never forget that you are a Jew." When my father himself is old, he tells me he wonders, Did I betray him?

You didn't, I think. You remember you're a Jew by remembering him. I remember I'm a Jew by remembering you.

"They Can't Both Be True"

A LIFE IN WORK, A LIFE AS WORK

"THERE'S SOMETHING THAT DOESN'T MAKE SENSE," A JOURNALIST who interviewed me calls to say. "I've been going over my notes, and two things don't fit together. You said you were raised working class, and you said your father was a lawyer. They can't both be true."

But they are. And why they are is fundamental to my father's view—and experience—of his life.

WHEN I SET OUT to understand my father's life, I focused on his relationships: the family he grew up in, his marriage, his children. But when my father sat down to write his memories, he began by listing the jobs he held, then set about writing or tape-recording detailed descriptions of each one. He regards this list, which totals sixty-eight, as a summary of his adult life. Its length reflects his pride in doing whatever he could—whatever he had to do—to support his family. It also reflects the bad luck and bad decisions that caused him to do so many different things before he reached the last item, "lawyer."

The prism through which my father viewed his life is the work he did and the decisions he made related to that work. If I want to understand my father, I need to see the world—his world—through that prism.

First page of my father's list of jobs

*

I'M A CHILD, ELEMENTARY SCHOOL AGE, HAVING DINNER (WE CALL it supper) with my family around the gray Formica-top table in our kitchen. Supper is when we talk, each of us telling what happened that day—and learning what to think about it from how others react. My

Jobs cont'd

34 On return to N.Y.C. from Providence = "selling" finance. Ad in Jewish Morning Journal
35 Selling Packard Lektro Shaver
36 Taking orders for store awnings. Betty DeBlowir to "good views"
37 Subway trainman
38 Shoe salesman
39 ~~Hans Pauline Rubin~~
40 Frederick Loeser
41 Thom McCann & Tom Dick & Harry
42 Gimbels' sold toys
43 Western Union
44 Fashion school for: sewing, grading, pattern making
45 Political jobs — unpaid   Just Described
46 Door to door soliciting
47 Sewing machines — Encyclopedias
48 Vacuum Cleaners
49 Knick Knacks for clarity (lipstick?)
50 Shapiro + Sons — 1st boy then in charge
51 F.C., Danbury — Custodial Officer, Parole Officer
52 ~~Foreman snow clearance~~ repeat
53 Welfare Dept. messenger
54 Knitted cuffs etc for Mrs Romfeld
55 "Row" Cigarette machines
56 Picking tobacco in Somers Conn
57 Raspberries @ a penny a box
58 Hoeing weeds
59 ~~Factory ~~ ~~Woods Lane~~ Cutter on shirts in Danbury
59 Treasury Agent (T-man)
60 ~~Selling fur coats~~ (Henig in N.Y.C., Danbury, Providence)
60 Bingo inspector
61 ~~Selling at Zoo Post~~
62 Export — Drayport for G. Barbour in Battery Park
       cont'd

Second page of my father's list of jobs

father's stories are about "the shop": he talks about the factory where he works and his fellow workers with good-natured affection. Many of his stories are funny, like the time a co-worker who everyone knows is a cheapskate is caught in an obvious expression of penury, and asks my father not to tell the other workers. My father recounts his reply: "I won't tell them you're stingy if you won't tell them I'm bald." Then he laughs and his eyes sparkle with amusement.

I NEVER FEEL SHAME about my father working in a factory. As a child growing up in Brooklyn, I see his job as of a piece with the work all men do: my best friend Cathy's father is an electrician; my parents' friend Bill is a garbage collector; Uncle Louie is a tailor. These jobs seem as natural to me, as worthy, as those that other relatives and friends hold, which I'd now think of as middle class: Uncle Albert is an organist and piano teacher; my parents' friend Ben works for the immigration authority. I see no difference among these jobs.

My father, I learn later, is keenly aware of the difference. I show him an essay I wrote about him, and he complains: "When you say I was a cutter, they'd think it's a very menial job. It was a skilled trade. I made ten thousand dollars when that meant something." I get a sense of what it meant to be a cutter in a book about the infamous Triangle Shirtwaist Factory fire. The author, David Von Drehle, explains that the fire was started when a cutter tossed a cigarette butt into a pile of fabric; though smoking was forbidden, cutters were the "divas of the garment district," their prestige so high that no one thought rules should apply to them. My father has another complaint, too: "You said I had a law degree. That doesn't mean anything. You have to say I was admitted to the bar. You go to court with a law degree, they'll throw you right out." I've corrected that omission here.

MY FATHER'S BEST FRIEND, Harry Rosenberg, is a cutter, too. Harry is a large, outgoing man with an outsized personality and a huge hearty laugh. I'm sure it's because of my father's and Harry's obvious love for each other that I adore Harry, too. I'm dazzled by his prizefighter looks, especially his dashingly flattened nose, and the way his laugh fills a room. Harry kisses my father on his bald head, and teases him for his foibles, like writing "toothache" on a to-do list. My father bears Harry's teasing with a self-effacing laugh of his own. When Harry dies, I see my father cry for the first time.

I sense in my father's friendships, and in his nightly stories from the shop, benevolence toward his fellow cutters, which I generalize to benevolence toward the work. So I'm caught off guard when, in one of the many conversations we have in his last years, I ask my father how he felt about working in the factory, and he says, "I hated every minute of it."

I HAVE MANY MEMORIES of my father the cutter and my father the lawyer, but no memory of his mood changing when he changed professions. He always seemed even-keeled and good-humored. The change that mattered to me was going from having a father who leaves the house while I'm still asleep to having one who is still asleep when I leave the house, as I'm the one who walks twenty minutes to the subway and catches the 7:15 A.M. local to arrive at Hunter College High School in Manhattan at 8:30. I regard this change, as I do the way my father's hands soften, as slightly embarrassing, a bit effete. I miss the feel of my father's callused hand, hardened by years of wielding a fabric-cutting machine.

*

THERE IS ONE WAY I KNOW HOW BITTERLY MY FATHER REGARDS THE thirteen years—he always refers to them by their aptly ominous number, thirteen—that he works as a cutter: the shroud of regret that cast a dark shadow over my childhood, and instilled in me a tendency to look backward in time through the lens of regret. At any moment, if you tapped me on the shoulder, I could give you a long list of decisions I regret, like invitations I turned down and should have accepted or accepted and should have turned down. None have consequences anywhere near the misfortunes caused by decisions my father made—especially one that looms larger than the others, larger than all the others put together. It can be brought to mind—often is brought to mind—by a single word, the name of a Connecticut town: Danbury.

"Danbury," in our family lore, is a Garden of Eden from which my father expelled himself and his family by making a disastrous decision. That single fatal mistake is what led to his thirteen years as a cutter, the purgatory he was trapped in, until he escaped the factory and began earning his living as a lawyer. Whenever my father mentions Danbury (which he does often) and whenever I think of it (which I do often) and when I write of it now (which I must), I feel an almost physical pain in my chest. That my own birth is intertwined with the terrible effects of that fateful decision, and with my father's consequent misery, complicates the story for me. My sister Mimi was born in Danbury. I've always felt that confers on her an angelic aura, as if her birth was accompanied if not occasioned by the wave of a fairy godmother's sparkling wand. I was "conceived" (that's how my parents always speak of it) in Providence, Rhode Island. The name "Providence" is as linked to misfortune as Danbury's is to glory. And that makes my birth seem ill-fated. I don't know if mention of Providence stabs because it brings back my father's piercing regret or because it reminds me of my own sense of guilt. It's probably both: in the tangled illogic of emotion, they're inseparable.

"I DIDN'T APPLY FOR a job as a prison guard," my father says. "During the Depression, I took so many civil service exams, I lost track. But so did everyone else. There might be hundreds, thousands of people taking a test for a handful of jobs. So it came as a surprise when, in 1941, on the basis of one of those exams, I was offered a job as a corrections officer at the federal penitentiary in Danbury, Connecticut."

It sounds odd today that working in a prison could be regarded as a golden era. But it was, for my father and his young family, because of the life that came with it. I also remind myself that the prison where my father was first a guard and then a parole officer, though it was surely a dreadful place to be for the prisoners, was different from the grim and ghastly images that come to mind when I hear the word "jail" today. Danbury Federal Penitentiary was a brand-new minimum-security prison, where inmates included a Hollywood mogul who arranged for prisoners to see first-run films, and the poet Robert Lowell, one of many conscientious objectors who refused to register for the draft because they were morally opposed to killing.

"They assigned me to guard the conscientious objectors," my father recalls, "because many of the other guards were so angry at them for refusing to fight that they mistreated them. I treated them with respect. I had many interesting conversations with them." One of those inmates is a civil rights activist I admire in my teenage activist days: James Peck. When I learn that Peck wrote a memoir of his time in prison, I eagerly read it, certain he will mention the guard who treated him with respect and engaged him in political discussions. I'm disappointed to read only about terrible guards who treated him badly. It's an early reminder that when people tell about their experiences— probably before that, when they recall them—they choose characters and scenes that support the point they want to make. I remind myself to bear this in mind with regard to my father's memories—and my own.

My father finds life in Danbury idyllic from the start:

> To be sure it will work out, I moved to Danbury myself and lived in the prison dormitory, then later got a room in the prison. I lived there in the institution for a couple of months to make sure that we were going to settle there, and I loved it. I had a room to myself with all brand-new furniture and enjoyed for the first time in my life the luxury of working at the same place where I was living without having to travel. When off duty I often sat in a grove of trees overlooking a great lawn in front of the institution, some distance away from it, and read and wrote letters to Mother and all over the world.

Not having to travel to work, having time to read and write letters in a grove of trees—these luxuries are precious. But the most precious to my father must have been "a room to myself." I learn, through his journals, that all the years he's supporting his mother and sister, the women share the only bedroom. When he's nineteen, he writes, "I am constantly dreaming of the pleasures of a private room, and a private free life." The two go together: in his impossible dream, he supports his mother and sister—an obligation he never questions—but doesn't live with them: "I imagine the little clean room I'd have, cozy in the winter, cool and airy in the summer, the sun shining in during the day and a lamp burning on my desk in the evenings at which I'd sit in my easy chair and study." Though he never had the pleasure of a "private free life," free of the obligation to support a family, that old longing must nonetheless have increased his pleasure in a private room—and the freedom to read and write—in Danbury.

When it's clear that my father will keep the federal penitentiary job, his family—my mother; her mother, Babi; and my sister Naomi, who was four—join him. Everyone is happy there.

> Mother and I had close friends, other Jews from New York who had gotten their jobs the same way I did. And we had a good relationship with our neighbors, the Tobiases. When we first moved in, we arrived before the moving truck. They saw us sitting on the porch steps and invited us in for lunch. Then they brought out a chair so Babi could sit more comfortably till the truck came. Naomi liked her school, which was very close to our house. It was a private house with a yard that had a gorgeous weeping willow tree. I liked the work, and—this is a funny thing—I liked wearing a uniform, maybe because I never had the right uniform when I went to school in Warsaw, since my mother didn't want to spend money on it.

As he often does, my father mentions his talents only through someone else's perspective, and uses someone else's arrogance to set his own humility in relief:

> The warden liked me. Others noticed it, too. One young man who started the training with me had been employed as a guard at the Metropolitan Museum of Art. He quit the training after a few weeks, and he said it was because of me. He said, "When we were walking in town and met the warden, he spoke to you for a long time and ignored me." Because of that, he was sure he wouldn't make it. I tried to convince him to remain, but he returned to his job at the Met. There was another person in our training group who happened to also be a lawyer. Where I felt the more humble because I couldn't get a better job despite having the advantage of a profession, this guy tried to lord it over the others for the same reason.

The young man was prescient. Not long after my father begins working as a guard, the warden promotes him to parole officer. In Danbury, at last, the work he's doing brings my father—and everyone in his family—a good life.

> To save gas, which was rationed during the war, we used to take turns driving to the institution, four or five of us in the car. It only took ten or fifteen minutes and I never could stop admiring the scenery, so different from the subway rides to work I used to take, or even from driving in the city among the drab-looking buildings. I used to get up so very early for the six-to-two shift. I used to stoke up the coal fire in the basement so that the family would have it warm when they get up. At the same time, I did it also for the Tobiases, who were so very nice to us when we moved out there.

Driving to work with a group, having a circle of friends, doing family-like favors for a neighbor: Danbury was a community. That's part of what made it a Garden of Eden. And part of what made my father's next move—the expulsion from Danbury, the move to Providence—such a terrible mistake.

> I was only earning fifty dollars a week as a probation officer, and I had to supplement my income through extra jobs. The work was six days a week, so I spent Sundays doing a lot of different things, like driving a taxi; selling fur coats that I got on consignment from a man named Henig in New York; and going door-to-door to get listings for a real estate agent. I'd taken many civil service tests and was on many lists. Suddenly I got an offer to be a T-man, a treasury agent, in the Alcohol Tax Unit of the Treasury Department, paying twelve dollars a week more. Looking back now, the difference seems piddling, but at the time it appeared as very helpful, so I decided to take it.

Salary is the only factor my father considers, in making this decision. His happiness—that he likes his current job, whether he'll like the new one—and his family's happiness don't figure in the equation at all. When I've had career choices to make, I've taken into account what I'd find satisfying or fulfilling, what I'd enjoy. When I got my PhD, I turned down several offers of tenure-track jobs to accept a three-year contract, renewable to five, at Georgetown University. I figured things might work out there (they did), but even if they didn't, I preferred taking a chance to taking a job I didn't really want. My father would never have rejected security for his personal preference. I could, because I was born in luckier times. Or maybe because I didn't have a family to support. My father says,

> When I told the warden, he was very upset and tried valiantly to talk me out of it. He argued that I was doing such good work that I will be appointed warden in the near future. I pointed out there was not a single Jewish warden in the service. He said that was because there were no Jews applying for work in prisons till recently and assured me I'll be promoted to that post. I didn't believe him, and I made the change.

I can understand my father's belief that, no matter how much the warden liked him and wanted to promote him, the higher-ups wouldn't go along. Denying opportunity to Jews was part of the landscape he'd inhabited his whole life.

> I was supposed to be posted to New Haven, a town not much farther than Danbury from New York City, where our families and old friends still were and which we continued to think of as home. At the last minute they changed it to Providence, Rhode Island, which is over a hundred miles further away from New York City, but it was too late to withdraw.

As if I were watching a thriller and the hero is about to walk into a trap, I shout to my father in my mind, "It's not too late! Don't do it! You can change your mind!" But he can't hear me. He takes the fatal step. At the age of thirty-six, he moves his family to Providence.

*

"I GRIPPED MY GUN HARD AND WAITED."

My father, the gentle giant, gripping his gun? This image astonishes me, but it also delights me. It reminds me of how I romanticized his prison work when I was a little girl. I was thrilled when he taught me how to escape if someone tried to choke me. Instead of trying to pry his hands from my throat, I should thrust my arms up between his, using the strength of my arms and the force of the thrust to break his hold. I loved practicing this move, with my father taking the role of assailant. It made me feel strong, and safer.

My father carries a gun in Providence because his job as an alcohol tax inspector entails chasing bootleggers. He never catches one, and he never fires the gun. In the scene that includes that tantalizing line, he's seated in his car, watching a door where a suspected bootlegger is visiting a woman. If the suspect comes out with a large quantity of sugar—a key ingredient in bootleg liquor—it will be evidence against him. As my father sits for hours in the car, gripping the gun, he thinks of what could go wrong: if the bootlegger knows he's there, he could have arranged for a hit man to take him out. In fact, "Nothing happened of course for he never did catch on. But I spent an unhappy night till I went home at daylight convinced that he wasn't there for sugar after all, but for sweets of another kind."

Just as the warden in Danbury singled my father out for praise and recognition, so did his boss in Providence: "The head of the office, O'Brien, favored me greatly, was impressed with my familiarity with politics, liked to take me with him on a job, like checking the stock of a licensed liquor store, just to hold conversations with me. And he liked me because I wrote good reports." Of course my father did well with his writing. Yet life in Providence was grim compared to Danbury: "We lived in an ugly housing project. There were very few Jews, and we didn't make friends. Then Mother got pregnant, and she wanted to give birth in Brooklyn, where her family was. So I left that job and we returned to New York. And for the next thirteen difficult years I was a cutter holding numerous jobs in that seasonal business."

———

THE FAMILY RETURNS TO New York, and my father is condemned to years of factory work, because Mother got pregnant. With me. That's how my father always explains this move. He never says it in a way that blames me: I was the result of the pregnancy, not its cause. But feelings aren't logical, and I always feel implicated in my father's thirteen miserable years. My birth spells disaster for my mother, too: having a newborn when my sister Mimi was not yet two is a burden that pushes her over a psychological edge. Years later, my father tells me that my mother had a nervous breakdown when I was born. Naomi, who was eight at the time, doesn't recall her having an actual nervous breakdown; it was probably what we'd now call postpartum depression. But she remembers our mother being overwhelmed by the demands of two small children. She'd say to Naomi, "I can't handle them. You take them." Naomi recounts this when explaining that she was a "parentified child": a child pressed into service as a parent to younger siblings. Naomi maintains she took pleasure in caring for Mimi and me. I believe her, because I never sensed resentment. And she credits that early training with leading to her successful career taking care of troubled children in a wide range of settings—including a school she established and ran, kind of like our grandmother did in Warsaw. Yet I still blame myself: my birth cut short my sister's childhood. And the move it precipitated caused my father's misfortune—and misery.

My father's comments on his list of jobs often refer to that misery, especially during the first three of those years, before he found steady work: "Of the thirteen years as a cutter, I worked about five years each on two long-term jobs and knocked about for only three, agonizing years."

"Knocked about." That phrase captures the anguish of holding a series of temporary jobs while searching for a permanent one. I hear it again in a letter my mother writes to her cousin Rose in January 1945, not long after they returned to New York from Providence. (Rose's son sends it to me after his parents die.) Rose has recently moved to Detroit because her husband, Ben, got a job there. My mother writes:

I'm certainly glad that Ben likes his new position. With his talents and resourcefulness, I'm sure he'll do very well both on the job and with "extra" work. I wish I could say as much for Eli, but so far he hasn't established himself yet. He's tried several things but nothing materialized that has any future in it. He now decided to learn a trade and is working as a cutter. How long it will last I don't know. He will probably go back to Civil Service after he's tried everything else. In the meantime it's discouraging to see him knock around the way he does.

THERE IS ONE MORE piece of this story—the way my father knew for sure that quitting the job in Danbury was a grievous miscalculation: "When I left Danbury," he says,

> the warden appointed my friend Frank Kenton to my job as parole officer. In a year, the warden became director of the Bureau of Prisons, and he made Frank the warden in Danbury. We visited the Kentons in their official residence in Danbury a few years later. Their home was spacious, surrounded by trees and a lawn. Frank's salary was nineteen thousand dollars a year compared to the seventy-eight hundred of guards and my high earnings of ten thousand dollars as a cutter. And Frank had many other perquisites, including the use of a car. He had also become an important personality in the community. I could have had all that instead of sweating overtime in a shop for thirteen years, with many taking it for granted that I simply couldn't cut it as a lawyer.

And Frank Kenton was Jewish.

*

AT FIRST, MY FATHER'S ACCOUNTS OF THE JOBS HE HELD AND THE work he did interest me in the way many children want to know what their parents did before they were born. But I also see, in his descriptions, why my father felt it was so important to list all the jobs and

types of work he did and count them: the sheer number is evidence of
how hard it was for him to fulfill his obligation to support his family—
and how he fulfilled it nonetheless. I begin to see that my sense of his
life as family relationships and his sense of his life as earning a living
are, in some ways, indistinguishable. Both story lines begin when he
begins his new life in this country.

I turned twelve a month after arriving in America and was
speaking English in six months, but I went to work before that.
I got a job delivering a weekly newspaper, *The Chat,* that came
out on Saturday. I'd go with my mother and sister to the synagogue, but women and men sat in separate sections. Instead of
going to the men's section, I'd go out to deliver papers. When
my route was done, the man in charge would drive me within a
block of the synagogue, and I'd meet my mother when the service was over, as if I'd been there the whole time.

When I was thirteen, I got a job delivering telegrams for
Western Union. The salary was negligible; what counted were
the tips, typically five or ten cents. A quarter was rare; getting
nothing was not. But on the day before Christmas, the tips were
bountiful. Two people were unimaginably generous: each gave
me a dollar. When I got home, I gave my mother the money,
counting it all out, including the dollar bills. It came to eleven
dollars. She was so grateful, she cried.

This is the only scene my father ever recounts in which his mother ap-
proves of something he did. In every other memory I've ever heard,
she's criticizing him, berating him, even beating him. How powerful
that moment must have been, basking in his mother's gratitude. For
once, he's made her happy instead of angry. For once, she thinks he's
done well.

What my father describes next is also unique: his mother working
in the United States.

During this time we lived in a single room at 473 Kosciuszko
St. in Williamsburg, which we rented from a widow named

Mrs. Wilner. Mother took a job as a matron at HNOH—the Hebrew National Orphan Home. It was in Tuckahoe, outside the city, and she had to live at the school, so my sister and I remained as boarders at Mrs. Wilner's during the week. On weekends, we took a long streetcar ride out to Tuckahoe.

Though my father was a boarder, he had a job at Mrs. Wilner's: washing dishes.

We all ate in the basement kitchen, and I remember standing over the sink for what seemed ages washing and scrubbing. Particularly onerous was trying to get the pots clean. That's why I'm so happy to wash all the dishes now. Every time I wash a pot, so easily, thanks to the materials they make pots out of now, like Teflon, I remember how I struggled to scrape pots clean back then.

This at last explains the context for something I heard my father say many times. After he retires at seventy, he takes over all dishwashing at home and never relinquishes the job, even when he needs a walker to get to the sink, and when he drags over a chair because his back hurts when he stands. He often says, as he washes a pot, what a pleasure it is, because he remembers how hard it was to wash pots when he was young.

We lived there about two years. After Mother ended her job she came "home" to us, where she engaged in the customary violent arguments with Mrs. Wilner. We moved out quickly. Around that time I got my first "regular" or "steady" job at a shoe store on DeKalb Ave. off Sumner Ave. I bought a pair of shoes there and got into conversation with the owner, Mrs. Pauline Rubin.

If this weren't my father, it would be surprising for a thirteen-year-old boy to get into a conversation with a woman selling him a pair of shoes—a personally revealing one, with the woman, not the boy, talking about her problems. Even in his memories of Warsaw, when he was a young child, my father is having long conversations with adults—that is, with women.

Learning that she's a widow, I displayed interest and sympathy, and returned in a few days to ask for a job. I was attending PS 25 at the time and was about thirteen, but she readily engaged me because she did need help and I came cheaply. I put in all my spare time including weekends. It was a ladies' and children's shoe store and I became quite expert at the job. After many months I quit when she refused me a raise I demanded.

This becomes a pattern my father repeats in explaining why he quits many of the jobs he recalls: he feels he's been treated unfairly. And another pattern is being established, too: his mother is relying on his income—and takes possession of it.

Mother went to her, unbeknownst to me, and asked her to call me back, which she did and gave me a heavy sweater as a gift but no raise. The most I got from her was twelve dollars a week, which was not bad for part-time but not nearly enough for the number of hours and amount of work I put in. I worked there for somewhat more than a year and learned the business very well. I turned over all I earned to Mother, and she gave me a weekly allowance from it.

My father tells me many stories of his time working at Mrs. Rubin's shoe store. One brief one sticks in my mind:

I was fitting a little boy, lacing the shoes by threading first one shoelace, then the other, from beginning to end. Boys then wore mostly shoes with high uppers, and using this method made a big difference in the time it took, rather than switching from one shoelace to the other with each eyelet. The kid objected I am not doing it the right way and pulled his foot away. No persuasion'd move him, and his mother sat by stolidly and silently. I wanted to tell her either to discipline him or do it herself because other customers were waiting. Had it been my business I'd have done just that but couldn't risk Mrs. Rubin losing a sale.

I recognize my father's devotion to efficiency, and his sense of loyalty to his employer, which he passed down to me. When I was in high school, I, too, worked part-time: as a sales clerk in Macy's camera department, Thursday evenings and all day Saturday. One day a customer told me that an item we were selling was cheaper at a store across the street. I later shared that information with another customer. At dinner that night, I told my parents about this, certain my father would approve of my watching out for the customer. But he didn't. He told me that Macy's was paying my salary, so I owed loyalty to them.

MY FATHER'S EARLY CAREER as a shoe salesman ends after a year, when he quits high school and goes to work in a coat factory in the garment district. That he had to leave school at fourteen to support his mother and sister was always key to my father's life story. Of all the surprises I find in his journals, letters, and memories, this is the one that most deeply shocks me: quitting high school and going to work full-time was not a self-evident necessity. The person he was doing it for—his mother—didn't think it was.

> I was in my fourteenth year, and in the first year of high school. As was always her custom, Mother complained unceasingly about her widowhood, her unhappy fate stuck with the care of two children and never enough money to subsist on. What I earned after school in addition to what my mother earned when she worked wasn't enough to maintain us even on a minimal scale. In retrospect I realize that even in those days she laid aside a few dollars due to her lifelong feeling of insecurity, which could be assuaged only by money in the bank. But at the time I only was aware of her constant complaints that we don't have enough for food and rent.
>
> I determined to work full-time while Mother, inconsis-

tently, vehemently opposed my decision and went to great
lengths to thwart me. She importuned me daily, lectured and
made awesome predictions for me, threatened and cajoled. Finally, she got everyone we knew to talk to me, going so far as
enlisting the persuasive powers of her friend's boyfriend, a rabbi.
He engaged me in an hour-long harangue, using every conceiv-
able argument, but couldn't budge me in my resolve because he
couldn't answer the question of how we'll manage on my small
earnings, other than to assure me that the almighty will provide.
My mother did everything she could to stop me, but the one
thing she wouldn't do is stop complaining so bitterly, so constantly, about the lack of money and her fear we couldn't pay
the rent or buy food.

This is new. I stop to take it in. My father's mother opposed his
quitting school to work? She tried to stop him? The more I think about
it, the more predictable her opposition seems. This is the woman who
established and ran a school in Warsaw, who graduated from college at
the turn of the twentieth century, whose sisters were educated, and
who had contempt for her brothers because they weren't. And this is
the grandmother who wrote in my album when I graduated from elementary school at twelve:

> *Dearest Debby,*
>   *On your graduation, I wish you that you should achieve perfection in*
> *your studies at every following graduation.*
>   *May you enjoy school for many many years to come, as the wisest is*
> *the one who always learns, and the happiest years are the ones spent on the*
> *school bench.*
>   *God bless you darling*
>
> > *Bubi*

The affection, the terms of endearment, surprise me, since I have
no memory of my grandmother being affectionate—or paying any attention to me at all. I recognize the love of learning she urges on me,
but I associate it with my father. No wonder she tried so hard to talk

him out of leaving high school. The wonder is that he did it anyway. Nowhere else in my father's memories does he openly cross his mother. My mother's brother Irving told me that when they were young, my father was terrified of his mother. If he wanted to do something she'd disapprove of, he'd try to keep it from her. If she discovered his plan, he'd abandon it rather than face her wrath. Where did he find the courage to defy her when she so adamantly opposed his quitting school?

I never questioned my father's claim that he had to work full-time to support his mother and sister. Never, that is, till now. Now that I think about it, my father mentioned several kinds of work his mother

My father at fourteen with his sister and mother

did. There were the two years she was a matron at the Hebrew National Orphan Home. She also worked as a seamstress. She was good at it, he said, but slow. She took a job as a bank teller at a window for customers who needed to be served in Polish, Russian, or Yiddish—but was fired because she refused to work on Saturday. Though none of these jobs worked out, they are all evidence that his mother assumed it was her responsibility, not her son's, to support the family. My father didn't have to dismiss his mother's insistence that he stay in school, and pay attention only to her complaints that there wasn't enough money for food and rent. It is stunning to think that his whole life story—the sacrifices he made to become a lawyer while working full-time in a factory, the "agonizing" years of uncertainty about how he'd support his family—might have resulted not from necessity but from a choice he made to take on the responsibility of supporting his mother and sister when he was fourteen.

Though his mother tried to stop her son from quitting high school and working full-time, once he does, she accepts his decision—and his salary. He takes a job as helper in the cutting room of a coat factory owned by two brothers, Harry and Louie Shapiro: "My salary, fifteen dollars a week, immediately put my family out of the constant worry of 'where will the money come from tomorrow.' I gave my mother probably—I don't remember exactly. I gave her probably fourteen dollars. And then I had a dollar. If it ran out, I used to borrow a quarter from Mrs. Dunkelman, a relative who lived across the street. I needed five cents to go to work in Manhattan and five cents to come home. My mother wouldn't lend me money. She'd refuse, saying I'd only waste it on soda and movies." Sometimes his mother was the reason he ran out: "She'd go through my pockets and keep any money she found there." He realizes years later that she didn't need all the money he gave her to cover their expenses; she'd put away enough to pay for a months-long trip back to Warsaw in 1931.

*

IN MY MIND, "MY FATHER WORKED IN A FACTORY IN THE GARMENT district" describes two different periods in my father's life: the five years between 1923, when he quit high school to work at Shapiro and Sons, and 1928, when the Shapiros hired him to run their finance company, and also the thirteen years he worked as a cutter after returning to New York City from Providence. But those two stints were fundamentally different—and the difference is due, in large part, to unions.

Unions were sacred in our household. Crossing a picket line was unthinkable. As a child, I asked myself what I would do if I were dying of thirst in a desert and reached an oasis that was being picketed. Would I cross the line to save my life? I wasn't sure. I get a sense of why my father so valued unions when he talks about his first stint in the factory, and how his working conditions differed from those of workers who belonged to the union—that is, the cutters.

The cutters were unionized, so they worked a forty-hour, five-day week. All the others, who weren't unionized, worked forty-eight hours over six days. The cutters' hours were strictly observed, because of the union. But everyone else's forty-eight hours could be extended at the employer's whim without additional compensation. They made us work on Saturday—no extra money. And a nephew of the boss Harry Shapiro was in charge. One day he told me, "Take the clothes from here and put 'em there." When I put 'em there he said, "Now put 'em back." I said, "I just did it." He said, "Well you gotta keep busy, so do it." I said, "I won't do it." When I came in Monday, Harry Shapiro calls me in and he said, "Were you told by so-and-so to take the clothes from there?" I said "Yes." "And did you do it?" I said, "No, I refused." And then I wanted him to ask me why. He didn't ask me why; he said, "Go to the office, get your pay, you're fired." I said, "Okay," and I left.

There he is again, quitting because he's been treated unfairly. And, as usual, he leaves without explanation. Why did he say only "I refused" without explaining that he'd been asked to do something pointless? The encounter, at least, doesn't end there. The brother who runs the cutting room, Louie Shapiro, sends my father a postcard asking him to return to work: "I went to see him and said, 'Come back to work? I was fired for no reason, all you do is, "Come back to work?"' He said, 'What do you want?' I said, 'Well I gotta get paid for this time that I was out.' And would you believe it he paid me for the time that I was out and took me back."

*

HOW ROTE AND ROUTINIZED FAMILY STORIES BECOME. HOW MANY
times have I said, "My father worked in a factory and went to law
school at night," never knowing, never thinking about, what that en-
tailed. Through an entry in his journal dated August 1, 1927, two
months before his nineteenth birthday, my father tells me: "After a day
of from 8–12 & 12:45–6:15 P.M. I have to go to school without supper.
This last I eat when I reach home at 10:30 for it to cramp my bowels at
night and all of the next day. Of course I can't go right to sleep for I
have homework to do, and yet after such a hard day and so little sleep
I am expected to keep my eyes open at the dry lectures in law school."

In a conversation we have when he's old, my father adds a visual
detail to the picture: "At law school, someone would say, 'What is this,
under your jacket?' " As he says this, he lifts his right hand to his left
upper arm and mimes the shape of a bulge. "I had my sleeves rolled up
working in the factory, and I didn't have time—I used to work late—
didn't have time to pull my sleeves down, so I put my jacket over them,
rolled up."

"When did you do your homework for law school?" I ask.

"Mostly I didn't," he says. "But when I did, I didn't get good marks.
I failed, you know, one year. I failed in two subjects, and I was going
to be held back. I pleaded with the dean, actually pleaded, to let me
make it up. It would be a tragedy. I'd have to be another year in law
school. Because I thought, As soon as I come out of law school I'm
going to start making a living. He let me make it up over the summer."

The long hours in the factory aren't the only reason for my father's
poor performance in school. In his journal, he writes that he manages
not to study even when he isn't at work: "I put off the studying from
day to day and from hour to hour. I intended to learn all the notes up
to date today but the day passed without my opening the notebook.
Instead I had gone to the movies in a veritable deluge of a rain with a
torn umbrella which seemed to attract the most voluble amount of the
liquid."

Going to the movies was my father's lifelong escape—until television was invented. So that doesn't surprise me. But not studying when
he had time? Not getting good marks? Failing? That does. At first. My
father's exceptional intelligence was taken for granted; he rarely spoke

of it. When he's ninety-two, I take him for a series of tests to evaluate the extent of his cognitive decline. The neurologist who discusses the results with us says he can't gauge whether age has affected my father's intelligence, because his score on the test is literally off the chart the neurologist has on his desk. So I always assumed that his intelligence helped my father become a lawyer by taking high school equivalency tests on his own and law school classes at night. But I assumed he studied hard, too. Then I think of how surprised people are when I tell them that I got C's and D's in college. It was a point of pride: I wouldn't memorize anything, because I believed, with the hubris of youth, that memorization is not education, and I didn't want to waste time learning anything I wasn't interested in. I wanted to get A's in courses I cared about, but was happy to get D's in those I didn't—or those in which grades depended on memorization. I was sure I wouldn't go to grad school—I didn't get that idea until years later—so I thought my grades didn't matter. Like my father, I just wanted to pass all my courses, so I could graduate on time. Even in graduate school, when it was time to study for my doctoral orals, I stayed home, intending to study, but somehow never did—and blamed myself, pretty much the way my father blames himself in his journal. I went into the exam knowing just what I had learned by taking classes and writing papers. So I shouldn't have been surprised that my father managed not to study even when he had time.

*

WE REFER TO PAST ERAS WITH LABELS THAT IDENTIFY ECONOMIC, political, or military events—the Depression, the Cold War, the Second World War—but convey little of what those events meant for the people who lived through them. My father's account of a job, one he speaks of often, is a story not only of how his own fortunes rose, then plummeted, but also of the human experience that lies behind one such label, the Great Depression.

"Manager-of-a-finance-company" was like a single word I heard so often, with the words so merged, that I don't know if it was "a" or "the" finance company. My husband heard it as just three words: manager-finance-company. My father speaks of the time he held this position as triumphant: he was doing better than he had thought possible, and he was able to move his mother and sister to a larger apartment. The way it happened begins with the same factory owner who fired him for refusing to follow orders. Apparently that insubordination has been forgotten.

In June 1928, Harry Shapiro called me into his office. He and his brothers were starting another business: a company that would buy the contracts for radios that people had bought on time. They'd pay a percentage of the price, then they'd either collect the full monthly payments or repossess the radio. A fellow by the name of McGreevy, who was experienced in the business, was in charge and I was to go there to be the assistant manager. However, instead of the thirty-five dollars I was earning at the factory, he offered me twenty-five dollars a week to start because I had no experience. I was nineteen, but I had just completed my first year in law school, which may explain their confidence that I could assist the manager capably.

I came down to the office for this McGreevy to show me the ropes. The office was actually two desks in the office of the Shapiros' lawyer, Kramer, 24 Snyder Avenue, Brooklyn, opposite the 95th Court, where this Kramer practiced criminal law. It was a hot June day, and I was wearing my Sunday suit, which happened to be a heavy black one, and a cheap straw hat, and met this McGreevy, who was inebriated and could teach me nothing. He was there only a couple of hours and left. I never saw McGreevy again.

My father went about setting up and running the finance company himself, while still studying toward his law degree:

I worked very hard, used to run around all day getting new business, looking after the old, and catching up with the office work at night after I finished with law school, which I attended every night from six to eight. I used to come home and gulp down my supper to run to law school and didn't get home till

eleven, twelve o'clock at night. Then I'd get up the next morning again at five-thirty, six o'clock in order to get to the office
early to do some more work. Within a year, I got so much new
business in all the five boroughs that I importuned Harry Shapiro to buy me a car, which he did, a 1923 Willys-Knight, for a
hundred and fifteen dollars, so I could run around and seek more
dealers. I wasn't twenty yet and it being a Depression, my having a car gave me great status among my friends and others, too.
On my block, you could never see more than four cars at a time.
In the country then there were only four million cars, as against
well over a hundred million today. Having a car at a young age
was no mean accomplishment in those days. I loved it so much,
I'd drive to the corner to buy a pack of cigarettes.

A car! In my father's stories, having a car is a sign of success and a
source of happiness; losing one signals humiliation, defeat. The sense
of excitement and satisfaction he feels the first time he buys a new car,
not a used one—which didn't happen until he was a partner in his own
law firm—is palpable. He never stops feeling that way—right up to the
last new car he buys, when he's ninety-one and calls it his going-away
present to himself. Shortly after he buys it, I'm visiting my parents in
Florida. When it's time for me to go to the airport at the end of the
visit, the taxi I called doesn't show up. My father insists on driving me,
and I accept. That is, I drive there and he drives home. I'm terrified
he'll get lost or have an accident (he does neither), but I love seeing him
drive off in his big new Lincoln Continental, because I know how
much he loves it—and because I know that buying an expensive new
car is the only extravagance he ever allows himself.

My father eventually gets a raise, but it's still far less than his work
is worth, as becomes evident soon. "Before too long, I got so much
business, we were doing, instead of eight thousand dollars annual business, a million dollars. Then Harry Shapiro decided that I was too
young to be responsible for such a large enterprise. I was then twenty-
two, earning sixty dollars a week—a princely salary in the Depression.
He brought in his cousin, Moe Rosenfeld, who had been in the real
estate business and failed due to the Depression, and put him in charge.

By that time, it was a complicated business: I had put in many methods and procedures. Moe was started in my job at a hundred dollars a week while I trained him in it."

This injustice is only the beginning. Moe brings in a man named Bush, who "had a cork floor installed in the office assigned to him and made other expensive improvements for his comfort. In all my years there I never thought of spending a nickel for my convenience." If this were a movie, the appearance of so self-serving a character would give you a sense of foreboding—and you'd be right. Bush promises to make the firm lots of money by buying foreign letters of credit and lending money to South American firms. But:

> The Depression continued and spread, enveloping also South America. South American countries no longer permitted sending out foreign exchange. Bush had ruined us with his schemes. He got us a lot of business, except that the people we loaned money to never or rarely repaid. The company didn't have the capital to function, and they started to liquidate, which I handled. It took a couple of years, and gave me a job at a reduced salary.

My father tells me many tales of liquidating the finance company. One stands out, for two reasons. The first is his ingenuity. One of the many businesses Bush invests in that go belly-up left the finance company with a large quantity of discolored, stuck-together mothballs. My father comes up with the idea of packaging them, and selling them cheaply to retail outlets. He designs and orders boxes, then invents and has a carpenter build a wooden "contraption," as he calls it, that separates the mothballs and sends them down a chute to be boxed and put into cartons for shipment. He finds and rents an abandoned warehouse in New Jersey, and hires a man to oversee the operation. My father's designing this "contraption" reminds me that he wanted to be an engineer. He always delighted in devising labor-saving systems, like when he built cabinets in our bathroom, installed a radio inside, and wired it so the radio went on automatically when the lights were turned on. He chose law instead because it was the only profession he could pursue at night.

The second reason the mothballs story stands out is a heartbreaking one: a reminder of the price poor women are often forced to pay to get and hold a job. My father tells it for the same reason: "I never alluded in any of these memoirs to anything connected to sex," he writes,

> only partly due to the paucity of my experience as a result of not having extra money and even less spare time. I will mention this incident only as a comment on the terrible effect a depression can have on morality. On one visit to the little "factory," my manager there pointed to three girls and said I can have any one of them "right now." I was shocked by what I concluded was the effect of poverty on the working poor, and charged him with compelling the girls to yield to him before he'd hire them. I knew he'd find girls willing to submit for the sake of a job, a low paying job at that. He swore to me he'd not seduced any of them. I didn't fire him though I was sure he lied.

How I wish my father had fired him.

> Once I helped complete the liquidation, in 1933, the Shapiros had no more need of me and I was again out of a job. Years later, I ran into Kramer, the Shapiros' lawyer, the one who rented them space in his office for the finance company. His thesis was that they exploited me to the full, took advantage of my talents and hard work, both of which he held in high esteem, then heartlessly threw me to the wolves without any consideration or compensation or even a word of regret. Perhaps strangely, I didn't feel that way then or since. I placed all blame on my ill luck in having been born at a bad time to the particular parents, to the onset of the war in 1914, to the loss of a father to TB, and, most disastrous, to the onset of the Depression at the very time I was completing law school and seriously beginning my career.

What a succinct summary this is of the outside forces—the ill luck—that shaped my father's life. As I hear this summary, I realize, in a new way, how drastically different my father's life turned out to be

from the way he expected it to when he entered law school. Of course
he expected to earn his living as a lawyer as soon as he passed the bar.
In June 1928 that expectation was still realistic: though only nineteen,
he had finished a year of law school and was manager of a finance company. He couldn't have imagined that less than a year and a half later
the stock market would crash, and his hope of finding work as a lawyer
would vanish—and become ever more elusive, year by year, till the
years stretched into decades. No wonder regret cast a dark shadow as
he looked back on his life.

Something else catches my attention in my father's description of
being fired by the Shapiros once he'd helped liquidate their company:
the date, 1933. That's the year my father married, earned a master's
degree in law, and passed the bar: all things to celebrate. Instead, 1933
begins a descent into difficulty:

> The period between the liquidation of the finance company
> and the move to Danbury—eight years, between 1933 and
> 1941—was bleak. I have a recurring memory from that time that
> never leaves me. I was walking along on the way home from a
> dispiriting day spent looking vainly for a job. I then had a wife
> and child whom I had to face penniless and hopeless while hid-
> ing these feelings from them.

"While hiding these feelings from them." My father says this not as
a decision he made but something he assumed: he would hide his despair from his family, to protect them. I realize this explains why I
never suspected that he hated working as a cutter during the first thirteen years of my life. How foolish I was to take his even-keeled temperament, his apparent satisfaction with his life, at face value. Hiding
his feelings from his family was one more way he supported us. He
goes on,

> I came across my mother, who was sitting outside her dwell-
> ing and greeted me pleasantly. I ventured to ask her to lend me
> five dollars, which she promptly and unhesitatingly refused
> with the usual accompanying indictment for being profligate

and irresponsible. Even now, when I think of it, I feel like crying. The next day, as always, I did get a job and could borrow
from the bank, where I had an unblemished record.

This memory brings to mind a remark my father made that surprised me, and hurt my feelings, when he made it: after reading the
play I wrote based on our trip to Poland—a play juxtaposing his childhood with mine—my father said, "I get it. I didn't have a father, but I
didn't miss him. You had a father, and you missed him. It's true. I had
more time at home when Naomi was small." I was touched, and grateful: he went right to the heart of the play. I expected him to go on to
say—I wanted him to say—that he was sorry his absence caused me
pain. Instead he said, "It was a good thing, because I was earning better." At the time, I could think only of my own perspective: a child
who missed her father. But now I can see it from his: how could he be
sorry that he was finally able to earn a living—in contrast to the humiliation of begging his mother for a five-dollar loan, and receiving
not only a refusal but an upbraiding. He needed that loan to support
his family; his absence wasn't because he didn't care about his children;
it was proof that he did.

I'm certain that painful memory never leaves my father for another
reason, too: talking about his life, and how long it took him to begin
working as a lawyer, he says, "If only my mother had been willing to
part with some of the money she had in the bank—money I had earned
and given her—I could have established myself as a lawyer and avoided
all those years of grueling physical labor and grinding financial insecurity. I could have repaid her many times over." His bitterness toward
his mother is never far from the surface, but this is one of the few con-
texts where he expresses it in such a straightforward way: it goes to the
heart of his lifelong regret.

*

MANY OF THE SIXTY-EIGHT JOBS ON MY FATHER'S LIST ARE FROM
those years between 1933, when the finance company folded, and 1941,
when he took the position in Danbury: eight years of the Great Depression. The details he fills in explain how he moved from one job to

the next, one business scheme to the next, because none panned out: buying motor scooters with a partner and offering rides for a small fee; selling sewing machines, encyclopedias, vacuum cleaners, and costume jewelry door to door; canvassing liquor stores, offering to take photos they needed to get newly required liquor licenses; selling plots in a Jewish cemetery; selling ads in a Jewish newspaper; working in a factory making kerosene lamps; working a variety of WPA jobs, including court interpreter. He wrote long accounts of each one, often explaining why he thought it might earn him enough to support his family—and why it didn't.

A galling (to me) development is one I learn indirectly: my father gets a job in a factory that makes cuffs for jackets. The owner who hires him is . . . Moe Rosenfeld. Yes, the Shapiros' cousin who was hired at nearly double my father's salary, was trained by my father to take over as manager of the finance company, then hired someone who drove the company into the ground. He walked away from that failure unscathed, and opened a factory. That's where my father is working when:

One day I returned home from work and doubled up in excruciating pain. It turned out to be a perforated ulcer. I was rushed to the hospital, and underwent emergency surgery. Of course there were no antibiotics yet; if infection had set in, I would have died. When I awoke after the surgery, I was surprised to find myself alive. As I recuperated, I couldn't go back to working in a factory so I took a job as a messenger at the Welfare Department. It was really a break, but I felt embittered, because here I was a lawyer in a menial job. In the debates I conducted with fellow workers, they looked to me for information and regarded me as best informed while they all held better jobs paying higher salaries. I worked there about a year, long after I had fully recovered, because jobs were still rather scarce. I had plenty of free time at work and managed to handle a little legal work, which enabled us to move to a much nicer apartment on Eighty-fourth Street. . . . And that's where I was working when I got the offer to be a custodial officer in Danbury.

Then, while he's thriving at Danbury, comes the offer to work for the Treasury Department's Alcohol Tax Unit, and the move to Providence.

I now have a sense of the twenty-five years between 1933, when my father passed the bar, and 1958, when he began earning a living as a lawyer. But there is a piece of that story that doesn't fit what I know about my father—the part that has such painful resonance for me: the move from Providence, Rhode Island, to New York City. I want to solve that mystery—a mystery that is small in my father's life story (the move he talks about is the one from Danbury), but big in my sense of my own.

*

"I CAME BACK BECAUSE YOUR MOTHER GOT PREGNANT AND DIDN'T want to have a baby in Providence. She wanted to have it in New York."

My father is ninety-five, once again telling me that he left his job with the Treasury Department because my mother was pregnant with me. This time, though, I question it. It doesn't sound like something my father would do: give up a secure job with no prospects for another. He values financial security above all else. When I was accepted into the PhD program in linguistics at the University of California, Berkeley, he tried hard to convince me not to enroll there. He was certain I should keep my secure job teaching remedial writing at Lehman College in the Bronx and work toward a PhD by taking courses at the City University Graduate Center at night.

"Wasn't it scary to go to New York without a job?" I ask.

"I was scared all my life," he says, "but I always managed."

This sounds more like an evasion than an answer. It doesn't sound right.

And it isn't.

I finally find an explanation in a tape recording my father made in 1981, when he was eighty-three and his memory was sharper. My impending birth was not the only reason he left his job in Providence and moved his family to New York, maybe even not the main one. Attributing the move to my mother's pregnancy alone is an example of the reductions and simplifications that collapse and erase events as they become memories and the memories become stories that are told and retold.

"When I gave up the job as treasury agent and returned to New York," my father recalls on the earlier tape, "it was for a twofold reason, or perhaps more than two reasons." He dispenses with the familiar one in a single sentence: "First, Mother was pregnant with Deborah, and she was very much disinclined to give birth in Providence." Then he moves on to two other reasons: one a surprise, the other a revelation.

My father didn't quit his job at the Treasury Department with no prospect for another. In Providence, as in Danbury, he's been supplementing his income by selling fur coats on consignment. The fur coat manufacturer, Samuel Henig, offers him a much higher salary to help out with his mail-order business, and promises that once my father learns the business, he can take over running it and eventually buy in as a partner. Leaving for a higher salary is exactly the sort of thing my father would do—did do when he quit his job in Danbury to take the one in Providence. But the new position lasts only a few weeks. Henig doesn't appreciate my father's suggestions for ways to improve efficiency and productivity; he resents them. Then my father learns that Henig doesn't trust him: he's keeping a lot of information secret. When Henig blows up for a reason my father considers unjustified—this, too, is a familiar pattern: his sense of justice is outraged—they agree to part ways. That's when—and that's why—he finds himself unemployed in New York.

Here's the third reason, the revelation:

I decided, as indeed I had erroneously decided when working for the prison bureau, that all the provisional civil service employees would be let go after the war, that there would be a depression like the one following the First World War, and that everyone entitled to civil service jobs would be flocking back to them. During the war, no permanent civil service appointments were made at all; all civil service appointments, including mine, were provisional.

This, at last, explains why he leaves what seem like secure jobs in Providence and also in Danbury: "I didn't feel secure with my jobs." That feeling wasn't unfounded; what he predicted is exactly what happened to the cousin who moved his family to Detroit for a job—the cousin whose "talents and resourcefulness" my mother praised in a letter to his wife: the job in Detroit had been vacated by someone who had gone to war; when the war ended, his predecessor returned and reclaimed the job.

I'm grateful to learn that my father quit his job in Providence and returned to New York for reasons other than my mother's pregnancy. I'm relieved to know I'm not the cause of that fateful decision. But I'm still its heir—as my father is heir to his history, and his mother's.

My father's expectation that World War II would be followed by a depression is a legacy of his experience of World War I in Poland, where the war was followed by worsening economic conditions, especially for Jews. And it's also a legacy of his mother's influence. My father makes this link in the same taped memories:

> My mother was a born Cassandra, abysmally pessimistic, and I recall all my days with her both in Europe and in this country as being under a shadow of impending disaster. She was able herself to tolerate this atmosphere, and when with her friends was quite charming, but it must have been an integral part of her character and perhaps could explain why she always saved, no matter how little she earned or how little she had or came into the home. . . . My recollection of my youth is that of living under the shadow of the unhappy events and the destitution that my mother forever anticipated.

This, I think, is how family legacies are passed down from one generation to the next: it isn't only property that can be inherited, but also states of mind and emotion. His mother's sense of impending doom pervaded the atmosphere my father grew up in, and shaped his decisions about work that led to his enduring regret. That regret pervaded the home I grew up in, casting a shadow that left me with a lifelong fear of making wrong decisions—and an inclination to question and regret decisions as soon as I make them.

★

AT LAST I GET TO THE HAPPY ENDING. AFTER THIRTEEN YEARS:

The call came. I got an appointment as assistant counsel to the Workmen's Compensation Board. There was great excitement. I felt vindicated. I worked under the head of the legal department, Mr. Hill. I was one of four assistants under him but the other three were appointed by the Democratic Party and came in only once biweekly, on payday to collect their check, when all of us sat together for an amiable chat. In reality I was the only one assisting him. I didn't have the nerve to imitate the others and was glad to learn the laws and regulations and practices of the organization."

I heave a sigh of relief: my father is saying he's pleased with his work—no hint of his being unfairly treated or of having made a fateful mistake.

How I loved the change in my circumstances at work. The day went so fast and the people I worked with were so different, as were the physical surroundings. Friends, relatives, and acquaintances regarded me, and treated me, differently. They had previously held me too retarded to do legal work. At least that is what I had suspected all along, and I never really blamed them. They couldn't understand, I am sure, that I wouldn't expose my family, first my mother and sister, then my wife and children, to the sacrifices they would have had to make if I were to go into law without a paying job in it. All the union people I knew as well as those in the Liberal Party talked to me differently, as did the managers of the locals, or so it seemed to me.

All those years, he was sure that others thought he was working in "menial" jobs because he wasn't capable of succeeding as a lawyer. At last he feels he's proved them wrong. "But the best part of the new work I was doing was the interest it evoked and the satisfaction in researching the law. The fact that I wore clean clothing and worked better hours, despite the extracurricular work I sought to make ends meet, pleased me a great deal."

But this bubble, too, is burst by a stroke of ill luck. After six months—that's right, six months!—the job he labored thirteen years to get is gone. The Democratic governor who appointed him—New York *always* had Democratic governors at the time—is unexpectedly defeated by a Republican. Out go all the political appointees, to be replaced by Republicans. "I was faced with the inevitable necessity to return to cutting. I had no financial resources of any kind yet immediate need to feed a family. Yet I also believed that this was my last chance to break into the legal field, and I decided to move heaven and earth not to miss it. Everyone advised me it was an impossible dream. Even Mother"—that's my mother, not his—"was convinced I was butting my head against an impregnable wall, but I persisted."

My father patches together a crazy quilt of disparate sources of income.

I revived a worker's compensation case of my own that I had won. I had suffered a herniated disk, but didn't receive benefits after I returned to work. Now that I wasn't working as a cutter, I was eligible for those benefits. I used my political connections to land a job as a bingo inspector. Many churches and synagogues had organized games of bingo in the evenings; my job was to visit them and make sure they were following regulations. It paid a hundred dollars a week, which helped but was not enough to meet expenses. So I finally talked to Mother about helping out till I got on my feet.

There's a world of meaning in that word "finally." Finally, after being the sole breadwinner through such difficult times—times that were so difficult in part because he was the sole breadwinner—he asks his wife to contribute to the family's support. In a recent conversation about my father, a cousin tells me that his mother fiercely criticized mine for not helping her husband break into law by going to work during the years that preceded that "finally." My father never hints that he ever thought she should. He does sometimes comment, when explaining that he couldn't establish a law practice because it required working for a time with minimal income, that men married to teachers were lucky because they could. It never sounds to me like he's complaining that his wife wasn't a teacher. Given his conviction that it's a man's sole responsibility to support his family, it must have been difficult for him to suggest that his wife go to work. But he found what turned out to be the perfect profession for my mother: "I convinced her to try electrolysis. The training was brief—only three weeks—and she would work out of our home. Though she was wary, she agreed. We borrowed to pay for the course and for an electrolysis machine and chair. The money she earned helped a lot. And it turned out that she liked the work."

So that's how my mother becomes an electrologist, and the room that was my grandmother's becomes her office. Behind the closed door of that office, my mother gets to know the women who come regularly, week after week, as she removes "unwanted hair" from their faces. To her regular "patients" she is something between a friend and a therapist. Now she, too, has stories to tell when we gather for supper: she updates us on her patients' lives. Though I usually trace my writing to my father, I hear echoes of my mother's stories about her patients when I write of women's lives in my books.

My mother's profession proves helpful to me in another way, too. I'm twelve when she puts up a sign by our front door, DOROTHY TANNEN, ELECTROLOGIST. One day, she sends me on an errand to the grocery store at the far corner of our block. When I reach the corner, a boy I've never seen before pins me against the brick wall of the store. I don't know what he intends to do: Kiss me? Just scare me? I don't know because my mother's profession rescues me. I say, "Did you see the sign on my house? Do you know what an electrologist is? It's a lady judge!" At that, he releases me.

———

WITH THESE NEW SOURCES of income keeping the family afloat, my father sets about establishing a practice in workers' compensation law, a field he now knows well. After only two years, he has more work than he can handle and goes into partnership with two other lawyers. As the work he brings in keeps expanding, they take on another partner and hire many other lawyers, some of whom also become partners. When my father retires at seventy, he's been practicing law for twenty years, and his firm is the largest workers' compensation practice in New York, which means it's the largest in the world.

In my view of my father's life—in my experience of it—the emphasis is on this happy ending. My father, too, takes great satisfaction in those last twenty years. He often marvels that he could retire and live comfortably without working at all. But he never forgets the struggle, hardship, and probably most of all humiliation, of the twenty-five years after he passed the bar, before he finally earned his living as a lawyer.

He tells me as much, when we're in the assisted living apartment where he moved after my mother died. He's ninety-six. "I'm thinking always," he says, "I was smart and I worked hard. Why did I remain in low positions?"

"You mean before you got the appointment to the Workmen's Compensation Board?"

"Yes, all those years."

*

REGRET, I GUESS, IS A HABIT OF MIND. THERE MUST BE PEOPLE WHO don't look back, reliving and revising what they did in the past like actors redoing scenes they flubbed. My father isn't one of those people. He keeps a mental list of mistakes he made. Even happy outcomes were delayed or darkened by mistakes, like the reason it was thirteen years before his ceaseless work for the Liberal Party was rewarded by a political appointment. That mistake is attached to a name that I heard, all my life, with a metaphorical hiss, as if a villain walked onto the stage of a play: Billy Weiss, the Liberal Party leader my father apprenticed himself to. When Billy kept promising my father that he'd be a judge next year, then the next, then the year after that, my father says,

> I believed his promises. I didn't realize until years later that he was actually holding me back. If I got the political appointment, he'd lose my services. I was writing his speeches, doing his bidding. Just being associated with him was holding me back. Years later Abe Dolgen, the fellow who headed the Queens Liberal Party, told me—boasted—that he was the one who talked Alex Rose [a founder and vice chair of the Liberal Party] out of his intention to make me a judge by threatening to pull the entire Queens club out of the Liberal Party if Billy were rewarded by having his protégé offered a judgeship.

I STILL ACHE WHEN I think of these mistakes: quitting Danbury, trusting Billy Weiss. Those are the ones my father keeps returning to in our conversations, when he's old. But I also think of the mistake he never mentions, the decision he never thinks of as a mistake but I now do, since I realized that his mother tried to dissuade him from quitting high school and going to work full-time. My conviction is reinforced by a document I find buried among his papers—and comments he made about it in memories he recorded—that makes me rethink the story of his life.

The document contains the results of a test my father took when he was fifteen, less than three years after arriving in the United States knowing no English at all. It shows that his verbal abilities are equivalent to those of a native-born college student, and that his intelligence is "very superior, considerably above that of average adults." (It also notes he is "less developed socially than intellectually.")

My father told me about this verbal ability test—he never mentioned the intelligence test—proud of how highly his English language skills were rated. But he never said how he came to take the test, and I never asked. In the memories he records for me, he explains that the test was part of an application for a high school scholarship from a Jew-

CUNY Educational Clinic report

ish organization: "The tests were very interesting to me, especially the mechanical problems, like a door lock in a zillion parts I was told to assemble." There again is his aptitude for engineering.

Multiple choice questions were easy, I thought, and I must have impressed the two teachers who worked with me because they exchanged comments about my being a short time in the country when they examined my essay and word association results. They filed a good report, which I showed you at one time boastfully, and I was awarded thirty dollars a month. But I did not return to school so the payment was stopped after two months and instead I was recommended for a job at Gimbels in the toy department.

I know about the toy department. My father told me that while working after the store closed, he came upon a music box that played a song he'd never heard before: "Silent Night." He liked it so much that he played it over and over until quitting time. But I didn't know about the scholarship. He mentions this so casually: thirty dollars a month. For going to high school. Why wasn't he tempted to take it? Why didn't he consider staying in high school, as his mother urged, and working evenings, weekends, and summers to supplement whatever income she could earn, rather than working full-time and taking classes at night? This thought is staggering: he could have finished high school; gone to City College, which was free; and become an engineer, as he wanted to.

WHY DID MY FATHER think, at fourteen, that he had to quit high school to work full-time, when his mother didn't—and did everything she could to stop him? Seeking an answer to this question, I recall the scene he describes from one of his first jobs: he's thirteen, counting out for his mother the tips he received delivering telegrams the day before Christmas, as she cries with relief. I find myself thinking this memory might hold a clue. It must have made a huge impression on him, that he could lift his mother's misery, lighten the burden she constantly bemoaned—her fate as a widow with two children to support—by handing over money he earned. At last he was able to please her. And maybe it goes even deeper than that. His mother always told him that he was "just like your father": ugly, irresponsible, and profligate. Her husband failed to support her—first by squandering her dowry in a failed business, then by dying of tuberculosis. By succeeding where his father had failed, my father proved his mother's judgment wrong: he was not like his father at all.

Though my father goes on to hand his mother all his earnings for fourteen more years—and some of his earnings for years after that—he never again earns her gratitude or approval. But maybe that scene helps explain why he never stopped trying.

*

I SAID AT THE START THAT WHEN I SEEK TO UNDERSTAND MY FATHER I focus on his family, while he saw his life as the jobs he held and the work he did. But that distinction is an illusion: family and work are no more separate than mind and body—though having different words for each, and no word for the two combined, makes it seem that they are. I see this in a remark my father made when, on a family outing, we drove across the Triborough Bridge, which links Manhattan to Queens. As we passed over the tiny island between the two boroughs, my father said, "During the Depression I applied for a job there, to be a janitor at the offices of the Triborough Bridge Authority. I'd be cleaning toilets. They refused to hire me because they said I was overqualified. I didn't feel that way. I would do anything to support my family." I heard this at the time as a reminder of my father's humility and work ethic, and of how the Depression reduced a lawyer to scrounging for work as a janitor. I see it now as a window on my father's view of the world: a man's obligation is, above all, to support his family. For him, that obligation, more than anything else, encapsulates the meaning of family.

My father's sense of family as fundamentally that obligation is part of his own family legacy. So are the beliefs and fears that led him to make the decisions he made, good and bad, to fulfill that obligation. And all this—my father's work life, the pride with which he looked back on it, as well as the regret—is part of the family legacy he passed on to me.

"Don't Tell Anyone Your Father Was a Communist"

"Don't tell anyone your father was a communist," I was warned as a child. "If you do, their parents won't let them play with you."

The only anyone I might have been tempted to tell was my best friend, Cathy O'Leary. Cathy lived in the apartment house directly across the street from our house in Brooklyn. If we were both home, we were together, though I went to PS 217, the public school, and she went to a Catholic school, St. Rose of Lima (which I thought was one word: St. Rosalima). Having a secret that might cost me my friend was scary. Other than that, my father's Communist past wasn't a big deal to me.

It was a very big deal to my sister Naomi. When Naomi was thirteen, one of the best things in her life—what made her happiest—was an art class she biked to on Saturday afternoons. She loved the art, and she loved the teacher, who taught her to paint and inspired her with idealistic values like the biblical injunction to "beat swords into plowshares." Naomi recalls painting a farm implement and a gun, with the words "This" and "Not that." She was devastated when our father told her she'd have to stop going because the class was sponsored by the American Labor Party, which the FBI considered Communist. There were "spies" all around. If they saw that his daughter was involved in the American Labor Party, it could be held against him. It was 1950, the McCarthy era, when people associated with Communism were being fired and blacklisted. My father was already five years into the purgatory of working overtime as a cutter while devoting every moment he wasn't in the factory to working for the Liberal Party. He believed he was on the verge of getting the promised political appointment and couldn't put that at risk. Naomi begged to at least be allowed to stay till the end-of-year exhibit of student work, and he agreed. When they went to the show, sure enough, across the street from the entrance was a parked van from which agents were taking pictures of everyone going in. Naomi never went back. But, even though she understood why, she never stopped regretting—and resenting—that she had to give up something that meant so much to her.

My father wasn't just worried that the FBI might open a file on him. He knew they already had one.

In 1991, when my father is eighty-three, a friend tells me she made a Freedom of Information request to the FBI and got a copy of her deceased father's file. (By reading it, she learned that her father had a years-long extramarital affair.) I ask my father if there's any chance the FBI has a file on him, and he says he knows they do. Though he doesn't seem all that curious himself, he agrees to request a copy. He predicts it won't contain anything very interesting—certainly no affair. The file arrives, and it's thick! But as I eagerly turn its pages, I see that many are not pages from my father's file, but forms in place of pages that have been left out. On each form, checked boxes correspond to section numbers that explain why the page was not included. I don't learn much from the pages that are included, either, because much of the text is blacked out.

Still, the file makes clear that the FBI investigated whether Eli Tannen was a Communist. The case was opened in 1944, when he was working at the federal penitentiary in Danbury. My father thinks he knows who denounced him: a fellow guard who seemed upset by some of the views he expressed. The investigation continued after my father was hired by the Treasury Department in Providence. Communists were forbidden to work for the federal government: if the FBI determined that he was or had been a Communist, he would lose his job.

In a memo dated August 18, 1944, the agent heading the investigation, whose name is blacked out, reports that the FBI has cleared my father of the charges and is closing the case. A memo dated January 23,

4-750 (Rev. 12-14-88)   (◯   XXXXXX
XXXXXX
XXXXXX

FEDERAL BUREAU OF INVESTIGATION
FOIPA DELETED PAGE INFORMATION SHEET

2   Page(s) withheld entirely at this location in the file. One or more of the following statements, where indicated, explain this deletion.

☒ Deletions were made pursuant to the exemptions indicated below with no segregable material available for release to you.

Section 552		Section 552a
☒ (b)(1)	☐ (b)(7)(A)	☐ (d)(5)
☐ (b)(2)	☐ (b)(7)(B)	☐ (j)(2)
☐ (b)(3)	☒ (b)(7)(C)	☐ (k)(1)
_____	☒ (b)(7)(D)	☐ (k)(2)
_____	☐ (b)(7)(E)	☐ (k)(3)
_____	☐ (b)(7)(F)	☐ (k)(4)
☐ (b)(4)	☐ (b)(8)	☐ (k)(5)
☐ (b)(5)	☐ (b)(9)	☐ (k)(6)
☐ (b)(6)		☐ (k)(7)

☐ Information pertained only to a third party with no reference to you or the subject of your request.

☐ Information pertained only to a third party. Your name is listed in the title only.

☐ Documents originated with another Government agency(ies). These documents were referred to that agency(ies) for review and direct response to you.

_____ Pages contain information furnished by another Government agency(ies). You will be advised by the FBI as to the releasability of this information following our consultation with the other agency(ies).

_____ Page(s) withheld for the following reason(s):_____

_____

☐ For your information: _____

☒ The following number is to be used for reference regarding these pages:
105-107632-2 p2 -p3

XXXXXX   XXXXXXXXXXXXXXXXXXXXXXXX
XXXXXX   X   DELETED PAGE(S)   X
XXXXXX   X NO DUPLICATION FEE X
     X   FOR THIS PAGE   X
     XXXXXXXXXXXXXXXXXXXXXXXX
     FBI/DOJ

Form indicating that pages were deleted from a copy of my father's FBI file

1945, reports that the Treasury Department will take no action—they won't fire my father—because the FBI "did not establish a basis for finding that Tannen advocates or is a member of an organization that advocates the overthrow of our constitutional form of government." My father recalls being questioned by his boss at the Treasury Department: "O'Brien called me into his office. He said, 'You've been accused of being a Communist. If you tell me you aren't, that will be sufficient

101-280

CONFIDENTIAL

By date of July 27, 1944, a letter was directed to the New York Field
Division requesting that the indices of that office be checked for any
information contained in their files concerning T.JEI.

PENDING   CONFIDENTIAL

A highly redacted page from my father's FBI file

for me.' I told him I wasn't, and that was the end of it. It was the truth.
I quit the party in 1939, when Stalin signed the pact with Hitler."

This makes the matter seem simple and unthreatening. But his file
shows that my father was called in and questioned—under oath—by
the FBI. It includes a transcript of the interview, showing that he was
asked directly if he had ever belonged to any of a long list of organizations, including the Communist Party. To each he answered "No." It
also includes an account of a follow-up conversation that took place

when he was called back to sign a transcript of the interview. At that time, the report recounts, he said he couldn't imagine why anyone would accuse him of being a Communist unless the complaint was made by co-workers at the prison, because many of them were anti-Semitic; were jealous of the promotion he received; and mistakenly thought that anyone who read the newspaper *PM,* as he did, was a Communist.

The FBI investigation must have been far more threatening and up-setting than my father let on in our conversations—except maybe he did let on, in a comment I took as a joke when he said it:

It's 1999. My father is ninety-one. I turn on my tape recorder and begin, "Today you're going to tell me about your political life."

"At the risk of arrest and deportation," he quips.

I laugh. "By the time I write my book, no one's going to care."

How naïve and thoughtless I was to laugh. During the McCarthy era, arrest wasn't as common as blacklisting and firing, but it wasn't uncommon, either. Nor was deportation—or instituting proceedings to deport, which was devastating even if successfully fought in court—of suspected "subversives" born abroad. At ninety-one, having been in this country nearly eighty years, my father was still aware that he wasn't born here and could, in theory at least, be sent back where he came from.

WHEN I TURN FIFTEEN, I take a summer job as a work camper—a teenage camper who also does work like serving food to the younger kids—at a summer camp in upstate New York. There I make friends who are more like me than any of my friends from the neighborhood or school. Some also have parents who were "progressive," which could describe Communists, Socialists, or anyone sympathetic to them. These friendships continue and deepen long after we return to our homes in Brooklyn, the Bronx, or New Jersey. It's 1960, the cusp of that transformative decade. Together we step into the worlds of folk music, peace marches, and civil rights activism. We recommend books to each other and have long conversations about them, and about how we can make the world a better place. Among these friends, my father's Communist past is a badge of honor. I learn a term for children raised by parents with Communist or Socialist leanings: red diaper baby. I'm happy to have a name for the background I was once supposed to hide; it makes me feel part of something larger than my family. I wear the label with pride.

My friends and I attend peace marches and civil rights demonstrations; I'm there when Rev. Martin Luther King gives his "I Have a Dream" speech in Washington. Some of my friends' parents disapprove; some even try to stop them. I feel lucky that my parents don't. My mother is indifferent; my father is sympathetic. I'm thrilled that he knows the union songs I learn from hanging around Greenwich Village and attending folk music concerts. He knows them because the American Communist Party was closely tied to the union movement: both were concerned with improving workers' lives. When he's old, we sing these songs together. My father is better at carrying a tune, but I'm better at remembering lyrics. We both especially like the ballad "Joe Hill," about a Swedish-born union activist and songwriter who became a martyr to the union cause. My father often asks me to sing the song's many verses, which tell the story of Joe Hill's execution in 1915 for a murder it was widely—and internationally—believed he didn't commit.

I'm visiting my parents in Florida. My father is ninety-five. I'm standing by, feeling helpless and concerned, while a nurse changes the bandage on his face for a large wound left by dermatologic surgery. I don't know if it's to give me something to do or to give him something else to think about, but I'm grateful that my father asks me to sing "Joe Hill."

A year later, my father and I are in the assisted living apartment he moved to when my mother died, singing union songs. "If people hear us singing," he says, "they wouldn't know that people got beaten up by thugs for singing these songs." Union songs reinforce assumptions I grew up with: idealizing workers, demonizing bosses. A story my father told over supper when I was a child encapsulates this. It was one of his many stories about "the shop":

> When I first started there, we were a small band of cutters. We worked hard, got all the work done, and did it well. We cut thirty, forty, fifty, sixty layers of fabric at a time. In two or three

hours, we cut a thousand garments. And we were making a living wage by working overtime. The owners figured that if they
bring in more cutters, they'll save money by not having to pay
overtime. But they cut overtime, we can't make a living wage.
So they went ahead and hired more cutters, but these men need
overtime, too, to support their families. So we all got together
and figured out how we can keep busy but make sure we need to
work evenings and Saturdays to get the work done.

My father demonstrates, with his body, gestures, and facial expressions, the way the cutters carefully smooth the patterns, adjust the layers of fabric, guide the electric knife that cuts the fabric, making a
show of working diligently yet keeping their productivity in check.
"The owners never caught on," he says. "They're so determined to cut
overtime—to deprive us of a living wage—that they keep adding cutters. There are twice as many of us now, but we still need to work
Saturdays and extra hours during the week to fill all the orders." The
moral of the story is clear: The workers triumph not only because
they're clever but because they stick together. And the owners are done
in by their heartlessness. They would have come out ahead if they'd
made common cause with the original band of hardworking cutters,
instead of trying to increase profits by depriving them of a living wage.
But now my father comments, "The workers are not angels. If they
had the power, they would treat the bosses no better than the bosses
treated them. It's human nature."

"WHEN DID YOU BECOME a Communist?" I ask.
My father answers the same way he answered my question about
when he became an atheist: He was influenced by his mother's youngest sister—the one who assumed a position high up in the Polish Communist government after World War II—and who, as a teenager, was
already an ardent and active Communist: "When I was six, listening to
my aunt Magda talking with her friends." Atheism is fundamental to
Communist ideology, which sees religion as keeping the oppressed
from rising up against their oppressors, and separates people who
should join together for the good of all. In the ideal Communist world,

all workers will unite: there will be no racism, and no anti-Semitism. So the idealistic fervor that swept up Magda and her friends, as it did many young Warsaw Jews at the time, lured them not only away from their parents' Hasidism but also toward Communism.

Through his aunt Magda, my father was influenced by that fervor and brought it with him to his new home:

> When I came to this country at the age of twelve, I considered myself a Communist. In Warsaw I belonged to a group already, a Zionist club. Which wasn't really contradictory. You could be a Zionist and a Communist, a Zionist and a capitalist. I wore the white and light blue cap, the Zionist cap. I don't know how I got it. I must have purloined it in some way. I couldn't have gotten money for it. In the club there were radicals and the other kind, too. I was the radical type. Because of my aunt Magda. It was natural for me to follow Magda, because when I lived in my grandfather's house, she was my protector against my mother. And she was only six years older than I. She had a group around her. The Jewish youth were dissatisfied, like many people. It was right in the Enlightenment, when so many Jews gave up religion. My grandfather's children, my aunts and uncles, seemed to have been caught up in that.
>
> Magda was the youngest girl, and she had all the influence already of her sisters, which was all secular. She was proud to say she knew nothing about Judaism. . . . The first time I remember that I was listening to what they were saying was on a Friday night. Friday night after supper, my grandparents went to bed early, and Magda invited her friends to the kitchen. It was a convenient place to meet. . . . Usually they held serious discussions about the state of the world and how they were going to change it through Communism.

Serious discussions about what's wrong with the world and how they're going to change it—make it better, more just—sound a lot like the discussions my friends and I had when we were teenagers trying to change the world through the civil rights and peace movements.

(Though my father never mentions this, and I don't know if he ever thought of it, I suspect that the reason his grandparents went to bed early Friday night is the belief of many orthodox Jews—it's specified in the Mishneh Torah, a set of Jewish laws dating to the twelfth century—that married couples are obligated to have sex as a way of observing the Sabbath, which begins Friday night.)

My father goes on,

These discussions were especially lively in 1917, after the Russian Revolution began. I was imbibing the things that they were saying. That I was for the workers, I was against the czar, I was against the capitalists. I don't know whether I knew already what capitalists were. But it was natural for me to be sympathetic to those ideas, because I hated the eight hours a day or more I was studying Talmud, and I hated the repetition that I had to do in the synagogue. I had to repeat the same thing and listen to it. Most of it I didn't understand yet. So I was ready to accept what I heard, the radicals' ideas.

My father's personal experience replicates the way Communism combined political idealism and atheism. And his family was a microcosm of that larger social movement:

What was happening in my family—all the discussions before, during, and after the First World War—reflected what was happening with Jews in Eastern Europe, and the changes in thinking which were taking place all over at the time: the older people, like my grandfather, clinging to their old ways and to their fanaticism; most of the children adopting new ways to a greater or lesser degree, ranging from what was called progressive clothes—meaning ordinary civilian clothes rather than the Hasidic uniform, like my uncle Bernard—all the way to revolutionary thinking and activities involving unionism, Bundism, nihilism, anarchism, and Communism. There was also socialism and socialist Zionism. So I had all that influence when I came to this country.

What fortuitous timing: my father came to the United States in 1920, just one year after the Communist Party was established here. And its establishment was the result of exactly the force that influenced him: the optimism and enthusiasm inspired in Europe by the Bolshevik Revolution, which led poor Russian workers and peasants to wrest power from an autocratic ruler whose regime exploited and oppressed them. World-changing forces work their magic—and their destruction—through individual lives. Because of where and when my father was born, his life was part of the cataclysmic effects of the Russian Revolution.

When I was young, I didn't belong to any Communist organizations, but I did go to the Workmen's Circle with my uncle Max, who belonged there. A lot of Jewish workers belonged to Workmen's Circle. They gave insurance, and sick benefits, and they helped each other out. They had literature, they had regular meetings, they supported strikes. They were quite radical in that branch, in Bensonhurst. And most of them were Communists, but not officially. The Workmen's Circle was never officially Communistic.

The Workmen's Circle. That's a name I recognize. The Catskill resort where my family had reunions when my parents were old—where my father asked everyone to say what it means to us to be Jewish—was Circle Lodge, still owned by the Workmen's Circle. It was his idea for us to meet there; he remained a member until he died. Now I see why.

KNOWING HOW FIERCE WAS the fear of Communism during the McCarthy era, I assumed it was a movement that must have swept millions of Americans up in its vortex. So I'm startled to learn how few Americans were members of the Communist Party. Various sources I find number them 75,000 or 85,000 at their peak. The highest number I find anywhere is 100,000. And my father was one of them. As was standard practice, since the Party was outlawed: "I took a false name, Edward Toler. Ernst Toller was a prominent German Communist. I kept my initials so I wouldn't forget it. I turned Norman to believing in Communism. We joined a Communist club. Part of it was a lecture on Sunday. We were like a class. There was a teacher, teaching us about Communism." This scene makes me think of a consciousness-raising group I joined in 1973, when I was part of another social movement, the women's movement. Though we had no teacher—the leader who brought the group together stayed only for the first meeting, leaving us to run our regular meetings ourselves—we were also, in many ways, like a class: we read and discussed and came to see larger forces shaping our lives.

"Around 1936," my father recalls, "not long after I stopped working for the finance company, the American Labor Party was formed, and I joined it." The American Labor Party—where Naomi took the art class she loved, and the FBI stationed a van to photograph people going in and out.

I still belonged to the Communist Party. They wanted me to use my influence in steering the American Labor Party in the right direction, following the Party line. I belonged to a club on Bay Parkway at Sixty-fifth Street in Bensonhurst. The Party gave me a large number of workers who would join and follow my direction. For a couple of Sundays I received these assignees at my home. They came singly, and I spent much time in training them for the role we were to play in politics, though only a couple of them actually joined and showed up at meetings. Still I worked hard for the Party, spoke at street corners, handed out leaflets. They sent me to Coney Island, to start conversations there under the boardwalk, to convince people about Communism.

I got myself appointed special assistant deputy attorney general for the election and toured the polling places to check on the legality of procedures. In some cases the election workers turned to me for advice in instances where they were genuinely perplexed as to the correct procedure in difficult cases. I had prepared myself by studying the law of course and was able to guide them.

My first thought, on reading this, is: How did he find the time? Then I remind myself: in 1936 my father was only twenty-eight. He was married, but had no children. And these are the terrible Depression years when he couldn't find permanent work—the years when he was doing one after another of the sixty-eight jobs he listed as a summary of his life.

"When I went to work as a messenger for the Welfare Department, I had plenty of free time, so I proselytized for the Party and tried, sometimes successfully, to direct their thinking towards justice and equality. Everything was directed toward protests against conditions of exploitation and injustice and waste of energy towards competition instead of cooperation for general welfare." There it is, summed up: the idealism of Communism—the yearning for social justice and equality—that inspires young people generation after generation: his peers, then mine, and so many young people today.

My father went to work for the Welfare Department in 1939, ten years into the Great Depression. Describing that time, he lets me know how he came to have a conversation that he told me about many times:

At work I was sometimes asked to substitute for the clerk or social worker in taking care of a client's problem. A conversation I had with a client regarding sales tax has stuck in my mind. Mayor LaGuardia had just instituted a two percent sales tax, the first in the nation, I believe, for a short emergency period. You know of course how that developed. Talking to this client, I said how unfair a tax that was, when the poor working stiff paid the same tax on his daily pack of cigarettes as the wealthy individual. "But I want to be fair to the wealthy." "Why in heaven's name do you worry about them? They are so well off and powerful, they don't need your help, and they certainly don't worry about you." "Because I expect to be wealthy myself someday, so I have to look out for justice to the wealthy. I'm not always going to be on welfare, you know." That was a lesson I never forgot.

The lesson was an explanation for why poor and working people might support policies that favor the rich: though it makes little sense from the perspective of their current lives, it reflects, and reinforces, their hopes for the future. That my father remembered and retold this conversation reflects and reinforces my sense of him as always trying to understand the world and the people in it.

AND NOW MY FATHER fills another gap: how an era of his life that I heard about but never experienced ended, and the era I lived through began.

"In 1941, I took the job at the prison in Danbury and lost all contact with the Party. When I became a cutter in 1945, back in New York, I met Billy Weiss at Wiesen's, where he was the chairman of the shop. The American Labor Party in the meantime had split. The Communists had taken control of it, so the unions, foremost among them the ILGWU, broke away to form the Liberal Party." Aha, I think, so that's how the Liberal Party came about. People like my father, who joined the American Labor Party to turn it Communist, had succeeded. So those who had no use for Communism formed an alternate party to improve conditions for working people. By this time, my father was one of them: "I freely chose to join the Liberal Party because I had in the meantime become disillusioned with the Communists, as I told you, when they made a pact with the Nazis in 1939."

This also explains the connection between my father's involvement in the Liberal Party and the ILGWU—the International Ladies' Garment Workers' Union, which I heard referred to as "the ILG," and heard so often, it was part of the landscape of my childhood. Because the ILG represented so many garment industry workers, the Liberal Party held the balance of power between Democrats and Republicans. Democrats needed the votes of Liberal Party members to win office. The Liberal Party could expect to be rewarded by policies that favored workers—and by political appointments. From time to time they reminded the Democrats of that need by running their own candidate. My father filled that role three times, running for Congress in 1956 and 1962 and for council member at large in 1966.

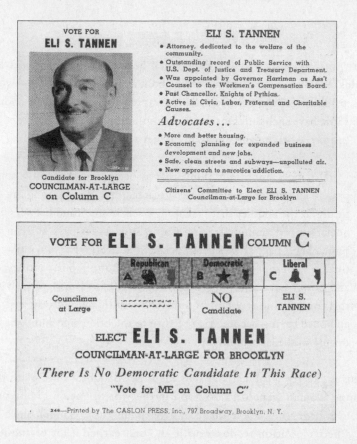

That's how my father's political activism and his longing to earn his living as a lawyer converged in the Liberal Party, as he came under the influence of the man who promised to get him a political appointment, but, he learned years later, was actually preventing him from getting one: Billy Weiss. "Billy was the head of the Brownsville–East New York Liberal Party, and I became the secretary, Billy's right hand, writing his speeches, and so on." So that's how my father started "being active," as I always heard it referred to, in the Liberal Party—the reason he was so often away from home when I was young. His political work for the Liberal Party that was so much a part of my childhood had evolved from the Communism that, by the time I heard about it, was just something in his past I was supposed to keep secret.

———

THE JOURNALS MY FATHER kept when he was young show that his plans for his life—what we now talk about as hopes and dreams—were inseparable from the political isms he was reading and thinking about, isms that have such different connotations now than they had then. In 1927, when he's nineteen, my father writes in his journal:

The most important thing that is occupying my mind at present and which I feel may be a great factor in determining my future, is the conflict that is shaping itself in my mind between Socialism or Communism and Capitalism. As far back as I can remember, I have always been socialistic at heart, always sympathizing with the lower or laboring classes. But of course money and power have always been inviting to me, so I made myself this comfortable program of amassing wealth any old way first and once having become rich to turn to the other side and fight openly in the laboring ranks.

This is exactly what a friend tells me is her daughter's life plan: the young woman wanted to do good in the world, but on graduating from college, she took a job at an investment bank. She felt she'd be in a better position to do good if she first earned a lot of money, which she could then donate to worthy organizations or projects. There's a difference, though. For my friend's daughter, it was a choice; for my father, the need to earn money first is an obligation—the obligation that drives every decision he makes after arriving in the United States:

The consideration of my mother forced me to decide to struggle for wealth even if I must thus act against my ideals and trample underfoot the altruism toward which I strive. For twenty years now she has been struggling for financial independence. She has never succeeded and now she is embittered toward life and is letting out her bitterness to us. The main object in this part of my life is to make her in the latter half of her life as independent financially as she ever dreamed in her life. To be able to place at her disposal the luxury and comfort of which perhaps our presence in this world deprived her.

The "our" refers to my father and his sister, the two children his mother had to raise on her own, the reason she was "embittered toward life," the reason my father feels, at nineteen—and continued to feel for the rest of his life—that it is his duty to make this up to her.

> And this is the reason I cannot follow the trend of my nature in striving for betterment of the laboring classes, in striving for helping the progress of the world, in striving to have a hand in the world revolution of workers which is inevitable, but must take my place in the opposite ranks, fight against my sympathizers and brothers in ideals, deter the world's progress, and trample my better nature underfoot in ruthlessly striving for wealth.

I'm certain that by "wealth" my father doesn't mean what this word means to me—being rich—but simply means having enough money for his mother to be comfortable, finally free of the financial insecurity that has darkened her, and consequently his, perspective on life.

In his journal, my father goes on to explain why, despite this obligation, his sense of social justice pulls him toward Communism—as it did so many others in the 1920s, when the Communist Party was the main social movement addressing not only the exploitation and poverty of workers but also social justice and world peace:

> I feel that in spite of myself I am being dragged to communism and either of two things will have to decide my future. I will either shake off by a superhuman effort my sympathy for labor or I will take some middle course between right and wrong as I now see and understand them.

I want to go back in time and assure the nineteen-year-old who would become my father that he did find a middle course: he earned a solid income as a lawyer laboring to get fair compensation for workers who'd been injured on the job. When he retired at seventy, it was be-cause his original partners were gone, and he felt that the young part-ners they had brought in didn't really care about the workers whose cases they were handling.

MY FATHER TELLS ME of a conversation he had with his aunt Magda in 1970, when our families met for a shared vacation in Yugoslavia, the only country at the time to which both Poles and Americans could travel freely. Magda, who had devoted her life to Communism and had spent eight years in prison because of that devotion, said of the Polish Communist system she had sacrificed so much to establish and worked so hard to administer: "This isn't what we fought for." I think my fa-ther is expressing a similar sentiment when he says, in the last year of his long life, "Communism didn't fail. It was never tried."

WHEN MY PARENTS WARNED me not to tell anyone that my father had been a Communist, it was still the McCarthy era, which didn't end till 1956, when I was eleven. Yet for many years after, the assumption still lingered that Communists wanted to overthrow our government. That is the charge of which the FBI exonerated my father. But my father's belief in Communism was about making our government better. Like many immigrants, he loved our country in a way that those of us born here couldn't—maybe in a deeper way, because he had experienced life elsewhere. I see this in a letter he writes to his mother when she's visit-ing Warsaw in 1931: he chastises her for not appreciating America as much as she should, as much as he does:

> I who complained of conditions here, who am so intent upon change for the better even in this wonderful land of plenty and freedom, nevertheless I always was grateful to the fate that brought me here and away from the misery of the old world. Over there one never knew when one will be without the bare necessities of life. Here one almost feels certain of one's daily bread. Here it is only the calamities of life such as accident or sickness that we dread, but are never really worried, no not even

in these hard times, about the daily sustenance of life. I have always appreciated this fact and have prized it accordingly.

DURING MY DAILY PHONE conversations with my father in his last years, I sometimes complain that we are the only industrialized country that doesn't provide health care for all its citizens, doesn't provide child care for small children, imprisons so many for so long. My father always dismisses my criticism: "It's still the best country in the world."

CHAPTER

NINE

Sex, Lies, and Love

THE MYSTERY OF
MY PARENTS' MARRIAGE

THERE ARE THINGS I THOUGHT I KNEW ABOUT MY PARENTS' MARRIAGE. I never noticed that they didn't match up.

From the time I was very young, I "knew" that my mother married my father because he was the smartest man she'd ever met, and he married her because she was the prettiest woman he'd ever met. Their wedding picture, which used to sit in a frame on my mother's dresser and now sits on a table in my living room, supports that story. My mother, twenty-two, looks beautiful in a lace-topped dress, white gloves that go up past her elbows, and an elegant, narrow-brimmed white hat. In other photographs, my father, six feet tall, dwarfs my mother, who's five two. In this one they seem to be the same height, because she's standing and he's sitting on the arm of a chair, serious and imposing, looking older than his twenty-four years.

I also knew that my parents married on impulse and in secret at City Hall. Their honeymoon was two weekends in the Catskill Mountains, where New York City Jews went for vacations. My mother stayed through the week because she had the time off from work; my father didn't, so he went back to the city after the first weekend and rejoined her for the second. Then they returned to their respective homes: he to the apartment where he lived with his mother and sister,

My parents' wedding picture

she to the house where she lived with her parents and siblings. I never thought to ask why they married in secret or how long they thought they'd keep it that way. Whatever they intended, by the time they returned to Brooklyn the secret was out. While my mother was in the Catskills, advertisements aimed at the new bride arrived at her home. Her father refused to recognize the marriage, not because he objected to her choice of husband (he didn't), but because a rabbi hadn't officiated—and couldn't, because it was a period in the Hebrew calendar when the Jewish religion forbids weddings. A month later they had a religious ceremony and a wedding celebration in the backyard of her home.

And the beautiful wedding photograph? When he's old, my father tells me that the picture wasn't taken at their wedding. "I knew a fellow who was a photographer," he says. "When he heard that I didn't have a wedding picture, he offered to take one. He didn't charge me."

My mother bought the dress, the gloves, and the hat not for the wedding but for the photograph.

I ALSO KNEW HOW my parents met: she was his best friend's sister. Two weeks after my mother arrived in the United States at the age of twelve, with her mother and three older siblings (her father and three other siblings had come several years before), her brother Norman went to work in the garment district at a factory owned by distant cousins named Shapiro. There he befriended my father, a boy his age— fourteen—who had been in the country for two years. So my parents knew each other from the time they were fourteen and twelve. When they married, a decade later, my father was running the Shapiros' finance company, and my mother was working there, as a secretary.

THESE WERE THE STORIES I heard when I was young. But when I got older and began asking my parents about their past—when they got older and had more time and inclination to look back—they filled in details that told a very different story.

"IT TOOK ME A LONG TIME to get him," my mother tells me. "I was after him for years. When we both worked at the finance company, we saw each other all the time. I was very possessive. I kept trying to get him to go to lunch and go out with me after work. I can't believe how aggressive I was. I was very much in love with him. I was pursuing him. He said he would never get married."

Why did my father suddenly change his mind? Here's how my mother explained it, when the woman I hired to interview my parents asked, "How did you meet your husband?"

He used to come to the house all the time. Eli wasn't very happy in his own house with his mother and sister, so any free time he had, he used to spend in our house. It was a very lively house. We had three men there—my three brothers. And he was just accepted as another member of the family. And I liked him right away. He thought of me as a kid and didn't pay any attention to me. But gradually as I got older I guess he started to

notice me more. I fell in love with him when I was about thirteen years old. That's not to say that I didn't have other boy-
friends, but as I got older I became more and more involved
with him. He was the one that I preferred to anybody else. I was
very impressed with his knowledge, and we would joke about it
a lot, his using big words. It seemed to me he knew everything
that was going on in the world, and I was very impressed with
that. He was a hero to me, because I thought he was so well educated, and he knew so much. I admired him greatly.

So half the story I'd formed in my mind is true: my mother fell in love
with my father because he was the smartest man she'd ever met. But if
that fits a romantic image of falling in love, the rest of the story
doesn't:

> We never had the kind of courtship where he would come
> and call and take me out. He was always there. I couldn't avoid
> him. We would be in the house, I would be there, and they
> would all be there, and then the boys would be playing cards and
> sometimes I was part of what they were doing, sometimes I
> wasn't. But when I was about nineteen and twenty, I started
> going out seriously with Eli. We became seriously involved, but
> he kept saying that he didn't want to get married. And there was
> a period where I was very upset, and I went through a traumatic
> time because I wanted to get married and he didn't. He always
> said if he married anybody, it would be me. He said he was in
> love with me but he didn't believe in marriage, and he wouldn't
> assume the responsibility and so on.
>
> But finally, I went through a stage where I was very upset,
> and I really became ill. It affected my stomach. I had a nervous
> stomach. Sometimes I would eat and then vomit. It was all due
> to the situation, because we worked together and I was seeing
> him constantly, and we weren't getting anywhere, so finally he
> decided that he would get married. Maybe he saw that I was
> very unhappy and then he started asking me to marry him and I
> refused. I said, "You're just asking me because you think I want

you to marry me." I think he proposed three times and the third
time I said okay [*here she laughs*], and we eloped.

That's why they married on impulse: my mother took to her bed,
couldn't hold food down, and was losing weight. My father took pity
on her—truly feared for her health—and gave in. And why could she
exert that pressure? It's implied in her comment "We became seriously
involved." I am certain that "seriously involved" means they were having sex.

How do I know my parents had sex before they married? They
both told me: my mother first, and my father only after he knew that
she'd told me.

I'M SIXTEEN. MY MOTHER tells me, with a laugh, that my father complained about my sister's boyfriend: "Daddy said, 'Imagine, he shows
up here like that—and he's sleeping with her, but they're not married
and have no plans to marry.' I said to him: 'But that's exactly what you
did!'" (And my sister went on to marry her boyfriend, too.)

MY MOTHER TOLD ME of the connection between having sex and her
hope to marry during one of the many conversations we had in the
nineties.

She's resting on the queen-size bed in my parents' Westchester bedroom, her back against the headboard, her legs stretched out before
her. I'm sitting on the bed cross-legged, facing her. She's telling me
about how things were when she was young. "All my friends were
sleeping with their fiancés," she says. "We didn't talk about it, but we
knew."

"But Daddy wasn't your fiancé."

"I guess I thought if we slept together, he would be."

THERE'S ANOTHER LAYER OF meaning behind my mother's comment
"All my friends were sleeping with their fiancés." My mother had a
fiancé, though it wasn't my father. She was engaged for a time to a man
named Nat. Among the books we had in our home when I was growing up was a large, thick poetry collection that Nat had given my

mother; on the flyleaf, he dedicated to her one of the love poems he copied from the collection. When my mother spoke of him, she always said that Nat was so crazy-jealous, she finally got fed up and gave him back his ring. She mentions Nat in the interview—and uses the word "serious" to describe their relationship, too.

> I had a serious boyfriend who was a cousin of mine, a second or third cousin that I was involved with. He wanted me to marry him, he was very much in love with me at the time, used to send me love letters a lot. And he knew that I liked Eli [*laughs*], and he was a friend of theirs, too—of my brothers and Eli, so it was a little complicated. I was sort of for a while stuck going with Eli and going out with Nat y'know, and all that kind of thing, at one point.

I HAVE ONE MORE REASON for believing that my mother means "having sex" when she says she and my father were "seriously involved": the story of sex and marriage and the woman my father might have married instead—the woman whose letters were hidden in the storage room of their condominium: Helen.

THOUGH MY FATHER HID her letters, Helen wasn't a secret. Both my parents refer to her casually. "She was my rival," my mother says, adding with a chuckle, "I answered the phone in the office where your father and I worked. When she called, I'd say he wasn't in." In another conversation, she says: "He had a girlfriend, Helen. He wouldn't sleep with her because he thought she was a virgin, but he learned later that she wasn't." This comment presupposes that my mother wasn't a virgin, or he wouldn't have slept with her.

This odd calculus about who was or wasn't a virgin undercuts my romantic vision of a couple falling in love. I realize that I'll never understand my parents' marriage if I approach it the way I view romantic relationships. To understand it, I have to grasp how different relationships between women and men were at the time.

*

MY FATHER AND I ARE IN THE WESTCHESTER CONDO, HAVING ONE OF our long conversations about his past. He's been talking about my mother, and I mention his "other girlfriend." He corrects me: "Your mother wasn't my girlfriend. Helen was my girlfriend."

IN ANOTHER CONVERSATION, he's telling me about Helen. I ask, "And so were you dating Mommy at this time, too?"

He corrects: "I wasn't dating—I never really dated your mother, just the last year. But I always used to see her, and we used to be together, and I used to be sort of like a boyfriend."

WHAT DOES IT MEAN to be "sort of like a boyfriend"? What kind of relationship did he have with my mother if they never really dated and she wasn't his girlfriend? I get glimpses in his journals and letters, and in comments he makes in conversation.

MY FATHER IS TALKING about how he got his law degrees. He says, "Mother typed my master's thesis."

Typing his thesis for him certainly is sort of like a girlfriend.

"It's funny that she was typing it," I say, "because in your thesis you argued against the idea of marriage, right?"

"Yeah!" He laughs. "That was my own personal idea, this idea that I was against marriage. I thought it's not a good idea, marriage, at all. But the curtain behind which I was arguing it was the Roman law on marriage. At that time I had studied it."

"Did Mommy comment on that?" I ask. I'm thinking she'd be upset by his opposition to marriage, since marriage is what she was hoping for, maybe even the reason she was typing his thesis.

"Not really," he says. "She sort of accepted the idea that I'm not the marrying kind. But she liked me anyway. I thought she made a big mistake. Well my other girl, your mother's competitor, Helen, also knew how I feel. But each of them decided apparently, 'Eh, let him talk. He'll do the right thing.'"

"He'll make an exception," I offer.

He repeats, "He'll do the right thing."

Then my father mentions a place that has taken on, for me, a magical aura, partly because of its exotic name, but mostly because he so often mentions it in connection with Helen: the Thousand Islands.

"And as a matter of fact, I was going to the Thousand Islands for my vacation by myself. And she, Helen, said she wants to come along. I said okay. Now, at that time—even in retrospect—I know that had she come with me, that she would no longer be a virgin, and once she's not a virgin, then I would feel obligated to marry her. So I would've married, and then your mother would've been faced with a fait accompli, that I'm married. And then she wouldn't pursue me anymore." He laughs, and goes on. "And Helen the same way. Once I got married . . ."

"Why did you make the decision not to go to the Thousand Islands with Helen?"

His answer rounds back to that tangled web: marriage and sex, sex and marriage.

"*She* made the decision. Her mother talked her out of it. The idea probably was, If you go with him, you'll no longer be a virgin, and he'll never marry you. Then it turned out that she never *was* a virgin. The whole three years I was seeing her. I got the card from her. Did I tell you about the card?"

"Yeah," I say, "the day after you got married. The card that said she wasn't a virgin."

"And I called up, 'I'm married.' "

"It must have been a hard telephone call to make," I say. "Especially since—you told me this in front of Mommy by the way—that if you had known she wasn't a virgin you probably would have ended up marrying her."

"Yeah," he says, laughing. "That's probably true. As a matter of fact, I have behind my mind, if she'd gone with me on that trip to the Thousand Islands, I probably would have done both. The one first, then the second." In other words, if Helen had gone with him on the trip, they would have had sex, and if they'd had sex, he would have felt obligated to marry her—just as he later felt obligated to marry my mother.

My father attributes this inevitable sequence to biology: "Which is how it is with young people, young men," he says. "I heard in public school, they told me that the libido, the urge to mate, is so strong in men . . . and in dogs, too. To get to a female they will actually go through fire. And the female is entirely different. Different entirely. Different entirely. They're just trying to get someone to——"

I expect him to say, "get someone to marry them," because I'm thinking of the social pressure on women. But he finishes the sentence: "see that they have babies. They don't think of it that way; it's nature that thinks that way. There may have been species that don't think that way, they were wiped out."

"It's an interesting calculation," I say, "that women had to do at that time."

"Yeah, I'm sorry for them," he says.

"You take a risk," I say, referring to women in general but thinking, too, of Helen and my mother.

"Yeah," he agrees. "You take a risk."

I finish my thought, "You might succeed in getting him to marry you, but if you lose the gamble——"

He finishes my sentence, "You could lose face, or there were some men——"

"Although you point out," I say, "she wasn't a virgin." I'm closing in on the irony: he believes Helen's mother thought he wouldn't marry her daughter if she wasn't a virgin, but he's saying the opposite: if he'd known she wasn't a virgin, he would have married her. This isn't because he didn't share the view that not being a virgin makes a woman unmarriageable. It's because he did.

He says, "I wouldn't have had—I never would—those days especially—it was a terrible thing. Especially for a boy raised like me. To deflower a girl who was a virgin. *Macht unglücklich* we used to say, made her *unglücklich,* unfortunate—ruining her whole life. Wasn't true but that's what——"

"Yeah, it wasn't true, because——"

"But it was more true then than now. A lot of boys then wouldn't consider fooling around with a virgin."

"You had to hope you gauged the person right," I say, using "you" to refer to women.

"That's right," he says. "I was sorry for her. I really was." Though I had widened the topic of our conversation to all women at the time, my father is still thinking of the particular woman we were talking about: Helen. Though "sorry for" is an odd way to put it, I think he means he felt empathy for her, given the unfair position all women were in with regard to virginity.

"So, did you know— You sort of knew in a way that once you slept with a woman you'd probably marry her."

"I suspected. I wouldn't have wanted to, but in retrospect I know that, uh—"

"You probably sort of knew."

"That I couldn't say—" he begins, then pauses and begins again: "I've got to do it right, I've got to make good. I did harm and I've got to pay for it. That's the way I would've felt."

Now I switch the topic from Helen to my mother, though the topic is really the same, because what he just said, that he did harm and has to pay for it, is exactly how he explains his decision to marry.

"How did it actually happen that you decided to get married?"

"Well, I decided it's good for her. It may not be good for me, but it's good for the woman. And I tell you it was. I was flattered also that she should want me anyway—any woman would want me. I thought she was crazy. I felt very unattractive."

This isn't a throwaway line. My father's belief that he was ugly was deep and pervasive, something he refers to again and again.

"She told me about it," I say. "She said that she got sick and she couldn't eat."

"She was vomiting," he agrees.

"Yeah," I continue, "she lost weight, she couldn't eat. Is that what did it?"

"Well yes! But after we were married, she had the same symptoms because I married her. She's not happy with me. I wasn't what she wants me to be."

I don't pursue this comment, because I know my mother is often unhappy, and that she usually sees my father as the cause. That's one of the reasons I thought he might have been happier with another woman—maybe Helen. I return to the moment when he chose my mother over Helen:

"So what did you feel when you made the decision to get married? In what spirit did you make that decision, since you really didn't want to?"

"Well, doing the right thing by my girl. But I had to betray the other one. I feel very bad, to this day I feel bad about it."

"Were you still seeing them both at the same time?"

"Yeah."

"So did you tell—"

"I didn't have any choice. You know that Helen moved to Benson-hurst. Did I tell you about it?" That's the neighborhood where my father and mother both lived.

"Yeah."

"She lived in the Bronx. And they moved to Brooklyn, to Bensonhurst—it's such a big move—for me. So I feel guilty toward all of them. Her whole family."

"Did you like Helen's parents?"

"I liked her mother very much. When I was in the neighborhood, in the Bronx, in connection with my business, if I wasn't too far, I would drop in; she would give me lunch. She'd treat me very nice. I didn't do it too often, and I didn't always eat the lunch, because I realized that she thinks I'm a prospect, and I wasn't. I felt I wasn't. But I was."

And now I ask the question I've been wanting to ask, knowing that I'm treading on thin ice:

"I have the feeling that you liked Helen better."

"Ah, I don't think so."

"No?"

"No."

"You wouldn't tell me," I say, and laugh.

He laughs, too. "I don't think so."

I don't know whether he means that he doesn't think he liked Helen better, or he doesn't think he would tell me. But he knows why I think he might have liked Helen better—at least one of the reasons, because he addresses it:

"I can tell you she was more intellectual than I. She'd gone to college. I was very flattered. I was flattered that your mother liked me, too. Very flattered. And surprised. I couldn't understand it."

"Did you ask yourself who you liked better?" This question, so important to me, has no resonance for him—at least none he speaks of.

"No. I just wanted to drop them both without hurting their feelings. I would have liked to get them both good husbands."

I offer, "Maybe Helen was not as, uh—"

My father finishes my sentence: "Depressive? She wasn't."

That's not what I had in mind, so I finish the sentence myself: "Manipulative."

"No," he says, still laughing, then equivocates: "Maybe."

"I'm not complaining," I say, "because I wouldn't be here if you'd married Helen."

I say this to reassure my father that I'm not criticizing my mother—or him. But the truth is, I do somehow wish he had married Helen. She represents, in my imagination, a woman who could have been my father's soul mate, as I assume a spouse should be, as I thought my mother wasn't and couldn't be. I hear the Thousand Islands story not as "If Helen had come with me to the Thousand Islands . . ." but "If *only* Helen had come with me . . ." Maybe it's because he tells this story so often that I believe he regrets—on some level, in some way—that he didn't marry Helen. But he says the opposite:

"So I don't think I need regret anything, because no matter what I did I couldn't have remained single. In order to remain single, you have to be heartless. But you know I was determined not to marry. I didn't want to marry because all my life, you know, all my life till that time, my mother and sister were my obligation. I used to hear about somebody who was alone and just himself—it's paradise! You didn't have to worry about anybody else. Suppose I don't have a job. Who cares. I told you, I'd stay in jail. They feed you, it's warm, nothing terrible. That's the worst thing that can happen. But I was always working. Just to have to worry about yourself? It was such a marvelous situation, to me that's what I wanted the rest of my life. My goal in life, my paradise, that I was looking for—heaven—was getting my mother and sister married. Let their husbands worry about them. And I'd be just worried about myself."

MY QUESTION IS ALWAYS whom should my father have married. But that's not what he's asking. His question is whether he should have married at all.

"If I had been single," he says, "there were a lot of things I wanted. I wanted to live in different countries, as soon as I got my mother and sister married."

"That's so funny," I say. "That was what I wanted. Maybe I got it from you without knowing it."

"I'd learn the language, I'd learn the customs, and I'd learn to live like them, and that's what I wanted to do. And I would learn different trades, different things. Different professions."

"My dream was to live in different countries, too," I say, "to learn the language, then move to another country and learn that language. I didn't think about what I'd do there. I didn't think about a profession. And I set out to do it, though I only got to one country—Greece."

I'm astonished to realize that what I dreamed of—and did—is what my father wanted to do. When I graduated from college, I had no career ambitions. I got a job, saved my salary, and went to Europe on a one-way ticket. I started by spending a month in Poland, visiting my great-aunt Magda and her family and traveling around the country with my Polish cousin, Magda's son. From there I traveled by train to Greece, where I was to meet up with one of my college roommates. We were going to travel overland from Athens to Turkey, Iraq, Iran, Afghanistan, and India, then take a boat to Japan, where we'd get jobs teaching English. But my friend didn't turn up to meet me as planned, so I stayed in Greece, taught English there, and learned to speak and read Greek. I remember waking up each morning, realizing where I was, and feeling deep satisfaction: I did it! I'm living in another country!

"But it's good I didn't do that," my father says. "I would have ended up like one of my cousins—a distant cousin. I only met him a few times. But I heard he got a girl pregnant and moved to England to get away. He died there, all alone."

"No," I say, laughing. "You would've gotten married."

"You're right, you're right. After all, if I can't live without women, one of them would get me. You're right about that. I should realize that." I'm pretty sure "live without women" means "live without sex."

I say, "I don't think it occurs to women anymore, that just because he slept with you he has to marry you."

"I know," my father says. "I read, I see movies. He doesn't feel he has to do the right— Even the girl doesn't think that, that he's obliged to do the right thing."

I was saying that men no longer have an obligation to marry a woman because they had sex. He's assuming that men still have that obligation; they just no longer have to make good on it.

In this conversation, as in others I had with him, I was trying to get my father to confirm my suspicion that he would have preferred to marry Helen. But he wouldn't. He never did—either because he was loyal to my mother, or because it wasn't true. The closest he ever came was one time—after my mother died—when he said, "I guess Helen would have been more appropriate."

Maybe what my father says next in this conversation, on the surface a digression, is his way of saying that he did regret marrying my mother but talked himself out of it. He says, "I developed the idea, which I haven't read, though somebody must have written about it— When people say they're not lucky, they don't have a lucky star, I would say to them, 'Look how lucky you are. You didn't win the lottery, but do you realize that you go backward without interruption to the time life started, when the bacteria, the one-celled animals, started to come out of the sea. If along the way there was a single break, you wouldn't be here. It's like every time, you have a billion sperm there. One—you—comes out. So you won a lottery from a billion, not from a lousy hundred million, from a billion you won. Then you have to do this every generation. One from a billion, one from a billion. You, by being alive, are that lucky.'"

I don't pursue this digression. Instead, I pull the conversation back to the question I've asked twice before: "So do you remember when you actually made the decision, 'Okay, I'm going to do it. I'm going to get married'?"

"Well, I said, you can't let the girl suffer like that. I proposed."

He's telling me what he was thinking, not what I want to know: how he was feeling.

He adds, "But I thought it'll be only for a few years."

"And then what?" I ask.

"And we'd have no children. But then we had a child, and once there's a child, it's already permanent."

"Did you make the decision to have a child, or was that, uh—"

"We made the decision to have a child."

"And how come you made the decision?"

"I saw, five years doesn't work. How can you leave the woman you love and the woman that you live with, make her unhappy?"

I notice he doesn't just say "the woman you live with" but also "the woman you love." He says "the woman you love" first. Why would he even consider ending a marriage if he loved his wife? His reason would have nothing to do with her personally; it would be to free himself of the obligation to support her and later the children they have together, because that obligation required him to work at menial jobs rather than go with minimal or no income while getting the experience that would allow him to practice law.

My father then returns to the proposition he started with: he isn't the kind of man who would make a woman *unglücklich* and abandon her:

"She might have married some nice person and now she's too late, she's no longer a girl. How can you do that to somebody? I wouldn't allow myself to think along those lines. I was for life."

Once he marries, my father never strays. He tells me that of all the men he knew, only he and one other, whom he names, didn't have sex with women other than their wives.

*

SO THE ANSWER TO WHY MY FATHER DECIDED TO MARRY MY MOTHER despite his obligation to support his mother and sister, and despite not believing in marriage, is sex. And sex is one way he was "sort of like a boyfriend" to my mother. At one time my thinking stopped there. But after my father dies, I find among his papers letters he wrote to his mother which show me that sex was part of a much larger picture that was sketched, then filled in, over many years. I see there were many other ways that my mother was sort of like a girlfriend.

IT'S 1931, TWO YEARS before my parents will marry. My father has just seen his mother onto a ship that will take her back to Poland for a months-long visit. In a letter addressed to her care of the ship's purser, he mentions my mother, using her full Americanized name, "Dorothy."

> By the way, do you know who had sent you that package by messenger? It was no other than Dorothy Rosen, and I don't mind telling you that I happen to know it cost her no less than five dollars [the equivalent of about eighty-five dollars in 2020]. I am enclosing herewith the card which she addressed to you. The package contained a mass of dried fruits and no end of all sorts of nuts.

IN A LETTER TO his mother in Poland, my father complains that her handwriting is illegible; as corroborating evidence, he says he showed one of her cards to Dorothy, and though the card was written part in English and part in Polish, "Dorothy . . . thought that it was all Polish and couldn't read it."

Sending a bon voyage gift to his mother, reading his mother's post-card—my mother is always there.

THESE TWO FORCES—MY MOTHER being always there, and my parents becoming "seriously," that is, sexually, involved—are inextricable. My father's journals give me a glimpse of how this happened, even though he wasn't her boyfriend—or didn't think he was. These are the journals he gave me: one that he kept between 1927 and 1928, when he was eighteen and a half to twenty, the other that goes from 1929 to 1931, when he was twenty-one to twenty-three. Getting to hear my father's voice, to learn his thoughts, when he was so young is a privilege—and a responsibility. He gave me these journals knowing I would write his life; that itself is a kind of permission not only to read them but to quote them here. And he said explicitly, in a letter dated 1996 referring to an essay I was writing about him, "Don't mind if some negative facets of my history and personality are included." Yet sometimes what I read makes me cringe, partly because it's private but even more because I'm put off by how much he focused on sex. I remind myself that I can't judge him from my perspective as a woman, let alone a woman in the twenty-first century looking back at a man born only a few years after the close of the nineteenth. I remind myself, too, that he's at the age when men's sex drive is the strongest it will ever be. The chance to understand him, and his relationship with my mother, is too tempting to pass up. I press on.

WHEN HE'S NOT YET nineteen and my mother is sixteen, my father writes in his journal about a weekend in the Catskills. He begins by mentioning my mother as an obligation. Using the diminutive form of her name, he at first lumps "Dotty" with her sister, Eva, who is eleven years older: "I rather enjoyed myself, although I was tied down to Norman's sisters Dotty & Eva who were with me." He doesn't mention Eva again, but has a lot to say about how he manages his obligation to her younger sister:

> I felt a little obliged to act like a boy toward Dotty and tried to do the foolish little things that girls (here at least) like boys to do to them such as pets, flirtations etc. Whether prompted by obligation or inclination, she rather responded and to a very small degree encouraged.

Really? I think. You flirted with her, showed romantic interest in her, maybe even made physical moves toward her—if that's what he means by "pets"—not because you liked her but because you thought it was expected? I'm also struck by my father's addition that he thinks it's expected by girls "here"—that is, in the United States, in contrast, I assume, to girls in Poland. This small parenthetical phrase reminds me that my father still feels rooted in the country he left seven years before.

What he writes next puts to rest my fantasy that my father fell in love with my mother because she was the prettiest woman he ever met—or fell in love with her at all, early on:

> She really doesn't appeal to me very much. I dislike her chin, her complexion and mostly her character which is of the kind that watches out that nobody harm her or hers or despoil them of anything.

He also writes what he likes about Dotty: "Her youthful bust however was not at all repulsive to me and perhaps a trifle inviting." He then describes a scene that both my parents talked about when they were old. They were on their way back to the city from the Catskills resort, which they called "camp."

> In our 9 hour bus ride from camp to N.Y. I took advantage of our sleepiness and the darkness and petted her to my heart's desire. She restrained me a little probably for fear that her older sister who sat right next to us might see, though I don't know how she could help seeing. I even kissed her several times as she lay on my shoulder and she didn't budge.

But his success doesn't make him happy. Instead:

> When I came home, as well as the next day a feeling of repulsion and nausea o'ertook me at the thought of this. I sorely regretted having shown these attentions, also having given her names of some immoral books to procure from the library. I wondered to myself whether I'll ever find again pleasure in such things with girls. I don't know what caused this feeling in me, perhaps the fact that my face swelled up from the sunburn? I suspect this because now the feeling is wearing off together with the sunburn. At any rate I will endeavor never again to act like that toward her and also never to refer to her about these actions or talk.

My father doesn't keep his resolution. A year and a half later, he describes a similar, though less serendipitous, scene.

> I took Dotty out last night. . . . I took her in my car. We rode through Prospect Park several times, freezing nearly to death because of the two broken windows. Then we parked the car in a luckily empty space and went to the Strand. I held her hand and she responded to my gentle pressure.

I expect to read once again that he's drawn to her physically but critical of her character. What he writes is very different:

> Somehow this girl likes me. There is no doubt in my mind that her high opinion of my personality and ability has an awful lot to do with it, but it seems to me that she has no aversion toward me physically. This makes me truly wonder, and I feel mighty good to think that here is a girl who, if I would marry her (and after all she could hardly hope to make a better match even from her own viewpoint probably) would be able to love me. Not be passionately in love with me, but would welcome my love and would like and appreciate it.

So the idea of marrying wasn't something my mother cooked up on her own, like a secret potion to slip into his tea. He's thinking about that possibility four years before he proposes under pressure. And he is touched—deeply touched—that she seems to find him physically attractive, when he's certain he is so ugly that no woman ever could.

My father then sums up his feelings about my mother:

> So while her liking for me flatters me quite often, it also sometimes discourages me. Sometimes I really wish that she wouldn't like me. Especially and specifically where I have to pay unwonted attention to her and pretend I like her more than I really do. I feel like a cad at such times.

I'm glad he realizes that he's acting like a "cad." Yet I think, You're encouraging her interest in you by acting like you're interested in her. And you *are* interested in her, even if you're ambivalent. She's everywhere in your life—even in your dreams:

> To return to Dot, on the way back from a show down Fourth Ave. I told her of a dream I actually had had the night before. The substance of it was that I saw her riding gracefully on a stallion chasing a mare. I had to start explaining to her what a stallion is which of course led to my usual and interesting topic. I would like to say some mean things about myself here but I am afraid that after all somebody might some day read this besides myself.

His "usual and interesting topic" is, obviously, sex. And that must be what he talks to her about in explaining the word "stallion." But what is most striking to me, and must have been to her, is that he's been dreaming about her—and tells her.

I take heart that my father holds back what he doesn't want anyone to read. That means it's okay for me to read what he goes on to say: He describes what seems to be their first significant sexual encounter. He also recounts their conversation, which recapitulates the dilemma facing women—and men—at the time, the one he talked to me about so many years later: a man will seek sex, but lose respect for—and therefore not marry—a woman who yields it, while marriage is the goal that women necessarily pursue:

> I went straight down Bay Parkway to the beach where there were only a few cars parked, because of the cold and lateness of the hour probably (It was 11:30). I discontinued my tale of the aforementioned subject and put my arm about her. She wore a heavy coat, so that it really was nothing. Yet she evidently guessed that I wouldn't stop there. She right away started protesting. She evidently harbors deep away some place as probably every girl does in regard to a fellow the hope that I might be a

matrimonial prospect. She said right away that if she behaves that way I'll think that she lets every boy that goes with her get free. I talked her out of it by subtle arguments and after she said petulantly "You don't like me." I had made up my mind to go in another minute and ask her to excuse me for putting my arm around her. But I happened at the moment to start joking and laughing, which left my way open. How could I resist taking advantage of the open road?

He recaps the joking conversation that opened the road. It begins with his question, "What would you do if I kissed you?" She replies, "I would sock you." He humorously interprets her threat as a proposed deal: "That's a go. You sock me in exchange for a kiss." She demurs, "I haven't got the heart," so he playfully helps her do her part: "I picked up her hand and hit my cheek with it." Having thus arranged for her to "sock" him in advance, he kisses her. But again, he later feels guilty; she is, after all, his best friend's younger sister, and not yet eighteen:

I felt nevertheless quite low taking advantage of her in that way. It is true I know that boys my age and perhaps some older have kissed her before, but still I ought to be more her guardian not equal or suitor.

He resolves not to do it again—and to make up for it:

Now I intend to take her out sometimes and not touch her all evening. I think this ought to square things up, for if I'll ask her to go out again she will without the shadow of a doubt think it's because I petted with her the last time and intend to do so again. It's now 7:15, the day is breaking and I guess it's time to go to bed.

SO I CAN'T HOLD on to the fiction that my mother became infatuated with my father on her own. He sounds like an addict who vows never to touch the drug again, but can't keep his vow. As for whether she welcomed his kiss, my mother gives me evidence years later that she did. She tells me, in her eighties, that the first time my father kissed her, she was so thrilled, she ran next door to tell her friend, "Eli kissed me!"

THOUGH HE'S TWENTY, my father's inexperience makes him sound like a teenager. And he sounds like a teenager when he writes, two months later, about going to Coney Island with Norman:

> Wherever one goes, one can see young men driving beautiful roadsters with pretty young women by their sides. Ah! This is the thorn in my present existence. I am woman mad. As we were walking along the boardwalk last night, or rather early this morning, I almost burst from envy and lost control of myself when I noted almost every bench occupied by a young man wrapped up in the arms of a girl. When I see a young girl with a comely bust or shapely pair of legs I become moody and weep within myself that I exist with the misfortune of a repulsive face, a displeasing personality and a poverty and consequent loneliness that permits of no search for a betterment of conditions.

Though my father's belief that he's too ugly and poor for anyone to love him may be extreme, I'm sure many young people feel envy and self-pity when they see couples. I did. But for me it was longing for romance and companionship. For him it was longing for sex.

*

FOR MOST OF MY LIFE AND IN MOST WAYS, MY FATHER'S REASON AND calm are a lifeboat in the turbulent sea of my mother's unreason and emotional flare-ups. She makes the world unpredictable and scary; he makes it predictable and safe. But when the subject is sex in relation to me, my father's reason and calm evaporate. Especially when I become a teenager, the subject of sex makes him act in ways I find inexplicable.

After I graduate from college I move back to my parents' house in Brooklyn, so my mail is forwarded there. One day a letter arrives addressed to Jay Lovinger care of me. When my father sees the envelope, he loses it. He tells me it was a grave mistake to let a boy receive letters at my address. "Jay isn't my boyfriend," I protest. "He's my boyfriend's friend. He stayed with my roommates and me because we had a couch he could sleep on. What harm could the letter do?" My father explains the potential harm: "You might meet a boy you want to marry, and the postman will tell the boy's parents that you received a letter addressed to another boy care of you, and they won't let him marry you." At the time I was baffled by my father's reaction, and his logic. Or lack thereof. Now it's obvious to me that he wasn't talking about a letter; he was talking about virginity.

THE TOPIC OF SEX makes my father turn critical—and irrational—even earlier.

For a science project in junior high school, I research the biology of earthworms. I put enormous amounts of time and effort into this project. First I try to dig up a worm in our backyard, but it's winter: the ground is too cold and hard. I take out the telephone book and call one after another fishing supply store in Coney Island until I reach one that has worms for sale. Despite my fear of taking the subway alone to a strange, distant corner of Brooklyn, I make my way there, and buy several worms. Though it turns my stomach, I dissect one and pin its splayed-open body to the bottom of a shallow box. I go to the public library and find a book that explains the earthworm's biological systems, with illustrations of each. Painstakingly, I copy the illustrations.

Most fascinating is the worms' reproductive system: each worm produces both spermatozoa and eggs but can't fertilize its own eggs. The drawing I copy shows two earthworms side by side, as spermatozoa flow from each worm to the other—outside their bodies. It's a marvel. The night before the project is due, I show my parents the results of my hard work. My father tells me I must not include the illustration of earthworms' reproductive system: if I do, my teacher will think I'm a bad girl. I can't bear the prospect of letting my work go to waste, or of submitting an incomplete project—especially since the worms' reproductive system is the most amazing thing I discovered. Yet I feel stymied—and sullied—by my father's view of the picture I drew. And I'm stricken by the inescapable implication that my father thinks I'm a bad girl for having copied it.

*

MY FATHER'S JOURNALS AND CONVERSATION CONVERGE ON THE PART played by sex in the story of how he came to marry my mother—and in relationships between women and men at the time. But the specific way that having sex led my father to propose—that is a skein wound by my mother, or maybe a skein wound around her by her personality and her past. To untangle the threads, I think back to the conversation I had with my father when I began a sentence "Maybe Helen was not as . . ." and he finished it for me: "Depressive? She wasn't." The word I'd intended to say was "manipulative." That word came to mind because it describes how I viewed my mother: I thought she manipulated my father into marriage. And it's how I experienced her. In a way, she manipulated me into marriage, too.

I've been living in Greece for a year and half, teaching English, when I decide to return to the States. I myself am not eager to move back. It's my boyfriend—a young man from the island of Crete—who wants to come to the United States, to get an MBA. I call my parents to tell them I'll be coming home, and he's coming with me. My mother says, "It's okay with me, but let us tell people you're engaged, so they'll accept his staying here with you. It doesn't mean anything; engagements are broken all the time." I see her point, and agree. But we haven't been in the States very long before she begins to say, "Everyone is asking, 'When are you getting married?' You can't be engaged forever!" Though we had no plans to marry, we soon decide to, and do—in a judge's chambers, on short notice.

I GET A STRANGE sense of satisfaction when I read, in his journals, that my father was frustrated by just that kind of bait-and-switch manipulativeness. One long account—one of many—begins when he's playing cards with my mother's three brothers, and my mother overhears them discussing plans for New Year's Eve. She interrupts their game and tells my father that she needs him to walk her to the store—now. He complies; calls a halt to the game, thereby annoying her brothers;

and walks outside beside her. She immediately begins berating him for not including her in his plans, and rejects his claim that he won't go out New Year's Eve at all, because he can't afford it. She informs him that he will go out—with her, and he accedes.

As the date nears, she suggests that they spend New Year's Eve with her friends Ida and Jack—and meet them on a given day at 4:15 to discuss what they'll do on the big night. He agrees, but makes plans to meet a friend named Joe later that evening. He explains his thinking—and how it backfired:

> If I meet D. at 4 PM I can spend with her till 7:30 & then have an excuse to get away. . . . I met D. as per appointment. We waited for Ida & Jack for an hour during which time in the course of light conversation I told her of appointment with Joe at 8. The result was immediate and startling. She assumed an attitude of the bitterest reproach as if I had asked [her] to go out with me or as if I had even agreed to spend the evening with her. The little schemer took it for granted I was bound to spend the rest of the day with her because I met her in the afternoon. The way she spoke & turned away and acted in general admitted of no doubt that I committed the gravest wrong against her.

My father's anger is fueled by his giving in:

> I started later calling my own & Joe's home to leave a message for him breaking the appointment. I could act no other way or she would have cried for hours and reproached me for weeks.

This tactic makes me think of a way my father phrased a similar observation more than a half century later, tinged with humor and irony but with poignant accuracy: "Mother," he said, "will weep me into submission."

MY FATHER WRITES IN his journal of many similar instances where my mother persuades him to do something brief and trivial with her, then insists he extend their time together, and he can't say no. The scenarios

he describes remind me of how my mother ruled me—whether I went
against her wishes and felt guilty for ruining her life or gave in to them
and felt I was ruining my own. I take shameful pleasure in my father
calling my mother "the little schemer," because that's the way I experienced her. She'd propose something inconsequential—just say you're
engaged; it doesn't mean anything—then reframe that commitment as
very consequential indeed: if you're engaged, you have to get married.
I am certain that this is how my mother manipulated my father into
marriage: I can hear her persuading him to have sex by saying, "I'm
not a virgin, so you won't be obligated." Then once they're having sex,
the obligation kicks in.

AT FIRST I THINK that "manipulative" is a different aspect of my mother's personality than "depressive." But now I see these two traits as inseparable. When my mother got my father to marry her by crying
constantly and throwing up repeatedly, she was being manipulative,
using her misery to get her way. But her misery was real, so how accurate is it to say she was "using" it?

My mother's manipulativeness and depressiveness—her tendency
to be deeply unhappy—are fundamental not only to my father's decision to marry but also to their life together after they did. And it was
fundamental to my life with my mother, too—both when I was a child
and when I was grown. That's probably why I develop the conviction
that my father would have been happier married to Helen—and somehow wish he had married her, even though that would mean I wouldn't
exist. By some twist of magical thinking, in my fantasy, if my father
had married Helen, I'd have had a different mother.

MY MOTHER OFTEN SAW me as the cause of her misery: because I was
a troubled and therefore difficult child; a rebellious teen; and a young
adult who failed to marry, as my sisters did, at nineteen and twenty—
and again when my first marriage ended before I turned thirty, and I
remained unmarried for another decade. I knew she blamed my father
for her unhappiness after he retired and my parents were together all
the time; when he's old, he tells me it was him all along, too. He implied this when he said, "But after we were married, she had the same

symptoms because I married her. She's not happy with me. I wasn't
what she wants me to be."

I find a long poem my father wrote to my mother on a birthday
card he gave her two years into their marriage. In his impossibly tiny
print, he begins:

> It may be true
> That to this day dear
> I've failed to bring you
> To happiness near.

Verse after verse goes on in this vein:

> The sighs you emitted,
> Touchingly, profoundly,
> The heartaches you suffered
> Unable to sleep soundly,
> Shall remain forevermore
> In my memory, my heart
> As a debt, to repay which
> I can't even start.

In later verses, he proclaims his love; says he can face any adversity
"because I know you are there"; promises that things will get better
economically and they'll "enter an order / For a little girl or boy"; and
closes with "My love, adulation, / My deep, deep devotion." His love
for her is palpable and moving. But his starting place—that he hasn't
made her happy, and is determined to keep trying—is like a script he
was trapped in for the rest of their marriage. And each of their children
in turn is written into the script.

My sister Naomi was the little girl my parents did soon "enter an
order" for, and my father enlisted her in the task of curing his wife's
unhappiness. In 1948, he goes to California, seeking work in the movie
industry. He writes in a letter to Naomi—an eleven-year-old child:
"You have made me inordinately proud of you by being such a help to
Dorothy. Thereby you are not only making her happy but protecting

Poem my father wrote on a card for my mother's twenty-fourth birthday

her health and improving her disposition." It's as if the child were the mother, and the mother the child. When Mimi and I came along, we felt the same way: we never told our mother about anything that upset us, so as not to upset her.

After my father retires, my mother's unhappiness becomes a major force in both their lives. My father tells me, "Mother's not happy when she's with me. We're talking nicely, like friends. Suddenly I say something she doesn't like. She turns cold, she gets angry. It just happened this week. She likes to take her temperature. She forgets that for her, normal is ninety-nine or a little higher. One day it was a hundred and two. The next day it was ninety-nine again. So I said, 'Maybe last night it was just an aberration.' That word made her so angry, she kept at me for days. She thinks I insulted her. I tried to show her what it means in

the dictionary, but she wouldn't look at it. She'd rather be angry."
What angered her is the very thing that attracted her to my father
when they were young: his using big words. I know it's common
among long-time couples to be irritated by qualities that were endearing at the start. But I think the depth of my mother's anger, of her
misery, go beyond that. My father tries to cheer her up with optimism,
but it makes things worse: "I try to tell her how lucky we are. We've
had no tragedies in our family. We live comfortably without working.
She gets angry at me: 'Oh yeah, I'm supposed to thank God because I
have a piece of bread to eat.'" And nothing makes her angrier than
what he loves most: talking about the past.

I OFTEN REBELLED AGAINST my mother's demands and argued against
her logic, but her unhappiness deeply affected me. It was as if an invisible cord ran from her chest to mine, transferring her emotions directly
to me. When her emotions spiked and plunged, they pulled mine with
them.

My mother is in the hospital in Florida. I always fly down there
when one of my parents is in the hospital, but this time I don't, because
my sister Mimi goes and assures me that our mother's condition is not
grave. Shortly after Mimi leaves, I call my mother to cheer her up, but
instead she saddens me down. She tells me she is worried about my
father, because he is all alone at home. "He said he misses me more than
I miss him," she says, and starts to cry. A tsunami of self-reproach engulfs me. I should have flown to Florida for the two days I could have
managed. When I hang up the phone, I pace my house, trying in vain
to grade the papers I must return to my students the next day. I call my
best friend to get perspective. Later I call my mother again. Now she is
in a fine mood. Her friends Sylvia and Lenny visited, she tells me in a
cheerful voice. As quickly as her grief plunged me into distress, her
raised spirits now lift me out of it. I was right not to fly to Florida; my
mother is all right.

The volatility of my mother's emotions—the depth of her misery
when it descended upon her—often caused me such emotional whip-
lash. It was at the root of one of the great dramas of my young life: a

decision I regretted so painfully that for decades any mention of the Peace Corps pierced.

In my senior year of college, I apply to join the Peace Corps, as many of my friends do and as my college boyfriend did the year before. I mail off the application and forget about it. After graduation, I live at home in Brooklyn, work in Manhattan, and save my salary until I have enough for a trip abroad, from where I have no plans to return. After several months traveling in Europe, including the month I spent in Poland with my relatives, I'm in Crete, where I meet a young man who gives me reason to stay. That's where I'm living when I get word that I've been accepted by the Peace Corps and assigned to Thailand. I leave Crete—and the young man—and fly back to New York, to prepare for the Peace Corps. I find my mother distraught. As the date for my departure to Hawaii for Peace Corps training nears, her anguish mounts. Whenever I return from having been out, she meets me at the door with eyes red and swollen from crying. She draws on a panoply of arguments to convince me not to go: I'll be killed by a stray bullet from the Vietnam War. I'll be doomed to the miserable life of an old maid, because by the time I return from two years in the Peace Corps I'll be twenty-three, and all the eligible young men will have gotten married while I was away.

Knowing that her arguments make no sense, I go about buying and packing the items recommended by the Peace Corps. But my mother's misery casts a spell over me. The night before I'm to leave, a cousin who is also a friend visits to wish me farewell. We sit at the kitchen table and talk deep into the early morning hours. I tell him of my misgivings, but say I can't change my mind, because the Peace Corps was the only reason I returned to the United States from Crete. He points out the fallacy in my thinking: it doesn't matter how I got to my current situation; what matters are my options going forward. I explain that if I don't join the Peace Corps, I will have to find a job, move to Manhattan, and rent an apartment where I'll live alone. These prospects frighten me. As I say this, I experience a surge of counterphobic conviction that has motivated many things I've done in my life, some wise, some foolish: I should do what I'm afraid of, to prove that I will not be driven by fear. I feel a great wave of relief to have found a path that makes sense to me—and will make my mother happy.

After my cousin leaves, I stay up until the clock strikes an hour when I can safely enter my parents' bedroom and wake them to announce my decision. My mother throws her arms around me, weeping, this time with joy. As soon as the Peace Corps office opens, I call and tell them I will not be going, then collapse into sleep. I awake a few hours later, stricken with remorse. I realize that the last thing I want to do is live and work in Manhattan. Several days later, still in the clutches of anguished regret (my father's legacy?) and equally anguished confusion (my mother's?), I call the Peace Corps to say I've changed my mind. They tell me they allowed someone to do that the day before, but today is too late. A friend who lives in Berkeley invites me to join her, and I do, immediately. I find a job in San Francisco and save what I earn until I have enough to buy passage back to Greece. As before, I have no plans to return. My mother is once again beside herself. "If I'd known you were going to go back to Greece," she says, "I would have let you go to the Peace Corps."

Many years later my father tells me, "I didn't see any reason why you shouldn't join the Peace Corps. I thought it was a good thing to do."

"Why didn't you tell me?" I ask. "If I'd had any idea—even a hint—that you didn't agree with her, it would have given me the strength to resist Mommy's pressure."

"I couldn't," he says. "Mother never would have forgiven me. If anything had happened to you, I would never have forgiven myself."

For years, I blamed my father for not sticking up for me in this struggle with my mother. After reading his journals, I see there is no way he could have: he couldn't stand up to her for himself—or couldn't stop hoping he could make her happy by giving in.

*

MAYBE IT'S BECAUSE OF THE EMOTIONAL TURMOIL OF THE WEEKS leading up to my Peace Corps decision that I always assumed the drama of my mother getting sick because my father wouldn't marry her, and his impulsive capitulation, also took place over a period of weeks. My first quick reading of my father's journal doesn't change that. But when I reread it carefully long after my parents are gone, I see that it takes place over a much longer period of time—not weeks, but years.

When my father is twenty-two and my mother has just turned twenty, he writes in his journal,

> Recently she is almost constantly in tears, and for the life of me I don't know what she wants. It is too lengthy to describe here. At any rate, she was so sick today that I really feared she may have a nervous breakdown. . . . She was in tears all day at the office and her eyes were red and swollen.

In tears all day, eyes red and swollen—just as she was, as her eyes were, when I was twenty-one and planning to go to the Peace Corps. And her tears, her suffering, have the same effect on my father that they had on me: "It nearly broke my heart." But he feels he can't let that show:

> for the girls and others would have sensed immediately my having something to do with her indisposition. I am sufficiently worried with fear that she may at any time create a scandal. God knows what I'll do if she does. I don't think I could marry her in that event for I would be very unhappy feeling that I was forced into it somehow and that people know it.

Though my father writes, "for the life of me I don't know what she wants," he clearly does know, since he goes on to say that he couldn't marry her if she revealed to her family and co-workers that he's the cause of her unhappiness. In other words, people would know that she forced him to marry her. To avoid that humiliation, he'd have to leave town, but he can't because of his obligation to his mother:

> I guess my only recourse would be to join the army. But then grief for my mother and knowledge that she is grieving would eat me up. How would she earn a living? All her hopes would be wrecked. They would sink into wretchedness and misfortune. The situation is indeed a complex one for me.

This is two years before he proposes—and a year into his relationship with Helen.

BUT MY MOTHER'S MISERY isn't the whole story. There is another reason my father can't bear the thought of disappointing her—the same reason he wrote, more than two years before, that it made him "truly wonder" and "feel mighty good" when he drove her in the freezing car through Prospect Park late at night: astonishment and gratitude that she finds him attractive and could love him. Here he writes, "She who is the only one who has ever loved me truly & for my own sake, my own worthless, ugly self. This will be my reward to her."

This comment reminds me of something my father writes in a letter to his mother during her visit to Poland: "Yesterday was my birthday, October 3d. I would have forgotten about it were it not for the fact that I received a card from Dorothy. She is the only one that ever remembers my birthday." The contrast is implicit: Dorothy remembered his birthday, and she always does. His mother didn't—and never does.

This is something my father says often: when he was a child, his mother ignored his birthday but elaborately celebrated his sister's. He refers to this again in a letter he writes to my sisters and me when he's in his eighties, urging us to call his sister, Ella, on her birthday. To convince us, he says how unfortunate Ella's life has been, made worse by

My father and his sister Ella in Warsaw

how far she's fallen from the heights to which their mother had hoisted her. Their mother, he writes,

> kept Ella on a pedestal, never let her forget she is a lady; gave her piano lessons during the war when there wasn't enough to eat, ever, and arranged birthday parties for her which took weeks in preparation. To this day, *szustego lutego,* the sixth of February, sounds like a holiday, like "the fourth of July," as it always did to my earliest memories. I never had a birthday party much to my delight. . . . I was happy to be left alone.

My father always ends descriptions of this contrast by saying he was glad to be ignored, but that claim is belied by how often he mentions it.

All this comes tumbling back to me as I read, in the letter my father writes when he's twenty-three, that Dorothy is the only one who ever remembers his birthday. The implication is that she's the only woman who truly cares about him. And it's the tip of an iceberg that I knew from my parents' comments was under the water, but couldn't envision—that's the thing about icebergs, you can't see them—until I read my father's journal from the time he was young: the situation that lay behind my mother's comment to the interviewer "Eli wasn't very happy in his own house with his mother and sister."

Such a simple phrase: my father "wasn't very happy in his own house." I thought I had a pretty good sense of his relationship with his mother: she exploited him financially and criticized him mercilessly. But the journals he kept when he was in his late teens and early twenties show me that his mother was far more damaged—and damaging—than I'd realized. In the journal, my father describes his mother not only insulting and berating him, but having screaming fights with him in private—and with strangers and neighbors in public. One day, coming home from work, he finds her standing in front of the house yelling insults about their landlady. When, in their apartment, he tells her she's wrong to do that, she threatens to "make a scene in comparison with which the last one was nothing." His mother's yelling and cursing, making scenes in public, probably explains why my father always shrank from attracting attention, and why I never—not once—heard him raise his voice. On the rare occasions when he showed anger, it was by silence.

Most astonishing is that his mother was physically violent. He is nearly nineteen—and has been the family breadwinner for five years—when, he writes, "she picked up a heavy stick and belabored me with all her might and kicked me so hard that the marks shall yet remain for quite a while." He describes a scene when she tracked him down at a friend's house where "with tears and yells she frightened all the people and chasing me around the house (a stranger's mind you) she struck at me repeatedly, viciously. Finally she exhorted an old man in that house (the father) to hold my hands while she smacked me."

In his journals, my father describes in detail these and many other clashes with his mother and sister, the anguish they cause him, and his belief that escape—even by suicide—is impossible:

> I might be driven to the point when I will go away and then I am full well aware that by cries and lamentations, by summoning help from the family and displaying to me a long haggard face she will get me back. Yes, I realize I am doomed, and had it not been for my hope that things will change soon and had I had the courage I would end my life. In fact I wish there is a leak in the gas apparatus of the kitchen next to which I sleep and thus pass away quietly, painlessly, and without the anguish that would be called forth at the thought of my mother's despair if I had contemplated voluntary suicide.

He's bound by and to his mother. He is so desperate to escape her that he wants to die, but it would have to be by accident, because doing it on purpose would cause her too much distress.

My father also feels responsible for Dorothy's distress, but he can't marry her because if he did, he could no longer support his mother, so her life would be ruined. And he believes that if he gives in to Dorothy's desire to marry, he would ruin her life, too:

> By marrying her I can only bring momentary relief and then far greater suffering must ensue for both of us. Finally her entire

life may be ruined even more than my mother's was. I sense a very ill omen for both of us, I feel I'd be fated to die a young, ignominious death, and she would have to struggle on thru life with a broken spirit and very little to live for.

Why? Where did he get the idea that marriage would lead to his early death and a life of hardship and despair for his wife? It's what happened to his parents. His father died at twenty-seven of tuberculosis, leaving his mother to raise two children on her own—and to bemoan her misfortune for the rest of her life.

Realizing that my father's strange ideas could be traced to his childhood, I wonder if my mother's childhood might help explain her "depressiveness" and "manipulativeness"—and how they are inseparable. My mother fled Russia with her family through a dark forest when she was nine, riding in a horse-drawn wagon driven over the border to Poland by a Polish farmer. She must have felt the fear of being caught that kept them from stopping to search for the shoe her mother lost in the snow. The only specific memory of her childhood that my mother ever recounted is emerging from a night spent hiding in a cellar in Minsk to find dead bodies strewn in the street. These early experiences must have helped create the deep well of fear and unhappiness that drove my mother to drive us to do what she wanted. They probably made her feel that what she wanted was necessary for her to survive.

*

MY MOTHER'S YEARS-LONG CAMPAIGN TO GET MY FATHER TO MARRY her—and his years-long resistance, then precipitous reversal—grew out of their own pasts, their own demons. But they played out their drama on a stage set for them by the world they lived in. Women at the time were drawn into a chancy game of sexual roulette. A woman's life, the belief went, would be ruined if she didn't marry. For a man, marriage meant assuming responsibility to support a family, so he'd be motivated to avoid what she sought. One way a woman could get a man to marry her was to sleep with him: his sense of obligation would lead him to marry. But she'd be taking a risk: if he didn't, her marriageability would be gravely compromised. In the competition between my mother and Helen, I used to think my mother won because she was craftier. But they both gambled with virginity. They just played the sex card differently. Helen hid the fact that she wasn't a virgin. My mother wasn't a virgin either, but she didn't hide it; she used it. My mother's was the gamble that paid off.

And what of my father's capitulation? His conviction that marriage would destroy his hope for happiness was dead wrong. It was his only hope for happiness. And only a woman who was willing to—and knew instinctively how to—manipulate him into marriage could have forced him to accept that happiness. His dream of becoming free when his mother and sister married was never realistic. His sister did marry, but not for five years, and there's no way of knowing when—or if—she would have, had her younger brother not married first. His mother never did. I am certain there was no chance she ever would. Does that mean my father was right that if he stopped supporting her, she'd be condemned to a life of deprivation and misery? No, dead wrong again. I believe my mother saved her, too.

I GET A SENSE of what it was like for my grandmother to stay home, supported by her son, in a letter my father writes to her in 1931; he's twenty-three and has been the family breadwinner for nine years. His mother's visit back to Poland (a trip paid for with money she saved from the earnings he gave her) is drawing to a close. He writes that while he of course looks forward to welcoming her home, he also somehow "dreads" her return. He then describes the behavior he hopes she will improve. What I see in his description is a woman immobilized by depression. (The similarity to my mother's disposition doesn't escape me.) He says that she spent her days lying on the couch. Only when he arrived home would she jump off it and make a show of tidying up. If he asked about dinner, she'd swear at him and complain bitterly of her fate. She didn't comb her hair, and always wore the same torn, dirty housedress and "wretched shoes" with her "stockings carelessly let down, one all the way and one only half way down."

Putting aside my surprise that my father would write to his mother this way—and he later expresses regret for having done so—I find myself thinking that my grandmother had good reason to be depressed.

Her life in this country—her position in her new world—was devastatingly reduced from what it was in Warsaw, where she established and ran a school. My father comments on this contrast in his journal: "How I regret and mourn for that mother-of-mine of old. That stately, dignified, clever woman of the days of Poland."

My grandmother couldn't hope to have a position in this country comparable to the one she held in Warsaw—her English, though fluent, was heavily accented, and her Polish education would have meant little. But that didn't mean she couldn't go to work. When my father could no longer support her, his mother became, like her brother Jack, a fundraiser for HIAS, the Hebrew Immigrant Aid Society. She must have been happier getting dressed each morning and going out to meet potential donors than she was spending days on the couch in a torn, dirty housedress with her hair unwashed and her stockings falling down.

By getting my father to marry her, my mother didn't condemn him and his mother to future lives of misery; she freed them both from the misery of the lives they had trapped themselves in.

IF SEX WAS THE TRUMP CARD that my mother played—the obvious way that her relationship with my father led to marriage—I think now it was only one of several forces driving him toward marrying her. In a way, their marriage was an inevitability set in motion when my father adopted his friend Norman's family as a substitute for his own. When he meets Norman, my father is fourteen and has been in the United States for two years. Only two years before, he was the youngest member of his mother's extended family—the household he said he loved for the "liveliness" of so many aunts and uncles. With his family now reduced to an unhappy three, no wonder he's drawn to Norman's, which my mother used the same word to describe: "lively," because of her three brothers. If I thought before that the net of forces driving my father to marry my mother was a snare, I see it now as a very different sort of net: one that scooped him out of the life he felt trapped in, bound to his mother and sister, and dropped him into a family—and a life—of his own.

And where did I get the story that my father married my mother

My father's mother in Warsaw

because she was the most beautiful woman he'd ever met? From my father.

It's 1996. My parents have been married sixty-three years—and will be married for eight more. In a letter to me, my father tells of a photograph he and my mother were looking at:

> Mom awoke to the fact she was so beautiful—something she'd forgotten. I wondered out loud why she accepted me so readily—a skinny, elongated, foreigner with a hooked nose. This time she admitted it was due to my mouthing a few big words unfamiliar to her.

Having read his journals, I know that this description really is how he saw himself, and why—from the beginning—he felt flattered and fortunate that my mother found him attractive.

I think now that he was.

READING HIS JOURNALS AND letters helped me understand how my father came to marry my mother even though she wasn't his girlfriend. But I still wonder about the woman who was—the woman whose letters he saved and hid for so many years, through so many moves. I turn to those letters to understand my father's relationship with Helen.

CHAPTER

TEN

The Hidden Letters

"ROMANCE OF A FLAVOR I HAVE NEVER YET TASTED BEFORE"

T HE THICK MANILA ENVELOPE I FOUND WEDGED BETWEEN A CARTON and the back wall on a high shelf in my parents' storage room is dirty and torn. On the outside, in blue ballpoint pen, my father's handwriting announces: "Mr. Lynch"—crossed out. Along one edge, in black felt pen, "ELI"—crossed out. In pencil, along the opposite edge and in the opposite direction, "Pictures taken at various trips abroad"—crossed out. And across the top in ballpoint pen—not crossed out—"Helen Feldman."

I can describe the battered envelope because I'm holding it.

I'M PREPARING TO SPEND a year in California, where I'll write the first draft of this book. I go through all the papers and notes and drafts and documents I've collected from and about my father, deciding which to take, which to leave behind, and which to scan and save in a computer file. Among the documents I scan are the letters inside that envelope—letters my father had kept hidden in each of the seventeen different homes he lived in from the time he married my mother. Then I have to decide whether to take them with me or put them in a fireproof safe along with other irreplaceable documents I'm leaving at home, and work from the scans. It seems risky and foolhardy and unnecessary to take the originals, yet I resist consigning them to the safe. I put off deciding and place the bulky envelope on top of the closed safe. On the morning of departure, I make my decision: I put the letters in my carry-on luggage. I'm doing what my father did, dragging these now-eighty-year-old letters from one home to another—only I don't have to keep them hidden. I just have to keep them safe.

Inside the envelope are two separate stacks. The thicker stack of letters, still folded in their stamped, postmarked envelopes, are what I was hoping to find when I went with my father to the storage room: letters from the woman he was referring to when he said, "Your mother wasn't my girlfriend; Helen was my girlfriend." The thinner stack of unfolded pages, most typed, a few handwritten—a gift beyond imagination—are drafts or copies of my father's letters to Helen.

In the years since I found the letters and my father told me to take them, I've read them several times. But I always read each stack separately. As soon as I got them, I read my father's, eager to hear his young voice. I found that voice off-putting and often baffling: his writing, always stilted and formal, went on at great polysyllabic length, as if intended to obscure meaning rather than convey it. When I got a chance to show my father the letters not long after we found them, he too began with his own—and, as he read, waved his hand over the page dismissively, laughing at his own verbiage. When I first began reading Helen's letters, I pulled one or another from her stack at random. Before long, I read them all. But I never read my father's and Helen's letters together, in chronological order, reconstructing them as a conversation. That's what I'm about to do now. I'm full of anticipation but also nervous. I feel as if I'm embarking on a new relationship, with all the promise and risk that entails.

*

THE FIRST LETTER, DATED MONDAY, JULY 21, 1930, IS HELEN'S. IT'S addressed to Mr. Eli Tannen, Oscawanna Gardens in Peekskill, N.Y. My father's first letter, typed and titled *COPY,* is dated July 22, 1930 – 2 A.M., Oscawanna Gardens. These addresses tell me that my father met Helen at one of the "camps," as the modest getaways north of New York City were called, where Jews went on summer weekends and vacations to escape the heat of the city. The addresses also tell me that Helen went back to the city after the weekend, while my father remained. It's a month after he graduated from law school—and nine months since the Great Depression descended. He's twenty-one and still manager of the finance company.

My father's letter begins with an apology for his handwriting (how is there a typed copy?), then tells me how they met—and that Helen has been unable to find a job:

> **You have changed my entire impression of my stay at Peek-skill. Ah, I shall never forget the good fortune I had in having gathered sufficient courage to ask you to have a turn with me that memorable evening when I first caught a glimpse of you. . . . What a pity you had to leave this place. My sorrow at your having done so and my deep desire and earnest hope that you will come back to Oscawanna and incidentally to me this coming Thursday, leads me to entertain the meretricious wish that you be unsuccessful in your search for a position, although as a general proposition it would please me very much indeed if your desire to find occupation would be fulfilled.**

I recognize my father's voice in his ponderous wording ("occupation" for "a job") and syntax, and his characteristic self-deprecation, saying he hopes Helen will return to Oscawanna only "incidentally" to him. I smile at the subtle trace of his first language: though he spoke English without an accent, he never adjusted to the way it uses what sounds like the past tense (it's actually a subjunctive) to refer to the future: "it would please me if your desire to find occupation *were* fulfilled."

I also recognize two aspects of my father's personality that he mentions: his extreme sensitivity to slights and his conviction that he's physically unattractive, though he's confident of his character in other respects. What moves me most is that the groundwork for their mutual attraction is laid by long, self-revealing conversations:

> **I must refer again to a topic I may have sounded in our short (to me) but rather exhaustive conversations; i.e. my supersen-**

sitiveness. In matters pertaining to the gaining of feminine favor I cannot combat competition. When a competitor, usually it is one with qualities vastly superior to mine for there are not many with inferior qualities (I am referring mainly to qualities in men looked for and valued by women and not such as e.g. ambition in life, filial and other related responsibilities and tenacity of purpose in unromantic pursuits, attributes of which a superiority in others I will not easily concede); when a competitor, I repeat, looms on the horizon, my wont is to slink into the shade and finally to retire entirely from the radius of vision, so to speak, of the object of attention. . . . But as an example of what ordinarily happens to my resolutions, when I met you and shortly after learned to know you I would have forfeited the fruits of fifteen years' labor for a kiss from you given as you might to one more blessed with the gifts of nature.

On the day that my father is at Oscawanna Gardens writing this letter to Helen, she is in New York City writing to him. In her letter, which covers seven pages, Helen tells of hitchhiking back to the city with a friend, of her job search, and of how hot the city is. She quotes a line of poetry from Edna St. Vincent Millay: *"Oh, world I can't hold thee close enough."* I know she's quoting from memory because she changes "cannot" to "can't." And she invites my father to visit her in the cottage where she'll be staying when she returns the following weekend:

> *This is in case you want to come. Anyway that's what you get for asking a strange girl to dance. Like the "Man of the Sea" of Sinbad's, I have become attached. A cruel word would drop me.*

I love that Helen knows, and quotes, poetry—and an Arab folktale. She writes so beautifully and fluidly, I'm afraid she'll be put off by my father's multisyllabic formality and convoluted syntax. I'm relieved that her second letter reassures me she isn't—and solves the mystery of the typed copy:

Your letter was delightful so I am not giving it up. But if you
want a copy I shall typewrite it for you.

The next letter is one my father writes three weeks later, responding to a letter he received from her, which I don't have. He's back in the
city, and apparently typed this copy himself: it says at the top "(Copy
of letter to Helen 8/7/30)." His writing has a quality I haven't seen
before. Though it's stilted, as his writing always is, it's somewhat less
so—and describes not only his thoughts but his feelings. And it's clear
what those feelings are: he's infatuated. His opening has already moved
from "Dear" to "Dearest":

Dearest Helen,

**I confess I was surprised to have received your letter (or
note is all it deserves to be called), but the surprise was of such
a pleasant sort that it had the effect of transporting me from a
state of tiredness and apathy to one of joyful enthusiasm.**

Though I wish he hadn't criticized her letter for being too short, I'm
glad he goes on to recall the weekend when she returned to the resort
where they met—and, not incidentally, to him:

**Romance of a flavor I have never yet tasted before fills me
now with an uncontrollable desire to give it expression (on
paper with pen and ink). . . . I've never before been made to
experience such thoughts as I do now. If you knew what a
havoc you wrought with ideas, theories and beliefs I thought,
till I met you, to be impregnable and unassailable. . . . Every
place I move and everything I look at is reminiscent of Oscawanna . . . Oscawanna to me of course is practically confined
to your cottage.**

So he did visit her there. And he called her when they were both back
home. He says that remembering the time they spent together at camp
rescues him from the bleakness of his surroundings and the challenges

he's facing, with the Depression closing in. His letter becomes a prose poem that builds to a perfect poetic ending:

> **I remember especially the night I called you from my office. I was reclining complacently in my armchair, smoking away the cigarets one by one, resting my feet on my desk and contemplating with sober mien the harsh, repellent to me at the time antipathetic walls and furnishings of the offices. . . . The look in my eye I imagined to have become wistful when slowly tho steadily the surroundings melted away from before me and in their stead there began to appear as if transported from the place of my imagination for my benefit, one scene after another of the transpirations of the two weeks then past. As each picture finally faded into oblivion with various emotions of joy, regret, sentimentality, hope, wistfulness, peevishness, pleasure, diversion, humor and at times sorrow, another took its place, at first appearing in a haze then gradually taking shape as if a magic wand was carving the objects into relief, There appeared, as if exorcised, the scene of our first meeting, the walk in the darkness of midnight, the climb thru the memorable path and the lovable strangeness with which it all filled me, my loneliness after your departure, the canoe ride of a Friday Eve, a game of gold, just you & I, and many other similar scenes. I must have spent an hour thus alone midst the four walls with my thoughts, but when they pertained to or contained you I felt as if you were there with me and I was happy.**

At twenty-one, my father is experiencing, for the first time, not just sexual but romantic attraction.

AS I READ THE LETTERS Helen writes over the next three years, I fall in love with her myself. She's contemplative, sensuous, thoughtful, playful—and she can write. She has his number and teases him: urging him to have photographs developed, as he has apparently promised but failed to do, she writes: *"Tomorrow instead of writing a 25 page letter to somebody, cut it down to 20 pages and the rest of the time do bring those pictures down to be developed.*" But there are months-long gaps between letters, and, I surmise, between their dates. They make arrangements to meet, sometimes with my father promising to bring a friend for her friend Charlotte. My father cancels arrangements, usually explaining that he has to study: he's now working toward a master's degree in law, which will qualify him to take the bar exam without first clerking at little or no pay. Sometimes he gives no reason, but Helen always replies that she understands. What a contrast, I can't help thinking, with my mother's imprecations and recriminations when he tells her he can't take her out or can't extend their afternoon meeting into the evening.

In his letters, my father speaks often of his unhappiness: his salary slashed, he has been training his boss's brother-in-law so he can replace my father as manager of the finance company at twice his salary, while my father is demoted and—a uniquely cruel blow—stripped of his cherished car. In a letter dated February 4, 1931, he writes, **"I gave up my car this week and I wouldn't like to go out without it. In fact I miss it so much that I loath to go anyplace and as a result hardly leave my office or home."**

Helen, too, is feeling the cruelty of the Depression: the price of a stamp—two cents—is an issue, and of telephone calls even more. She tells of taking, once again, an annual exam to qualify for a teaching job, while acknowledging the futility by saying she took leave of her fellow test takers with a wry, *"Same time next year."* She proposes outings, always promising that she will cost my father nothing: they can go "Dutch treat." She complains that he makes cryptic references to things he will explain in future letters, but never does: *"You always hint about what you will write in your next letter that isn't the letter that I receive."*

Two years after they first met, my father returns, in a letter dated May 1932, to their romantic beginning. He contrasts it with the time they've spent together in the two intervening years, which he describes as "disappointingly mundane." Then he refers to their most recent meeting as once again romantic—even passionate—but ill-fated:

I have been turning over in my mind the whole cycle of events since we first met. The idea struck me that it began very romantically for me. I am sure that it was more like romance

for me than <u>any</u> other experience that I enjoyed ever before. I am convinced that never again in my life will I approach so closely the real thing. . . . I next meditated on a subsequent period in our acquaintance which was rather drab. It must have been worse than that for you. I have reference to the evenings we spent in your home in company with another couple. Mind you—I don't mean to convey the impression that those evenings were utterly devoid of pleasure for me. Compared to most evenings that I spend alone or in company those were very enjoyable. It is only when I compare them with some other evenings that I spent with you that I can characterize them as drab.

The situation we find ourselves in after our last meeting appears to me to be easily adaptable to romance on a grand scale. Perhaps admixed with a touch of tragedy. Thus the cycle is completed. I am now confronted with the grave question of whether the cycle will prove to be a perfect circle or will break or deviate from its destined course into a foreign direction. This is a problem the solution of which is both enticing and foreboding.

How maddeningly enigmatic is his circumlocution! What does he mean by "a perfect circle" and "a foreign direction"? Is he referring to whether they will have sex, or marry, or part ways?

As I ponder this mystery, I realize that the dates hold a clue—to this and to another question that puzzled me. My father told me that he was "sort of like a boyfriend" to my mother "only the last year." This letter to Helen is dated a year before he marries. He writes in the letter that the intense infatuation of his and Helen's romantic beginning subsided: though they continued seeing each other, it was to do things like playing cards with another couple. Might this explain how my father could write in his journal, a year into his relationship with Helen, that my mother is "the only one who has ever loved me truly & for my own sake, my own worthless, ugly self"? And might it explain why he mentions Helen in his journal only once, and fleetingly: when he's about to have an operation on his nose, and lists the people whose reactions to the change in his appearance worry him? His journal ends in 1931, two years before he married, and a year before the romantic beginnings of his relationship with Helen are reignited—and, I surmise, just as he has begun having sex with my mother.

This letter, like most of the letters my father writes—to Helen and to others—is very long. There follow many pages about his concern for Helen and thoughts about her, and about how unhappy he is, before he asks:

> **Helen, did you feel that I wasn't sufficiently pleasant while speaking to you on the phone? I will admit I was in a sad mood. This you can probably judge by what preceded. But this mood was completely dispelled when I heard your cheery voice except for a slight continuance of the erstwhile gloom by inertia. Then too you know the problem I have to contend with in the office when you call. I spoke to you about it before.**

This has to be a reference to my mother: she's a secretary in my father's office, and part of her job is answering the phone. If my mother knows he's talking to Helen, she will find a reason to interrupt. Sure enough:

> **That was the cause of the interruption which must have annoyed you. You cannot know how inordinately glad I was to hear you so cheerful. Maybe it was because I felt relieved after having received your inexplicably sad letter. However that may be you made my day perfect and I am grateful.**

It's clear to me that my father genuinely cares for Helen—and that he's torn. He never writes like this to my mother. But then he never writes to her at all, because he sees her at work every day and also in her home when he's visiting her brothers. How different his tone is from the way he writes about my mother in his journal. But that's not a fair comparison. Like many people, he tends to write in his journal when he's frustrated or upset. It's possible, maybe likely, that he sometimes—often?—enjoys time he spends with my mother but doesn't write about it.

———

IN A LETTER HELEN writes two months later, a place name jumps out at me: Thousand Islands. From the many times I heard my father say— and the few times I heard my mother say—that he probably would have married Helen had she gone with him to the Thousand Islands, that exotically named place assumed a magical aura. I imagined my father inviting Helen to join him on a trip to the Thousand Islands as a last-ditch attempt to be obligated to marry her instead of my mother, the drama of the proposed trip concurrent with the drama of my mother getting physically ill and repeatedly throwing up because my father wouldn't marry her. Reading this letter, I see that the story I concocted is not how it happened: Helen refers to my father's planned trip in a letter dated July 1932—a year before he marries. This, too, fits with my father's comment that he was "sort of like a boyfriend" to my mother "only the last year." If I'm right that "like a boyfriend" refers to their having sex, the Thousand Islands trip would have taken place—had it taken place—shortly before my father began having sex with my mother.

But my father's recollection about why Helen didn't go is not how it happened either. My father told me that Helen turned down his invitation because her mother talked her out of it. Her mother, it turns out, did not disapprove, and Helen did not decline to go away with him, though she did decline his original invitation. In three letters addressed to Eli Tannen c/o Eager Mountain House, Catskill, N.Y., she lets me know that my father went there instead—and that she kept offering to join him, for ever-shorter periods of time. Apparently, he didn't respond. It seems that he wrote to tell her where he was spending his extended vacation—probably at least three weeks, judging from the dates of Helen's letters, which would explain why he originally planned a trip as far away as the Thousand Islands.

In a letter dated July 22, 1932, Helen writes,

> *My map tells me that you are not so far away. How come?*
> *Catskill is a far cry from Thousand Islands. Where-ever you are—*
> *I hope it's good for you.*

I love Helen for always thinking of my father's welfare, hoping he's happy. She goes on to ask about the place where he's staying, including a playful question about whether "eager" describes the mountain or the people staying there. And she asks if he'd like her to send him books to read—or to deliver them in person.

FIVE DAYS LATER SHE writes again, reminding my father that he invited her to go with him on his vacation to the Thousand Islands. She says that she reconsidered and would like to accept, even though it would now be only for the last week. And she says that her mother does not object:

> I told my mother that you asked me—and she said it would be very nice. So nonchalantly, too. I thought I would ask for a week off—go up and come back by car with you.

This offer is part of a long letter, in which she describes how deeply moved she was by nature on a previous trip to the country with a friend—a description that renews my appreciation of her writing and my affection for her:

> I felt those stirrings inside at the beauty. I just wanted to lie on my back and gaze and gaze, to take into myself—imbibe some of that splendor.

She then tells of a long walk she took through Harlem, describing the people and places she saw there, and says that it "seems ages" since he left, though it's only a week—and two weeks since she last saw him. She closes by assuring him he needn't write to her if he hasn't time because he has to write to so many friends—a teasing reference to his obsessive letter-writing, which she immediately rescinds, saying she'd miss his letters if he didn't write to her.

APPARENTLY, MY FATHER TOOK Helen at her first word and did not answer her letter. Six days later she writes again, now offering to join him for the last few days of his stay. With poignant self-deprecation, she writes,

*I promise you that I won't bother you one bit—that is unless you
want me to. O.K.?*

Helen then does something that is endearing in its whimsy but searing
in its humility. She encloses an index card on which she has typed a
series of options, so my father can compose a reply simply by putting a
check mark beside a word or phrase in each set. She explains that she is
resorting to this method *"because I see from your response(?) to my other letter that you are not in the writing mood."* The card says at the top, under-
lined, "Check the word that best conveys your meaning." The options
are lined up vertically with ( ) next to each.

(Dear/Dearest/Darling) Helen:

*I am (very/not very/just) well and am very (sorry/happy/glad) to
hear that you will be able to spend some time up here. It will be (very
nice/terrible) if you come. I would prefer that you do (come/stay home).*

*If you are coming here is the information. I am going home on or
about Aug. . . . (date). The cost is $. . . . per day here.*

Tell me (when you are/you are not) coming.

(Love/Sincerely/
Devotedly) Eli

Since I have this card, I assume my father did not check the options
or send the card back to Helen. Whether he answered in another form,
I'll never know, but I'm fairly certain he did not take her up on her
offer to join him for the last few days of his vacation, as he didn't accept
her previous two offers. Why he didn't, and why he didn't reply to her
letters after he wrote to tell her where he was, is a mystery. Perhaps he
wanted company to brave a trip to a place as foreign and far away as the
Thousand Islands, but felt no need for company on the closer, familiar
Catskill turf. Is it possible my mother joined him in the Catskills, and
that's why he didn't respond to Helen's letters? Could that be where
their relationship became sexual? That might explain why the Thousand Islands stuck in my father's mind as the trip that might have led to

his marrying Helen. Whatever the reason, that card is the last word I'll
ever hear on what really happened with the Thousand Islands trip that
never took place—and the chance for my father to be obligated to
marry Helen instead of my mother.

I WAS WAY OFF in imagining that my father asked Helen to go with
him to the Thousand Islands just before he agreed to marry my
mother. It was a year before. And his recollection that she turned him
down wasn't accurate either. Memory is like that. We mix things up,
we get things wrong. But what matters is how a memory fits into the
story of our lives. From that point of view, the timing has exactly
the significance I thought it had. If I'm right that when he said he was
"dating" my mother "just the last year," my father was referring to
their having sex, then the meaning that the Thousand Islands had for
him is true: it's code and metaphor for having sex with Helen. He
said of the Thousand Islands trip, "I know that had she come with
me, that she would no longer be a virgin, and once she's not a virgin,
then I would feel obligated to marry her. So I would've married, and
then your mother would've been faced with a fait accompli, that I'm
married. And then she wouldn't pursue me anymore." In other
words, he would have married Helen if he had had sex with her before he began having sex with my mother. The moment he does, his
future is sealed, even though it will be another year before he marries, and since he proposed on an impulse, before he knows that he
will—and even though, by some twist of fate, or of the complex and
mysterious workings of human emotion and will, romance reenters
his relationship with Helen six months after he begins having sex
with my mother. And it's obvious from her letters that Helen doesn't
know it's already too late.

THE LETTERS HELEN WRITES to my father in the six months following
his stay at Eager Mountain House—at least those I have—are brief
and businesslike. The first is dated a month after his vacation in the
Catskills. On a postcard-size blank card, she asks if, on his way upstate, he could drop her off at a "camp" she's going to—if it wouldn't

inconvenience him—and signs off, "As ever." A month after that she writes with birthday wishes—it's his twenty-fourth—and includes the poem "Barter" by Sara Teasdale. She signs it with an even more distant *"Sincerely."* Shortly after this she writes a note about tickets she bought to a German film, assuring him that they can be returned if he doesn't want to go; the brief next note acknowledges logistics, so it seems he went.

Then, following a three-month gap, Helen's letters completely change in length, tone, and content—and they hold another big surprise: Helen, too, tries to convince my father to have sex. Astonishingly, I get to listen in on their arguments. And I get to see how close they came. The transformation in their relationship leaps off the page at the start of a letter Helen writes in January 1933—six months before my parents marry:

> *I am so deadly tired I could drop to sleep, cradled in your arms,*
> *to one of your Polish lullabies.*

This scene stops me in my reading tracks. It recalls one of my father's most evocative memories of his childhood in Poland: being sung to sleep by his adored grandmother. Even more moving than the image of him lying beside Helen, holding her, is the image of him singing to her as his grandmother sang to him in the language of his childhood.

Helen writes that she has been happy in my father's arms, and cares nothing about the future that he won't stop talking about. She says, *"I've never asked more of you than your friendship and love."* I believe her, and I love her for it—and for again quoting a Sara Teasdale poem, this one including the line "Child, child, love while you can." When she complains that my father dismisses her arguments and her offer of love, I can hear the persuasion she's referring to: his claiming that he cannot, must not, take advantage of her reassurance, because the obligation would be there whether she acknowledges it or not.

MY FATHER'S REPLY TO this letter is three tightly packed typed pages. It begins:

Very dear Helen,

It would be vain for me not to admit that I was deeply moved by certain portions of your letter, despite the fact that I claim to be impervious to sentiment.

He then says that he forces himself to resist her entreaties because he can't forget inescapable reality; then he adds:

I plead in my defense the fact that most often it is not the jeopardy of my own interest or the threat to my own social standing or reputation which deter me from giving way to my impulses. It is the welfare of those others who might be affected adversely which frightens me.

He goes on at great length, repeating more or less the same thing in slightly different ways: If he and Helen have sex and do not marry, her life will be destroyed. If he makes good on his obligation, his own hopes for happiness will be dashed. At one point, he says,

You are in so much of a better position than I am. Your stand is consistent, positive and unequivocal, while I am in a contradictory and wholly untenable position and what is worse I am powerless to change it.

I'm certain that the situation my father feels powerless to change is his obligation to his mother and sister, who he believes would fall into destitution if he stopped supporting them.

Finally, my father lays out the dilemma he's facing in a single interminable, anguished sentence:

Wouldn't this position stigmatize the man even more? Might it not finally make him very unhappy, verily being hurled into a maelstrom of misery either from a sense of having inflicted ignominiously grave and irreparable injustice and injury or as a result of an effort to repair the harm by changing the whole course of his life from the plans he had cherished for

it destroying all the hopes he had built for his future often having found them the only excuse for holding on to what otherwise seemed an utterly purposeless and worthless life, thus giving up at one stroke all his hitherto dearly held convictions and ideals thus embittering him to an extent that might cause to but hurt even more deeply the thing he had made all these sacrifices for, hurt it though unwittingly and involuntarily?

This devastating prediction explains why my father feels he must not give in to Helen's—and his own—desire to have sex: if he succumbs and does not marry her, she'll be, to use the Yiddish word he used when he explained this thinking to me, *unglücklich*—and her life will be ruined. If he does marry her, he will ruin his own, because marriage entails a permanent obligation to support others, and his only hope for happiness is the freedom he'll finally win when his mother and sister marry. In that case, his bitterness would ruin his wife's happiness, too. This description of the doom he believes would result if he marries Helen applies equally to his marrying my mother, which he has no idea he will do six months later.

My father asks Helen to destroy his letters as he says he will hers:

for our own protection although I would want to keep them forever as I am convinced that never again in my life will I receive any similar to them in what they contain. It would be asking too much of fate to expect a recurrence of the accident wherein a woman will imagine herself possessing toward me the sentiments you express.

That is a temptation my father did yield to: he did keep Helen's letters forever, and he kept this copy of his own. But I think he was right that he would never again feel such selfless, passionate love from a woman.

THOUGH MY FATHER REMAINS steadfast in his determination not to compromise Helen's virginity, he has not foresworn intimacy with her. Her next letters are dated two months later, in March. Again they are short, mostly arranging times and places to get together. It saddens me that Helen is still assuring him that their meetings won't cost him money, and it moves me that she also suggests they meet in the evening so he'll have time to study. The contrast with my mother is stark on both points: in his journal, my father bitterly complains that an evening my mother insisted he spend with her—tricked him into spending with her—cost him half the five dollars he had for the entire week's expenses. His journal also describes many exchanges where my mother brushes aside his protests about needing time to study. Helen's letters also continue to display her playfulness and attunement to language. In one, she addresses my father as *"you old moth ball,"* then adds, *"Very dangerous weather for a moth ball to be out in (isn't that a funny idiom)."*

THE NEXT LETTER I have from Helen takes my breath away. Postmarked a little less than two months before my father marries, May 3, 1933, it's the thickest in the pile: twenty-five pages written in green ink over several days. It includes, for the first time (and Helen says she is telling him for the first time), a long account of how difficult things are at home because her father is out of work. Graphically, heartrendingly, she describes her parents' despair and her struggle to hide her own distress so as not to worsen theirs. In another section of the letter, she says that my father has wanted to convert her to Communism but did not tell her which books to read, so she has found some on her own and is taking notes, preparing questions to ask him. I'm captivated by these and other parts of the letter, so full of details about her life and her thoughts. But most of all, I am riveted because this is, in its beginning and its end, a gorgeously evocative and deeply moving love letter.

My father told me that he spent an entire night with Helen yet managed not to compromise her virginity. Helen must have written this letter after that night. She begins by describing her happiness waking up and remembering their time together, feeling contentment not only in her body but also in her mind because she and my father *"had met as individuals—merged as individuals and had come out as individuals."* She writes that *"all morning—every time the telephone rings I hope that it is you feeling a similar longing for me,"* but finally accepts that he won't call— and says that's all right. She refers to a weekend in the country that they have apparently talked about; says how much she looks forward to uninterrupted, unhurried time with him; and wonders if he desires it as much as she does. The letter begins, *"Darling,"* and ends, *"I whisper to you 'Good-night,'—kiss you fondly and turn to dreams of you."*

As I transcribe this long letter, transforming page after page of Helen's round green handwriting into harsh uniform black letters on the screen, I feel far closer to her than to my father. I picture her as if she were still somewhere in New York City, still feeling the emotions of a night spent with a man who has never felt so close to a woman before, yet still is beyond her reach. And I realize that I have been rooting for Helen all along, even though had my father married her, I wouldn't be here.

THIS IS THE LAST LETTER I have with a Bronx return address. Helen's next letter, postmarked less than a month later—and a month before my father marries—has a Brooklyn return address. A month! When my father said—as he often did—that he felt guilty because Helen's family moved to Bensonhurst for him, I never thought this happened so close to the moment he made the decision to marry—a decision, in the words he used when he told me about it, to do "the right thing by" my mother but required him to "betray" Helen, which he said he still felt "very bad" about. When she writes this letter, Helen clearly doesn't know that the end of their relationship is near, and I am certain that my father doesn't either. The letter confirms a boat outing they have planned—and beseeches my father not to oversleep.

HELEN WRITES THE NEXT LETTER three weeks later. Though she doesn't know that my father will marry in eleven days, she does seem to suspect—to know—that she's losing him. Written at two o'clock in the morning, the letter begins, *"Darling,"* but immediately asks, *"(May I still call you that?)."* She has to be hurting: she says she'd wanted to call but didn't because she couldn't be cheerful, so is writing instead to *"stretch toward you a seeking hand—just to create a contact between us."* Her letter has no hint of bitterness. Instead it's dreamy, contemplative:

> *The house is so still and brooding. The furniture stands upright as though waiting for everyone to go to bed before it begins a midnight*

dance. Awfully weird thought to have when you are all alone in a
sleeping house.

She closes with concern for my father: *"My womanly intuition tells me*
that something is wrong. What is it?" and signs with her name unadorned.
Then she adds a postscript that evokes the intimacy, now gone, that
they so recently shared: *"Good-night just heard the milk man. Remember?"*

AND NOW A LETTER dated Thurs. 7:30 P.M. I know from the post-
mark that it's Thursday June 29, 1933, the day my parents marry in City
Hall. In this, and in the letter that follows, Helen refers to letters from
my father that I don't have—and she answers the question I could
never get my father to answer: how he felt when he made the decision
to marry. He has apparently told Helen that he can't see her, without
telling her why, and described his own psychological state as so
wretched, she feels driven to speak to him—to assuage his pain. She
says she's been calling him but no one was home—and that she'd been
trying to reach him even before she received his latest letter, which
"hurt me very much. I had hoped that at least you were happy." She says she
will continue to try to reach him, and tells him when and how she will
try; then she says, if she fails to see him, she'll write again and closes
"Keep well."

Reading this letter, I sigh audibly. Helen is trying to reach my father at home, but he's in the Catskills—on his honeymoon.

HELEN'S NEXT LETTER IS written several days later. She's on vacation in
upstate New York. Again, her concern—at least the concern she expresses—is not for herself but for him. She's writing, she says, because:

> *your letter sounded so—so desperate (?)—no—so hopeless and because*
> *of some odd notion of mine I always felt even if I never removed any*
> *trouble you may have had I helped to alleviate it—I tried to change your*
> *uncompromising view of it.*

I love Helen for caring about my father's feelings, even as he has deeply
wounded hers. Later in the letter, she again invites him to join her—

and, as usual, assures him it will cost him no more than the $1.70 fare
to get there. It must have been after he got this letter that my father
called to say "I'm married."

After that, he never called or wrote to her again.

THE STORY I HAD formed in my mind of the Thousand Islands drama
taking place just before my father proposes to my mother, is false. But
my vision of a drama involving Helen as my father nears the decision
to make that proposal is closer to the truth—and closer to the moment
that he married—than I ever imagined.

Helen's letters reinforce my sense that she was better suited to my
father than my mother was. She was more like him: a kind, compassionate intellectual who shared his love of ideas, reading, and books—
and wasn't given to depression. But my mother had an insurmountable
advantage: ubiquity. She was always there, from the time she was
twelve and my father began hanging around her house to be with her
brothers. That advantage was sealed when she worked in the same office as my father at the finance company—a job she had because my
father hired her, as he hired her brothers, when he was manager and
jobs were scarce because of the Depression. There's another way Helen
probably never had a chance: she didn't have the temperament—or the
deep well of need—to pressure my father to marry her. Maybe my father would have been happier if he'd married Helen. But he surely
would not have been happier had he not married, clinging to the fantasy that one day his mother and sister would marry and set him free.

Finding My Father Finding Family

IN THE SMALL ASSISTED LIVING APARTMENT WHERE HE MOVES AFTER my mother dies, my father pins up—where he can see it while lying in bed—a small photograph of my mother already old but looking youthful and cute in a straw hat, smiling right out at him.

One day I ask him what he thinks about. "Mother," he says. "And I remind myself ninety-three is a good age." He means that he has no right to curse fate for taking her from him. Yet in a way he does. Five months after her death, he writes in a letter to old friends that Dorothy died

> at the tender age of 93. I wanted her to live at least to 110. She, on the other hand, said she only wanted to avoid being a widow. But I am just as distressed as a widower. I don't know how I can go on without my Dorothy. We've been married only 71 years, but I loved her since she arrived in America at age 12. Truth is I do not know what I'll do, what I can do, without her. To me her loss is equivalent to the loss of a saint, the kind that may never again walk on earth.

Though it may be a stretch to say he loved my mother from the time they first met, when my father was fourteen and she was his best friend's kid sister, it's true that he knew her since she was twelve; that he loved her in some way in the years before they married; and that he loved her deeply, without reservation, for seven decades after.

———

MY MOTHER IS TELLING me about the time she was in the hospital giving birth to Naomi, their first child. My father was confined to the hospital waiting room. "He wrote poems to me," she says, "and sent them up to my room."

I find these poems, and others he wrote during her weeklong stay in the hospital, in my father's files: slips of paper he covered with tiny print. One includes the rhyming lines "I'm in love with married life" and "I'm in love with loving my wife."

A CHILDHOOD FRIEND OF Naomi's recalls a scene from when they were teenagers: "Your parents were chaperoning a party," she says, "and your mother was sitting on your father's lap. He whispered something to her, and she laughed. Naomi asked her what he said, and she said, 'It's a private joke.' I was impressed. It gave me the impression that your parents had a romantic, sexual relationship, which my parents didn't."

MY SISTERS AND I go with my parents to Poland when my father is eighty-three and my mother eighty-one. Their hotel room in Warsaw has two single beds. On the morning following their first night in that room, my father is limping. He hurt his leg while trying to push the two beds together, so he and my mother could sleep as they always do, embracing.

MY FATHER, EIGHTY-SIX, IS trying to rise from an upholstered chair. My mother is watching, with an expression of extreme anxiety. The first two times he hurls his weight forward, he falls back into the chair. When he succeeds on the third try, he reaches his long arms toward her, takes her face in his two big hands, laughs, and reassures her, "I'm fine."

MY MOTHER AND I are in the living room of their Florida apartment. My father comes in, pushing his walker before him. But instead of heading for the upholstered lift chair, he heads for his wife.

"Where are you going?" she asks.

"I'm going to give you a kiss," he says. This he does, before making his way to his chair.

MY PARENTS ARE BOTH in wheelchairs—she recovering from a fall, he from surgery—waiting for the dining room to open in their Florida senior residence. They're holding hands across their wheelchairs. They always hold hands. It's something about them that I take for granted.

I'M VISITING MY PARENTS in Florida to help celebrate their sixty-sixth anniversary. My father is ninety, my mother eighty-eight. They're opening cards they've given each other.

She has written on the envelope of his card, "ELI."

He has written on the envelope of hers, "To ever so sweet Dorothy."

Inside his card she has written the date, "Dearest Eli" at the top, and, at the bottom, "Dot."

Inside her card he has written: "Dear Dorothy" at the top and, at the bottom, "Yours (and yours alone), Eli." On the facing page he has written a poem that ends with "everlasting deep devotion / Full of feeling, genuine emotion."

The day before, I drive my mother to Eckerd's, the local chain drugstore, so she can buy a card to give my father, and I can buy one for him to give her. She stands for a long time before the greeting card display, picking up one card after another, reading it and returning it to the rack. She picks up a card that she holds longer than the rest, and reads its printed message aloud to me: "You are my one and only love." She says, "That's true. He's always been the only one. I'll take this one."

*

I HAD MANY GRIEVANCES AGAINST MY MOTHER GROWING UP. HER unhappiness played out more often and more painfully with me than with my sisters, for several reasons. Yes, there was the fact that she didn't want a third child, and I unfortunately turned out to be a difficult one. Which was cause and which effect I don't know, but I had a tendency to be unhappy much like hers. I was also the youngest, and therefore easiest to focus on. I was the only one left to focus on after Mimi got married when I was seventeen—and in the grip of sixties culture that prompted me to act in ways unthinkable to a mother born into an orthodox family in Minsk. Then I caused her misery by not getting married until the advanced age of twenty-three—and again by getting divorced and staying single for a disastrous (from her point of view) decade that spanned my thirties. On top of all that I was, like my father, sensitive—prone to overreact to slights and to absorb others' emotions. But all this changed as my mother aged, especially after I remarried and was no longer causing her sleepless nights by failing to find a husband.

I comment to my father that my mother seems much happier since we children no longer live at home.

"No," he says, "she's still unhappy most of the time—unless she's in company."

"She seems happier to me," I say.

He says, "Now, you're company."

So I was the lucky one, getting to be with my mother when she was happy, which means she was funny, loving, and effusive.

When my mother is old, I also come to treasure the quality my father praises in the journal he kept when he was young: her unassuming ways. And I bask in the expressions of love she is generous with. It was her example that led me to write, in my book *You're Wearing THAT?* about mothers and grown daughters, that love between mothers and daughters is in many ways like romantic love. I discover I can make her happy by sending affectionate notes and buying her small gifts. She responds in kind. "Dearest Deb," she writes in a letter when she is in her eighties and I have just left after a visit, "You brought sunshine into our lives. What a thrill to wake up and get that smiling, big hug. I shall miss it terribly! But I'll survive and cling to those memories—till we meet again." And another, written when she was eighty-one: "Darling, you're probably not yet at the elevator but the emptiness has already set in. The stillness in the house is shattering. . . . I shall think of you every minute of the day and do everything you ordered! (to do) I'll be counting the days till you return. With endless love, Mom."

When she's old, my love for my mother is also endless. And my father's is, too.

*

AFTER MY MOTHER DIES AND MY FATHER MOVES TO AN ASSISTED living residence near Naomi, my sisters and I hope he'll find companionship in his last years. I harbor hope he will find a woman with whom he has the intellectual rapport he didn't have with our mother. My father hopes to find a companion, too. But what he's looking for isn't what I have in mind.

MY FATHER DEVELOPS A relationship with a sweet and kind woman who lives in the same residence. During one of my visits, he suggests that we call on her. I walk beside the bright red scooter that has replaced his walker. When she answers the door, I am moved, though also caught off guard, that he calls her "sweetheart" and takes her hand. The entire time we're there, he keeps his hand on the arm of her chair. We sing songs together: "America the Beautiful" and "The Star-Spangled Banner." She sings some songs alone, and my father asks me to sing the union song "Joe Hill." When I get to the line "They shot you Joe, says I," she winces and says, "That's terrible." When I sing the line "Says Joe, I never died," she heaves a sigh of relief and says, "Oh, good, that's better."

Much of the time that my father spends with this friend is in her room with the door closed—and locked. He's ninety-six; she's in her sixties. That's why he picked her: he isn't interested in women his age. But there's a reason why she is younger than the other women in the facility: she has Alzheimer's. My father doesn't realize this at first. When she forgets their appointments, he gives her a watch as a gift. She wears it, but still forgets. When he realizes she has dementia, he calls a halt to their relationship. He doesn't want to take advantage of her.

NAOMI KNOWS A WOMAN she thinks my father would like—should like: a fellow New York Jewish leftie. She arranges for them to meet. Though he is respectful and cordial, he has no interest in seeing her again. I ask why.

"Why should I?" he asks.

"Because you have so much in common: shared backgrounds, similar experiences and views."

"There's no point in talking to people who agree with you," he says. "What's interesting is to talk to people who disagree. You find out how they think."

I admire this explanation, but I believe it's a quick-witted way to satisfy me without really answering my question. The reason he has no interest in pursuing a friendship with this woman is that he isn't sexually attracted to her. And I must, at long last, acknowledge how different my father's view of relationships with women—and of marriage—is from mine. My assumption that marriage is about finding a soul mate is not his. I finally see he might really have meant it when he said, "It doesn't matter who you marry. The difference is between being married and being single. If you're single, you're free. You can do what you want in your life. If you're married, you're responsible for other people. You can't do what you want. You have to make a living." When he said this, I took it as my father's way of deflecting my question about whom he would have preferred to marry. I hadn't yet begun writing this book, and didn't fully understand how his life was shaped by the struggle to support first his mother and sister, then his wife and children.

So I have to give up both story lines I formed about my parents' marriage: the romantic one of the prettiest woman and the smartest man falling in love, and the cynical one of the conniving woman who ensnared a man she didn't deserve to marry. After reading my father's journals and letters, after countless hours of conversation with both parents as they aged, and after having lived over seven decades myself, I arrive at what feels like a truer understanding of what was, and maybe still is, a common story: the inevitable interplay of two young people thrown together by circumstance; the temptations of sex (for him); the desire to marry (for her); and the scaling back of great, often unrealistic expectations by circumscribed opportunities. In the end, what leads to lasting love—with couples who find partners on their own as surely as with arranged marriages—comes less from having chosen the perfect partner than from the accumulation of days spent side by side, caring for and talking to each other, and something my parents did a lot of: laughing together. When my father wrote in his teenage journal that Dorothy would be able to love him and welcome his love, that really was what he was looking for, and what—not to his misfortune but to his great luck—he found in her.

My parents at my wedding in 1988

*

JUST AS I'M FINISHING THIS BOOK, MY SISTER MIMI SENDS ME LINKS to two videos that her husband, Bruce, took in 1988. The first shows our family gathered for Thanksgiving at Mimi's house. When it starts, some of us are already there. Then others come into view as they step off the staircase leading to the floor we're all on: first Mimi herself, carrying a bag of groceries; then one of Naomi's daughters, then my parents. Each person, on arrival—before taking off their coat—goes from one to another family member already there, hugging and kissing in greeting. In a later scene, we're all sitting around Mimi's living room, talking in pairs or small groups. Several people compliment the new couch, which Bruce built himself—and tease that it isn't very comfortable. My father tries sitting on it, slouches into a near-recumbent position to dramatize that discomfort, and needs someone to help hoist him out of it.

In the next scene, everyone is seated around a large table. My father begins dinner by slicing a loaf of *challah* and saying the Hebrew prayer, but he doesn't hand out slices in order of age, as his grandfather did, and no one says a prayer before eating. Instead, there's a din of overlapping voices and laughter. My mother announces that she's going to say a few words about everyone in the family. Reading from note cards, she teases each of us in turn, caricaturing our phone conversations with her: "Mimi is a devoted daughter. She's eager to talk—for three minutes. After three minutes, you have to hang up. Naomi loves to chat. She'll tell what she had for breakfast, name every vegetable in her garden, and what she did during the day. Deb calls from all over the world. When Daddy has a cold, she gets the name of a doctor for him by calling her doctor friend—in Greece!" My mother then mocks my father's preference for doctors who are willing to be paid directly by Medicare: "Of course Daddy won't see the doctor, because he doesn't take assignment." She goes on to tease each grandchild in order of age. Throughout, my father and others toss in asides. After each of her pronouncements, and every aside, the table erupts in bursts of raucous laughter.

The third scene takes place after dinner. My sisters' kids, whose ages range from seven to twenty-five, perform for us: wearing outlandish outfits, they dance and sing the then-popular Bobby McFerrin song "Don't Worry, Be Happy," with new lyrics they just composed. Each sings a verse making fun of family members—or themselves. Between verses, they sing in unison the chorus, which ends, "Call Mary!" mocking my father's relentless attempts to get them to call his uncle Bernard's widow. As I watch this video, it occurs to me that twenty-five is kind of old to be grouped with "the kids." Then I recall that they thought so, too.

Soon after this video was taken, at a family gathering in the Catskills, "the kids" rebel against our suggestion that they prepare one of their usual skits to entertain us. They're no longer kids, they protest. Why don't we elders put on a skit for them? And we do. Each of us takes the role of another family member, dons their clothes, and makes fun of them. Wearing Bruce's jacket, I enter the room with his lumbering walk and greet the first person I see with his characteristic "Hiya!" and sideways hug. Wearing my father's jacket, Bruce plops into a big chair, then repeatedly tries to propel himself out of it, each time failing and falling back down. My husband, wearing my turtleneck sweater and vest, leaps onto Bruce's lap, throws his arms around him, and exclaims, "It's true! I do love you, Daddy, more than Mommy!" The only thing getting in the way of our performance is one after another of us collapsing in laughter.

A family gathering at Circle Lodge in 2002

All this came back when I saw the old video of our Thanksgiving gathering at Mimi's: three generations showing—creating—our love for each other by teasing and laughing. And the video shows who started it, who modeled it: my mother. The second video that Mimi sends shows where she learned it: the family she grew up in. This one was taken at our parents' house in Florida. Mimi is visiting, and my mother's brothers Irving and Norman, who live nearby, have come over with their wives. The aging siblings and their spouses are sitting around the living room, telling stories—and laughing. Norman tells how he tormented his brothers when they were young. "I was always hollering," Norman says. "I was a bad boy. Every family needs a bad boy, so I was the bad boy." His wife, Millie, jokes that the friend who introduced her to Norman is no longer a friend. His brother Irving says Norman was not such a bad boy when he went to a doctor to fix his eye, and fainted! My mother joins in, "You passed out in the dentist's office once also!" Watching this video, I see that my mother learned from her brothers to show affection and spark laughter by telling stories and teasing. Watching these videos, I see—literally, see before my eyes—what drew my father to his friend Norman's family, so lively and warm, in such stark contrast to the grim atmosphere of his life with his mother and sister.

THIS IS THE HAPPY ENDING to my father's story. He did manage, finally, to earn a living as a lawyer while staying true to his ideals, helping workers get compensated for injuries they suffered on the job. And also, together with my mother—thanks to my mother—he found in this country what he lost when he left Warsaw; what he wrote in his journal that he yearned for; what he recalled about his childhood when he said, "That was what I loved most: the liveliness, the warmth, of so many aunts and uncles." By marrying my mother, he gave me and my sisters "so many aunts and uncles" (if not quite as many as he had), and created a family full of liveliness, warmth, and love.

Epilogue

"My problem wasn't having no father," my father says. "My problem was too much mother. I didn't miss my father because I never knew him. I never missed having a father because I never had one." But every now and then a comment he makes gives me an inkling that he did miss his father—missed having a father—more than he let on. He tells me that Mrs. Wilner, the widow he and his sister boarded with when he was thirteen and his mother was working in Tuckahoe, caught him reading in bed at night. (His bed was a cot in the passageway between two rooms in the basement. Mrs. Wilner, her two daughters, and my father's sister all slept upstairs.) To stop him from using electricity, she replaced the white bulb with a blue one, so he wouldn't be able to read. "I read anyway," he says. Then he adds, "That's what happens when a boy doesn't have a father. If I'd had a father, he might not have let me read at night, but he wouldn't have put in a blue bulb."

My father never knew his father because he was two when his father moved out, having contracted tuberculosis; he died of it when my father was six. My father says,

I have only four memories of seeing my father. One night my mother woke me out of a sound sleep, and I saw that my father was there; he must have come by to discuss something with her. She had cooked frankfurters for him, and she woke me up to give me a bite. She knew I loved them, and they were so rare during the war. I guess I was still sleepy, because when I tried to swallow the frankfurter chunk, it got stuck in my throat. I don't know if I remember this because it was one of the few times in my life that I saw my father, or because I nearly choked.

In two more memories I have of my father, he's talking to my mother. In the earliest one, I'm standing with my mother, holding her hand, at the enormous arch that led into our court-yard. My father is on the other side of her—a tall, reddish man, saying things I can't understand. In the other memory, he's sick in bed in a room just big enough for a bed and space to walk around it; a staircase went right into the room. My mother is talking to him at his bedside. I was in the room with them, but I couldn't get near. Because of his illness, my mother made me stand at the door.

The only other time I remember seeing my father is also the only memory in which he spoke to me. I was walking with him in the country, and we came to a brook. He wanted me to cross it with him, but I was afraid. I was convinced the bottom was quicksand and would suck me in. He picked up a large green pinecone and threw it into the water, to show me that it didn't sink. For some reason, that reassured me, and I crossed the brook with him. Later we came to a field of wheat. I still recall it as one of the most beautiful sights I've ever seen: the yellow wheat curved in the breeze as far as I could see. I asked my father if the wheat field went to the end of the world.

I like to think that my father's sense of the beauty of the wheat field reflects a feeling of comfort to be walking with his father. I love that he asked his father if the wheat field went to the end of the earth. By asking that question, I think he was asking his father if that sense of comfort—of his father's presence—might stay with him after his fa-ther was gone. Maybe it did, in his memory of the wheat field, the walk, and the conversation. I know he was comforted to learn, as an adult, that his father was thoughtful, intelligent, generous, and kind—a wonderful person—not the terrible person his mother had led him to believe his father was.

Maybe I'm projecting. Had my father not lived nearly thirty years after he retired, I might have titled this book *Missing My Father*. How lucky I am that he lived so long; that he spent so many hours talking to me about his past; that he wrote down his memories when he was old and wrote journals when he was young, and kept them, and kept so many of the letters and papers that came into his life—and gave it all to me. I'm grateful, most of all, that he gave me the assignment to write this book, so he could continue spending time with me a dozen years after he died. By writing it, by having written it, I ensure that he'll stay with me till the end of the earth.

My father's father, Symcha Tenenwórcel

Appendix

CHILDREN OF CHAZKIEL KORNBLIT
(IN BIRTH ORDER AS CLOSE AS I CAN DETERMINE)

Jack (Jakob, Jakub, Yankel, Rachmiel, Yerachmiel, Jakub Rachmiel), born to his father's first wife, Chana; first to come to America; sponsored those who came after; fundraiser for the Hebrew Immigrant Aid Society (HIAS)

Ruchcia (Rozia, Ruchul, Rose), married a Hasid, mother of five children; died in the 1918 flu epidemic

Eva (Ewa, Chava), first woman dentist and first woman periodontist in Newark

Sarah (Chai Sura, Salome, Salomea, Sala, Helen Sarah), my grandmother; established and became first principal of Warsaw's first school for Hasidic girls, Chavaceles

Dora (Dvoyra, Dorota, Dorotea, Dorothe, Dorothy), mathematician, physicist; student and lover of Einstein

Bronia (Bronka), went to Russia to help establish Communism, died of tuberculosis in the Crimea

Zosia, the only one I know nothing about; her name appears in only one place: the list my father made after visiting his aunt Eva

Max (Mates), a cutter, got my father his first job in the garment district

Sam (Schmuel Eliyahu, called Schmul-eli, like my father: Samuel Eli), worked at a bank in Philadelphia

Regina (Rivka), because of severe epilepsy, lived with her parents until she killed herself by jumping off the balcony

Dina, burned to death at fourteen after her apron caught fire while she was cooking

Joshua (Schia, Jehoshua Leib), killed in Auschwitz with his wife and five children

Bernard (Boruch Zishe, Bob), worked for the Hebrew Immigrant Aid Society (HIAS)

Magda (Malka, Malgosha, Magdalena), high-ranking official in the Polish Communist government

NAMES IN NOTES ONLY

Esther, died at age four
Nathan, died at a year and a half of spinal meningitis

UNNAMED

twins born after Magda who died at birth
possibly another set of twins who died at birth

Chronology

OCTOBER 3, 1908: Schmuel Eliyahu Tenenwórcel, my father, is born in Warsaw, Poland

MAY 3, 1911: Dina Rozin, my mother, is born in Minsk, Russia

FEBRUARY 13, 1912: Jakub Rachmiel, Uncle Jack, arrives in New York

SEPTEMBER 2, 1912: Schmuel Eli, Uncle Sam, arrives in New York

AUGUST 5, 1913: Mates, Uncle Max, arrives in New York

JANUARY 11, 1914: Ewa, Aunt Eva, arrives in New York

JULY 1914: World War I breaks out

1914–1918: Germans occupy Poland

1915: Salomea (Sala) Kornblit Tenenwórcel, my father's mother, is hired to set up and become the first principal of the Chavaceles School; moves there with her children

1919: Leile (Leah) Finkel Kornblit, my father's grandmother, dies in Warsaw

AUGUST 18, 1920: Nachan Chaim Rozin, my mother's father, arrives in New York with a son and daughter

AUGUST 26, 1920: Boruch Zishe, Uncle Bernard, arrives in New York

SEPTEMBER 18, 1920: arrives in New York with his mother and sister

NOVEMBER 3, 1920: Dvoyra, Aunt Dora, arrives in New York

1923: quits high school to work full time; goes to work at Shapiro and Sons coat factory

SEPTEMBER 5, 1923: Dina Rozin (my mother) arrives in New York with her mother, sister, and two brothers

1926: becomes a naturalized citizen through his mother's naturalization

1927: begins law school at night

1928: helps establish and becomes manager of the Shapiros' finance company

October 24, 1929: stock market crashes

June 1930: graduates law school

July 1930: meets Helen Feldman

1933: receives LLM degree in law; passes the bar exam; marries Dorothy Rosen (née Dina Rozin)

1935: finance company liquidates

1937: first child, Naomi, is born

1941: goes to work at Danbury Federal Penitentiary in Danbury, Connecticut

1943: second child, Miriam (Mimi), is born

1944: goes to work for the Alcohol Tax Bureau in Providence, Rhode Island

1945: returns to New York City; third child, Deborah, is born

1956: runs for Congress on Liberal Party ticket

1958: appointed assistant counsel to the Workmen's Compensation Board

1959: goes into private law practice

1962: runs for Congress on Liberal Party ticket

1966: runs for Kings County Councilman-at-Large on Liberal Party ticket

1974: moves to Westchester

1978: retires from law

1997: moves to Florida

July 28, 2004: Dorothy Tannen dies

September 20, 2006: Eli Samuel Tannen dies

Acknowledgments

MY DEEPEST DEBT IS TO MY FATHER, FOR TRUSTING ME WITH THE stories of his life; for passing down to me his love of writing and of words; and for bequeathing me so many of his—the written words of the journals, letters, and notes he kept throughout his life, and the spoken words of the hours upon hours of conversation he graced me with, especially after he retired but also throughout my life.

I am also deeply grateful for the trust of my sisters, Mimi Tannen and Naomi Tannen, since my father's stories are theirs as much as mine, and for sharing their own memories and helping me make sense of—and sometimes question—my own.

I know far more about my father's and his family's history because my friend Paul Gordon generously located the immigration records of my parents and their relatives and the records about my father's aunt Dora in the United States. I'll always be grateful to him. I also want to thank Alice Calaprice for putting me in touch with Robert Schulmann, and to Robert Schulmann for locating the records of Dora's matriculation at the University of Zurich and for helping me place them in relation to Einstein's time there.

I owe an early and earnest debt to Emily Mann, whose 1992 invitation to write something for the theater led me to write a one-act play about a trip that my husband and I took to Poland with my parents. The play, *An Act of Devotion*, intersperses my father's memories of his childhood in Poland with my memories of my childhood with him; it became a seed for this book that germinated over all the years since. For assurance that the story I tell there might be worth the telling I am grateful to Joyce Carol Oates and Ray Smith for publishing the play in *Ontario Review* (No. 41, Fall/Winter 1994–95); to Howard Stein and Glenn Young for including it in *The Best American Short Plays 1993–1994*; and to Leslie Jacobson, founder and director of Horizons Theatre, for mounting a full production of it. I have adapted and included a few passages from the play here. The same is true for my essay "Daddy Young and Old," which is included in *Family: American Writers Remember Their Own*. I thank the editors, Sharon Sloan Fiffer and Steve Fiffer, for inviting me to contribute to that collection.

I wrote a first draft of the material shaped here while a fellow at the Center for Advanced Study in the Behavioral Sciences at Stanford University. I thank the center for providing the expansive physical and mental space that made that possible.

For invaluable comments on earlier drafts I thank Domenica Alioto, Kate Arnold-Murray, Sally Arteseros, Alan Bakalinsky, Suzanne Gluck, Cynthia Gordon, Harriet Grant, Molly Levine, Michael Macovski, Micah Perks, Susan Philips, Joan Silber, Mimi Tannen, and David Wise. For this book, as for many of the books that preceded it, Naomi Tannen has been my uber-reader, giving detailed comments on draft after draft.

I owe a debt to Georgetown University, which has been my academic and intellectual home since 1979. I want to thank those who helped with transcription, including Nancy Blaney and Jeff Deby. Gwynne Mapes digitized my nearly two hundred cassette tapes of interviews and conversations with my father, and scanned documents; and Kate Arnold-Murray, my dedicated assistant, helped in many ways, including last-minute fact-checking, short-notice transcribing, and manuscript formatting.

I am grateful, as well, to my editor, Sara Weiss, whose comments and suggestions made this a much better book.

I also thank the gifted copy editor, Susan Brown, for her close attention and astute queries—and her light touch.

For this and every book I've written since the stars aligned in my favor and led her to become my agent, Suzanne Gluck has been my literary guardian angel and wise guide. I owe her my deepest thanks.

Last and first is my boundless gratitude to my husband, Michael Macovski, who has been by my side on this quest through decades, always offering unwavering support and patient counsel. My gratitude to and for him is forever and for everything.

DEBORAH TANNEN is the author of *You Just Don't Understand,* which was on the *New York Times* bestseller list for nearly four years, including eight months at number one, and has been translated into thirty-one languages; the *New York Times* bestsellers *You're Wearing THAT?,* about mothers and daughters, and *You Were Always Mom's Favorite!,* about sisters; and many other books. A university professor and professor of linguistics at Georgetown University, she appears frequently on national television and radio. She lives with her husband in the Washington, D.C., area.

deborahtannen.com

This book was set in Bembo, a typeface based on an old-style Roman face that was used for Cardinal Pietro Bembo's tract *De Aetna* in 1495. Bembo was cut by Francesco Griffo (1450–1518) in the early sixteenth century for Italian Renaissance printer and publisher Aldus Manutius (1449–1515). The Lanston Monotype Company of Philadelphia brought the well-proportioned letterforms of Bembo to the United States in the 1930s.